Transition In, Through and Out of Higher Education

Transition In, Through and Out of Higher Education: International Case Studies and Best Practice recognises that the initial steps into undergraduate education mark only the beginning of the journey for students, and that the journey involves other significant transition points that students need to negotiate. By providing theoretical knowledge alongside practical guidance and resources, this book helps those involved in university teaching to guide students through their experiences and develop into autonomous, reflective learners.

Putting student engagement at the centre of teaching, *Transition In, Through and Out of Higher Education: International Case Studies and Best Practice* includes case studies to illuminate best practice, with resources and activities that can be used and adapted to address the individual needs of students. Addressing a wide range of themes, it considers:

- active learning
- promoting engagement
- encouraging independence and autonomy
- coping with change and increasing complexity
- the need for belonging and identity
- social and academic integration
- developing partnership working
- evaluating the effectiveness of developments to teaching practice.

From exploring the underlying pedagogy related to the theme to identifying the major challenges for students at key transitional points, *Transition* offers a comprehensive grounding to generate and inspire creative teaching that in turn enables students to better engage in the transition process. A highly practical and accessible resource, this book is suitable for all higher education staff involved in supporting students' transition in, through and out of university.

Ruth Matheson is Head of Learning, Teaching and Student Experience for the Faculty of Life Sciences and Education at the University of South Wales, UK, National Teaching Fellow, and a Principal Fellow of the Higher Education Academy.

Sue Tangney is a Principal Lecturer in Academic Development and Programme Director of the PgCert in Teaching in Higher Education at Cardiff Metropolitan University, UK, and a Principal Fellow of the Higher Education Academy.

Mark Sutcliffe is Postgraduate Programme Director at Cardiff School of Management, Cardiff Metropolitan University, UK, and Senior Fellow of the Higher Education Academy.

Transition In, Through and Out of Higher Education

International Case Studies and Best Practice

Edited by Ruth Matheson, Sue Tangney and Mark Sutcliffe

LONDON AND NEW YORK

First published 2018
by Routledge
2 Park Square, Milton Park, Abingdon, Oxon OX14 4RN

and by Routledge
711 Third Avenue, New York, NY 10017

Routledge is an imprint of the Taylor & Francis Group, an informa business

© 2018 selection and editorial matter, Ruth Matheson, Sue Tangney and Mark Sutcliffe; individual chapters, the contributors

The right of Ruth Matheson, Sue Tangney and Mark Sutcliffe to be identified as the authors of the editorial material, and of the authors for their individual chapters, has been asserted in accordance with sections 77 and 78 of the Copyright, Designs and Patents Act 1988.

All rights reserved. No part of this book may be reprinted or reproduced or utilised in any form or by any electronic, mechanical, or other means, now known or hereafter invented, including photocopying and recording, or in any information storage or retrieval system, without permission in writing from the publishers.

Trademark notice: Product or corporate names may be trademarks or registered trademarks, and are used only for identification and explanation without intent to infringe.

British Library Cataloguing-in-Publication Data
A catalogue record for this book is available from the British Library

Library of Congress Cataloging-in-Publication Data
A catalog record has been requested for this book

ISBN: 978-1-138-68217-7 (hbk)
ISBN: 978-1-138-68218-4 (pbk)
ISBN: 978-1-315-54533-2 (ebk)

Typeset in Goudy
by Swales & Willis Ltd, Exeter, Devon, UK

Contents

Case studies vii
Foreword xi
Acknowledgements xiii

Introduction 1

PART I

1 Transition through the student lifecycle 5
RUTH MATHESON

2 Identifying student need 17
SALLY BROWN

3 Developing belonging, community and creating professional identity 31
RUTH MATHESON AND MARK SUTCLIFFE

PART II

4 Managing and setting expectations 49
LORETTA NEWMAN-FORD

5 Promoting engagement, active learning and student ownership 81
SUE TANGNEY

6 Developing academic integration 113
CHRIS DENNIS, JAKE BAILEY AND STUART ABBOTT

7	Developing social integration MARK SUTCLIFFE AND RUTH MATHESON	139
8	Developing self SUE TANGNEY AND VALERIE CLIFFORD	166

PART III

9	Evaluating the effectiveness of transition activities LIN NORTON	199
10	Student stories	216
	Contributor biographies	226
	Index	240

Case studies

1 Pre-arrival orientation programme to increase
   retention and success   58
   LEONIEK WIJNGAARDS-DE MEIJ, UTRECHT UNIVERSITY,
   UTRECHT, THE NETHERLANDS
2 Using a structured timetable to manage first-year students'
   expectations of independent study   60
   REBECCA TURNER, VICTORIA HURTH, DEBBY COTTON,
   SEBASTIAN STEVENS, SAMANTHA CHILD, DAVID MORRISON
   AND PAULINE KNEALE, PLYMOUTH UNIVERSITY, PLYMOUTH, UK
3 Promoting student engagement and managing study
   expectations: *Passport to Success @ SCU*   63
   SALLY ASHTON-HAY AND ROBYN CETINICH, SOUTHERN CROSS
   UNIVERSITY, LISMORE, AUSTRALIA
4 Masters carousel: an experiential approach to equip
   transitioning students with key academic skills for level 7   67
   SAM DAVIS, KATIE PECK AND TANEFA APEKEY, LEEDS BECKETT
   UNIVERSITY, LEEDS, UK
5 Recoding academic expectations: the use of
   storytelling-as-pedagogy in supporting the transition
   of level 5 students   71
   DAVID ALDOUS AND DAVID BROWN, CARDIFF METROPOLITAN
   UNIVERSITY, CARDIFF, UK
6 Supporting the student experience from the outset   74
   WENDY JOHNSTON, LIVERPOOL JOHN MOORES UNIVERSITY,
   LIVERPOOL, UK
7 'Mind Your Own Business': enterprise education –
   going beyond the classroom   77
   RICHARD MORRIS, CARDIFF METROPOLITAN UNIVERSITY,
   CARDIFF, UK

8	The transition tube	90
	MARK SUTCLIFFE, CARDIFF METROPOLITAN UNIVERSITY, CARDIFF, UK	
9	'Technologising' the postgraduate classroom	94
	SARA SMITH AND MARTIN KHECHARA, UNIVERSITY OF WOLVERHAMPTON, WOLVERHAMPTON, UK	
10	Encouraging reflective practice through action research process models	97
	STUART ENGLISH, NORTHUMBRIA UNIVERSITY, NEWCASTLE, UK	
11	Increasing student engagement in a biomedical science award: peer-supported learning through video	99
	SARA SMITH, LIZ O'GARA AND MARTIN KHECHARA, UNIVERSITY OF WOLVERHAMPTON, WOLVERHAMPTON, UK	
12	Deepening engagement through problem-based learning (PBL)	103
	ALASTAIR TOMLINSON, CARDIFF METROPOLITAN UNIVERSITY, CARDIFF, UK	
13	Assignment design for students on international mobility	107
	GARETH BARHAM, CARDIFF METROPOLITAN UNIVERSITY, CARDIFF, UK	
14	Supporting the transition of mature learners into higher education	121
	JOHN BUTCHER, THE OPEN UNIVERSITY, MILTON KEYNES, UK	
15	Aiding active learning through pre-arrival, student-led resource for international students (student pre-arrival induction for continuing education [SPICE])	124
	MONIKA FOSTER, QUEEN MARGARET UNIVERSITY (FORMERLY EDINBURGH NAPIER UNIVERSITY), EDINBURGH, UK	
16	The biscuit game	127
	SALLY BROWN, INDEPENDENT CONSULTANT, UK	
17	In praise of patchwork assessment: creating a more flexible process that effectively supports the learning of part-time and in-work students	129
	STELLA JONES-DEVITT, SHEFFIELD HALLAM UNIVERSITY, SHEFFIELD, UK	
18	Learning to think outside the square	132
	LIZ DITZEL AND JOSIE CRAWLEY, OTAGO POLYTECHNIC, DUNEDIN, NEW ZEALAND	

19	Use of screen recording software to promote engagement with assignment feedback and feedforward in undergraduate studies	135
	HENRY DAWSON, CARDIFF METROPOLITAN UNIVERSITY, CARDIFF, UK	
20	The T-shirt exercise: developing rapid integration and social cohesion among first-year students	149
	JARKA GLASSEY, NEWCASTLE UNIVERSITY, NEWCASTLE, UK	
21	Peer mentoring on a Masters programme in Ghana	151
	RUTH CROSS, DIANE LOWCOCK, JERRY FIAVE, SARAH AYIKU AND GRACE KAFUI ANNAN, LEEDS BECKETT UNIVERSITY, LEEDS, UK	
22	The PodMag: podcasting to promote academic community	154
	KAREN FOLEY, THE OPEN UNIVERSITY, MILTON KEYNES, UK	
23	Student induction and graduate attributes: the outdoor problem-solving residential	156
	BILL DAVIES, CARDIFF METROPOLITAN UNIVERSITY, CARDIFF, UK	
24	Normalising a campus culture of safe mental health difficulty disclosure and support through mental health awareness (literacy) training: developing sport student mental health ambassadors	160
	MIKEL MELLICK, CARDIFF METROPOLITAN UNIVERSITY, CARDIFF, UK	
25	Networking approaches to integrating mid-programme entry undergraduate musical theatre students	163
	LOUISE H. JACKSON AND VICTORIA STRETTON, TRINITY LABAN CONSERVATOIRE OF MUSIC AND DANCE, LONDON, UK	
26	A picture is worth a thousand words: stimulating nursing students to reflect and make sense of their experiences in a professional context	176
	CATARINA LOBÃO, HEALTH SCHOOL OF LEIRIA, PORTUGAL; ANA BAPTISTA, QUEEN MARY UNIVERSITY OF LONDON, LONDON, UK; AND RUI GONÇALVES, NURSING SCHOOL OF COIMBRA, COIMBRA, PORTUGAL	
27	The role of public engagement in enhancing transition at postgraduate level	179
	DUDLEY SHALLCROSS AND TIM HARRISON, UNIVERSITY OF BRISTOL, BRISTOL, UK	
28	Transition as metaphor: how building with Lego helps students navigate team working for an external client	181
	ALISON JAMES, UNIVERSITY OF WINCHESTER, WINCHESTER, UK	

29 Design futures: a trans-active curriculum community-based approach to the development of student self-confidence, empowerment and entrepreneurship 185
STEPHEN THOMPSON, CARDIFF METROPOLITAN UNIVERSITY, CARDIFF, UK

30 Designing a student-led framework for pre- and post-mobility intercultural skills development as part of the curriculum 188
MONIKA FOSTER, QUEEN MARGARET UNIVERSITY (FORMERLY EDINBURGH NAPIER UNIVERSITY), EDINBURGH, UK

31 Culturally appropriate assessment strategy 192
HAZEL HOROBIN, FORMERLY SHEFFIELD HALLAM UNIVERSITY, SHEFFIELD, UK

Foreword

The question 'What is a successful higher education?' is surprisingly often only implicitly addressed. While this is indeed a slippery idea with which to grapple, it is nevertheless fundamental in a field that is increasingly replete with well-meaning 'one-off' interventions and 'success support' programmes that regularly are found to be not generalisable or transferable. Conceptual frameworks that synthesise the developmental pathways and constellations of contested, and often competing, identities and capabilities (e.g. intellectual, social, personal and professional) that characterise the contemporary student lifecycle provide the necessary fabric for the next generation of systemic design and development. What is required is the theoretical, empirical and political basis for better contextualising findings, posing well-formed inquiry, developing systematic evaluation and, most critically, reliably understanding the underlying needs and factors that influence the questions: 'What works?' 'And why?' This book is a timely contribution to such a meta-organising discourse. Here, you will find an accessible and rigorous evidence-informed conception of the student learning journey. You will find a persuasive narrative that speaks from and to both theory and practice and brings to clear light the implications for facilitating the success of diverse cohorts of students in the modern higher education system. Most refreshingly, it is not silent on the wicked challenges inherent in this aspiration, and indeed invites deep interrogation from multiple perspectives: case studies, staff accounts and student voices. One of its outstanding features is that it does not locate its discourse in terms of reductionist 'performance indicators' (e.g. retention, employability). While these imperatives are honestly acknowledged and practically addressed, they are framed as outcomes of a holistic and critical approach to higher education.

It is a widely acknowledged sad reality that educators and students can often disappoint each other and fall short of each other's expectations. Given that education at its core is a relational process, this is more than just an unfortunate social dynamic; it in fact diminishes the efficacy of the whole enterprise. One of the benefits of this text is providing guidance in ways to avoid the easy and mistaken assumptions that both educators and students can make about themselves and each other and, more critically, the purposes of higher education. Here, you will find the 'university laid bare' and the beginnings of a shared language that offers the promise for more honest and effective working relationships in the service of a 'higher education'.

Relatedly, there are also opportunities here not just to reflect on better ways of helping students to succeed, but also to assess our own practices. One of the unacknowledged reasons for the failure of so many student success interventions has been that they have lacked a critical appraisal of the roles and culture within which they are conceived and delivered. Thus, you will find here an opportunity to consider ways of both assisting our students to enrich their identities and capabilities and also reviewing and refreshing our own identity claims as 'higher educators'. In a time of transition, it not just our students who are on a journey of becoming, but also ourselves: in terms of our roles, our authority and our required expertise. The language of active, authentic and flexible learning that we readily apply to our students is also required of us if we are indeed to be agents of a successful higher education. This text is an invitation to a more sophisticated and self-involving conception of the agenda of 'student success'.

Professor Alf Lizzio
Dean (Learning Futures) and
Director (Learning Futures)
Griffith University, Australia

Acknowledgements

We wish to acknowledge and thank Nicola Poole and Mikel Mellick for their insightful and formative comments and discussions about Chapters 4 and 7, respectively. We would also like to say a warm thank you to Richard Matheson for his assistance with the copy-editing.

Introduction

Transitions occur throughout our lives, some major and others relatively minor. Making the choice to come to university is the start of one of these major life transitions. It has many costs and benefits as students take a "leap of faith" (Macfarlane, 2009: 221) that the benefits of university will outweigh both the personal and financial costs. There is already some literature addressing transition *to* university with emphasis on the first year. We, as editors, identified the need for a book that recognised that transition into university is only the beginning of a journey that continues across the student lifecycle and beyond into the world of work or further study.

This book seeks to illuminate this ongoing journey, highlighting both the nature of transition points through the student lifecycle, and the ways in which practitioners can use these to more purposefully challenge students' thinking, and enable them to develop as autonomous, reflective learners ready for the twenty-first century. We chose to address transition thematically rather than chronologically, enabling us to introduce pedagogic theory and related practice that could, in most cases, be transferable to different levels and subject disciplines. We have gathered practice in the form of case studies from across the globe to bring you a variety of ideas from a diverse range of disciplines.

The book is divided into three distinct parts. Part I provides three chapters grounding the book with the underpinning theory of transition within the context of contemporary higher education. Part II, consisting of five chapters, focuses on specific pedagogy related to each chapter's theme, with practical suggestions for meeting students' needs. These chapters provide a range of 'off-the-shelf' case studies that lead you through tried-and-tested learning activities step by step. Part III includes two chapters: one on evaluation of transition activities and one documenting students' own personal stories of their transition.

We have sought to make this book highly practical and accessible, both for those academics who are starting out on their journey of teaching and supporting learning and for those further down the track who are seeking to try something new.

Reference

Macfarlane, B. (2009) A leap of faith: the role of trust in higher education teaching. *Nagoya Journal of Higher Education*, 9, 221–238.

Part I

Chapter 1

Transition through the student lifecycle

Ruth Matheson

Introduction to the chapter

There has been a dramatic increase in the number of students entering higher education over the past 50 years. In 2000, 99.5 million students entered tertiary education across the globe. Fourteen years later, in 2014, the number of students entering this sector had more than doubled to 207.2 million (United Nations Educational, Scientific and Cultural Organization, 2016). Predictions estimate that by 2030, the number of students entering higher education will rise to 414.2 million (Calderon, 2012). This rise has been driven by government policies across the globe that have recognised and sought to address the need for a knowledge-based society to meet the changing demands of a globalised economy. Universities are seen as key agents in enhancing knowledge, ideas and abilities, leading to an increase in global competitiveness. Many of these government policies have focused on widening participation to increase both numbers and diversity of a previously demographically narrow student population (Gale & Parker, 2013). Two main factors have dominated the widening participation agenda: first, the need for a highly educated workforce that can compete in globalised economies; and second, a recognition of the importance of social justice and the provision of opportunity for all.

The need for a highly educated workforce that can compete in a globalised economy

Within the UK, higher education has long been recognised as having connections with the economy. As long ago as 1963, *The Robbins Report* (Committee on Higher Education, 1963) recognised that one of the aims of higher education was to provide skills for the labour market. Highlighted again in *The Dearing Report* (National Committee of Inquiry into Higher Education, 1997), higher education was seen as having a vital role in the modern economy. Dearing stated that "Education and training [should] enable people in an advanced society to compete with the best in the world" (National Committee of Inquiry into Higher Education, 1997: 7).

In recent years, this focus on employability has come to the forefront of higher education, with an emphasis on the development of graduates with relevant attributes, skills and knowledge. Australia and the US are also currently looking at how best to support the development of graduate attributes in the curricula, and the subsequent transition to the world of work (Bennett, Richardson & MacKinnon, 2016). However, research demonstrates that the UK is leading the way due to central support provided by funding bodies, highly advanced employability initiatives, extracurricular practice and the sharing of embedded careers practices (Department for Business, Innovation and Skills, 2011).

If students are to develop graduate attributes, they need to have opportunities to engage with employers, experience authentic assessment, and participate in pedagogies that promote active engagement and the development of teamworking skills. These opportunities need to be developed throughout the student lifecycle and embedded in both curricular and extracurricular activities if students are to be enabled to transition through and out of university into the world of work. This requires academics to actively engage with future employers or service users when designing curricula, and to give greater consideration to how entrepreneurship and enterprise are fostered within higher education.

The importance of social justice and providing opportunity for all

Traditionally, universities had a narrow demographic, with students entering higher education from similar socio-economic groups and having had similar educational experiences. The early 1990s saw existing colleges and polytechnics in Australia and the UK being transformed into 'new universities', widening both the student population and the nature of the programmes of study being provided (King, 2004). This widening of population within the higher education sector demanded that often small, elite universities had to expand rapidly to meet this increased demand. No longer did one size fit all, but by the very nature of an increasingly diverse student population there was an impetus to consider the different needs of students and ask the question: "Who are my students and how can we work together to maximise student learning outcomes?" (Hunt & Chalmers, 2013: 180).

Today, students coming from wider sociocultural and academic contexts bring with them different expectations. These expectations need to be recognised and reflected in a curriculum design that allows for flexibility in learning opportunities, values inclusive assessment and provides appropriate support (Barnett, 2014). This also demands an awareness of the different transitional pathways that students may take through their student lifecycle and the relationship between successful transition and student retention.

The importance of retention

With an increase in the student population and the diverse nature of the student group comes the increased risk of withdrawal from university. Early studies on attrition, pre-1970, largely focused on the "students' characteristics, personal attributes and shortcomings" (Aljohani, 2016: 2) drawing on the field of psychology. It was in the early 1970s that the first sociologically framed student retention model was developed, which recognised that both academic and social factors contribute to students' decisions to withdraw.

Tinto's Model of Institutional Departure (1993), as cited by Aljohani (2016), has held a prominent place in the literature on retention since first developed, recognising the need for students to be integrated both academically and socially, and placing responsibility on institutions to provide opportunities to enable this. According to Tinto, students enter higher education with pre-entry attributes (family background, skills and abilities, and prior schooling) and these shape their initial goals and commitments. Their experience of the academic system and the social system, both formal and informal, impact on their ability to integrate academically and socially, and this in turn leads to a re-evaluation of their goals and commitments. If lacking social or academic integration, or both, students are at risk of making the decision to drop out. Understandably, this danger is most prevalent in the first year.

"Roughly two thirds of premature departures take place in, or, at the end of, the first year of full-time study in the UK" (Yorke, 1999: 37), with students struggling to make the transition into university. This withdrawal rate is significantly higher in students from low socio-economic backgrounds, mature students and disabled students (Yorke & Longden, 2004). Students withdraw for multiple reasons that are often complex and diverse. Some of these reasons have been highlighted by Morgan (2012):

- poor subject choice;
- course structure;
- student demographics;
- previous educational experiences;
- an inadequate student experience; and
- personal reasons.

(pp. 9–10)

The complexity surrounding retention and withdrawal requires us to be mindful of being inclusive in all aspects of curriculum design, assessment and feedback in order to support the differing needs of our students. This book seeks to provide ideas that can be adapted for different levels, and which help to integrate all students, whether they are home-based, international, direct-entry, returning, or students learning at a distance, through all stages of the student lifecycle.

The student lifecycle

To understand the complexity of student transition, it is important to appreciate the different stages of the student lifecycle. While there are numerous frameworks and models of student transition into and through higher education (Lizzio, 2011; Morgan, 2012; Bridges & Bridges, 2017; Burnett, 2007), they all recognise that transition is complex, placing different demands at different times, with students experiencing frequent disruption as expectations and their environment change.

Understanding the student lifecycle is vital in designing curricula that meet student needs and enable successful transition. To guide this development of curricula and to integrate co-curricular design, Lizzio (2011) developed an 'integrative framework' of the student lifecycle. This framework is useful in helping to illuminate the different stages of transition and the nature of student thinking and actions at each stage. He describes the student lifecycle as "the constellation of evolving identities, needs and purposes" (Lizzio, 2011: 1). These identities, needs and purposes help us to have a better understanding of the concerns and motivations of our students.

The student lifecycle, according to Lizzio's framework, can be viewed as a series of transitions that will be summarised here and expanded on later in the chapter. Beginning with 'transition towards' university, the main thoughts and actions of future students during this period focus on the process that leads to the choice of course and university, defined as aspiring and exploring, clarifying and choosing. At this stage, institutions need to provide opportunities that enable potential students to make informed choices, and to begin to explore and orientate themselves towards their chosen subject and future aspirations. 'Transition in' (focusing on commencing students) recognises students' priorities as committing and preparing, joining and engaging. The need for active engagement, opportunities for social integration, and early formative assessment and feedback underpin the success of integration into this new student world while also promoting retention. Lizzio (2011) defines 'transition through' as continuing students. These students are working for early success and building on that success. Often neglected in the literature, this stage is vital in ensuring the continued engagement of students through the creation of authentic curricula and assessment that challenges students, develops graduate attributes, and ultimately leads to high student satisfaction.

Finally, Lizzio (2011) identifies 'transition up, out and back'. This includes those students who are graduating or returning for postgraduate study. Their focus is on future success, partnering and continuing. Here, our responsibility as educators is to provide opportunities for students to develop skills for their future employability, inspire higher study, and support transition into the workplace or back into higher education. Through our own research into postgraduate transition (Matheson & Sutcliffe, 2017), and echoing the findings of Tobbell, O'Donnell and Zammit (2008), we have found that students returning to university at a postgraduate level often re-enter the student lifecycle from the beginning, bringing with them new academic and social concerns. These concerns can be further accentuated if coming with English as a second language or having previously experienced a different, less participatory educational culture.

Transition through the student lifecycle 9

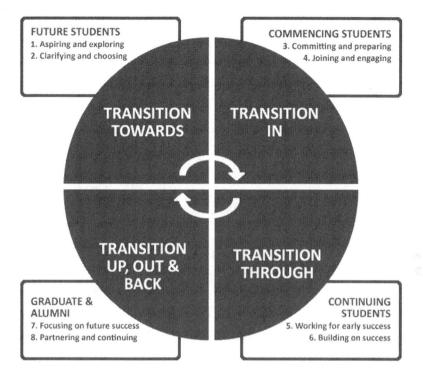

Figure 1.1 Student Lifecycle Framework
Source: Lizzio (2011), reproduced with permission from the author

Students are constantly adjusting to not only a changing academic identity, but also a changing social identity, which requires them to negotiate their way through a maze of new expectations, partnerships in learning, and new academic competencies, while integrating socially and dealing with a changing sense of self. Is there any wonder that students often find this transition challenging and sometimes troublesome? As those teaching and supporting learning, it is our role to help students find their way through this maze.

Transition stages

There are many models outlining student transition in higher education. Most of these models outline the stages of transition through the student lifecycle. We have taken the decision not to structure this book through the stages, although we will make reference to them. We will instead focus on themes that impact on transition and that serve to inform teaching practice and course design. However, at this stage, and to provide a backdrop to the subsequent chapters, especially those within Part II, we feel that it is important to draw attention to the identified stages of transition and a number of the existing models and theories. Although often presented as a linear process, there is common agreement that students often leave and re-enter the stages at different times throughout their transition into, through and out of university.

Pre-entry

With a growing expectation that the majority of young people will enter the university sector, there is a clear need to enable future students to develop a sense of purpose, and have the necessary resources to feel that they will be able to succeed and make social connections. Initially, it is helpful if students view themselves as valued members of their future learning community and feel secure in their choice. This is a new world they are entering, which Menzies and Baron (2014) describe as pre-departure, where they consider students as being in neutral mood. Lizzio (2011) challenges educators to develop curricula that begin prior to arrival, with activities that promote a sense of inclusion, inspire a belief in the ability to achieve, give a clear idea of what it will take to achieve, and develop a sense of aspiration.

Burnett (2007) and Morgan (2012) identify an even earlier transition stage, pre-transition, which requires engagement with students from the age of 14 to 18 to enable them to make informed decisions regarding their future direction. This first contact is important in getting students to shape their aspirations and expectations, with questions such as: 'Is university my only option?' 'What will be expected of me as a university student?' 'Which course and university are right for me?' (Morgan, 2012).

On entry (induction)

Research on transition illuminates the importance of induction in promoting retention and student achievement (Sheader & Richardson, 2006), with poor retention linked to students who encounter poor-quality learning experiences, have little opportunity for in-class interaction, and lack opportunities to make friends (Yorke & Longden, 2008). There is a need for a more holistic view of student engagement, developing curricula and extracurricular activities that embrace both academic and social dimensions (Krause & Coates, 2008), enabling students to come to terms with the expectations of university, and to reshape their self-identity.

The Student Adjustment Model (Menzies & Baron, 2014) identifies three phases that students go through on entering higher education. Menzies and Baron (2014) describe the first four weeks as the honeymoon period, with students arriving full of excitement and expectations. This is followed by what they have labelled as 'Party's Over', where the reality of a new academic and social environment becomes real. It is during this time that students often suffer from homesickness, feel isolated and confused, and experience high levels of stress. This phase is clearly associated with early withdrawal from university, where students have failed to gain a sense of belonging and have not engaged either academically and/or socially (Thomas, 2012). Thomas (2012) highlights early engagement, which continues throughout the student lifecycle, as crucial to student retention and success. Curricula need to provide opportunities for students to engage socially, learn from and about each other, and promote belonging (to the course, to the institution and to each other).

Induction provides an ideal opportunity to open the eyes of students to the benefits of cultural and educational diversity, as well as demonstrating that hopes, fears and aspirations are shared across cultures, ages and gender. This is also the phase where students need to learn the rules of engagement and to navigate institutional norms and procedures. Early formative assessment and feedback opportunities allow students to identify gaps in their skills and knowledge, and it is within this period that strong support mechanisms are crucial. Gale and Parker (2014) provide suggestions to aid this transition, including orientation activities for both facilities and staff, "just in time information" when meaningful for procedures, curriculum and assessment, and the embedding of active pedagogies (p. 738).

First-year experience

Menzies and Baron (2014) note that having negotiated the 'Party's Over' phase, students move into healthy adjustment. They see this as occurring around week 11 and beyond. It is at this point that students gain a "sense of positive student identity" (Lizzio, 2011: 8). This positive student identity requires students to examine their social interactions and how they are developing friendships and connections with other course members, faculty staff and the wider institution (closely linked to establishing belonging). Students also need to be able to see their capabilities, identify where gaps occur and be able to judge themselves against institutional requirements. In addition, students need to be resourceful in finding ways and means of addressing any gaps, meeting their own and institutional expectations, and managing their learning and social environment. Finally, students need to be able to identify the *what next?*, fuelling future aspirations.

Findings from the Quality Assurance Agency for Higher Education (QAA) Scottish Enhancement Theme exploring the first-year experience (Whittaker, 2007) highlight the need for universities to address the multidimensional aspects of transition (social, personal and academic). This can be difficult for academic staff with time, content delivery and learning environment pressures. However, the first year needs to be viewed as a longitudinal process of induction, with opportunities for the student to receive formative feedback, assessment that provides opportunities to identify gaps, a curriculum that provides opportunities for social learning and networking, teaching methodologies that encourage engagement and challenge, and active learning that develops the skills of self-directed enquiry and application. In addition, peer and tutor support should enable further opportunities for personal and academic development.

Reorientation and reinduction

The middle years are often a neglected period in the transition literature, with students expected to pick up any new rules and expectations, but with little acknowledgment of the adjustments that they need to make. During these middle years, Burnett (2007) states that students experience a loss of well-structured and appropriate support. Returning students need to be reorientated to study and have time and opportunities to consider the changing expectations of a different level of study. Many students experience significant periods of absence from the academic environment due to holidays, placements or periods of intermission. International students are returning from their home countries with the need to reorientate themselves once again into a different culture. Morgan (2012) recommends that students be reorientated at the start of each level of study. This is also the case for students returning or entering postgraduate study (Tobbell et al., 2008). This reinduction takes place over a significant period of time, with Morgan (2012) suggesting this should occur over the first term/semester.

The 'middle years', as identified by Burnett (2007), can be a time when students feel that they are a long way from the start but there is also a long way to the end. Expectations on students have risen with higher workloads and increased demands. For many students, this results in confusion, uncertainty and impatience as they try to adapt to the new. Bridges and Bridges (2017) refer to this as the 'neutral zone', where students suffer increased anxiety over their role and identity, often resulting in low morale and productivity. Our job as educators is to enable students to see through this stage to the 'new beginning' (Bridges & Bridges, 2017), through providing students with frequent feedback, helping them navigate the 'maze' and see the end point.

During this time, students should be engaged in activities that enable them to reflect on their past academic and personal learning gains, identifying how they can build on these in the coming year. Expectations will have changed as students move to a different academic level of study, and these expectations need to be explored and understood to enable the students to recognise what they must do to achieve and realise their aspirations. There may be a reduction in scaffolding and signposting, with students needing to develop independent learning skills, more complex working relationships, leadership capabilities, and to recognise the importance of developing graduate attributes (Chalmers & Partridge, 2013; Lizzio, 2011). This requires academics to examine the opportunities that students have within the curriculum to develop these skills and attributes, through well-crafted learning activities, feedback and feedforward, engagement with complexity and unpredictability, authentic assessment, and opportunities to develop themselves as global citizens.

Up, out and back

Within the final year of undergraduate study, students not only have to focus on the 'here and now', but also are looking towards the future and life after university or return to study. Students are having to build on their success to meet current academic targets towards gaining their degree, while forming and actioning their future plans. There is currently little research into the latter years of undergraduate and postgraduate study (Gale & Parker, 2014). This is despite the sector placing great emphasis on the identification and development of graduate attributes to prepare students beyond their undergraduate study.

To address this need, Morgan (2012) suggests that students should be given the opportunity to explore how the skills that they have developed throughout university can be transferred into the workplace or back into study. Having the opportunity to ask 'What next?' and examine the options open to them is also vital in enabling students to make informed choices and recognise their own personal and professional developmental needs. What this adjustment entails and how students are going to make the necessary adjustments also need consideration and should form part of the curriculum (Morgan, 2012).

For those returning to postgraduate study, there is also a need for reinduction to university. Having successfully completed undergraduate study, returning students are often viewed as 'experts'; however, the reality is that postgraduate students need support to further develop academic skills and understand the new practices required of them in order to succeed (Heussi, 2012; West, 2012). From the literature, it has been identified that postgraduate students also value curricula that offer learning opportunities with other students that are facilitated by staff, an informal atmosphere with emphasis on group interaction, and support to understand new practices enabling academic identity (Tobbell & O'Donnell, 2013).

Considering the diversity of the student body

It is important to consider the individuality of the student and the diversity of the student body. It is this diversity that affords us as educators the opportunity to introduce students to a global world and all that it has to offer. However, with this diversity come challenges in meeting the needs of students who come with different language, culture, educational backgrounds, and with different life and home experiences. Our aim is to provide case studies that explore and utilise many of these differences to enrich the student experience.

Towards becoming

Gale and Parker (2014), in their review of 24 Australian Learning and Teaching Council projects and fellowships and other international literature on transition, identified three broad conceptions of transition: (1) induction; (2) development; and (3) becoming. They categorised all references to student orientation (defined periods of adjustment) and institutional expectations as *induction*; all references to the formation of student identity (distinct stages) as *development*; and references to the 'lived experience of students' (fragmented moments) as *becoming*. They found that 1 and 2 tended to focus on institutional systems and the requirements for fitting into the institutions, and these formed the majority of their findings. Little literature relating to conception 3 was identified, so drawing on the work of Hockings, Cooke and Bowl (2010), Gale and Parker (2014) identify four transition pedagogies that emphasise this becoming:

- Creating collaborative and inclusive spaces, in which students are encouraged to share their beliefs, knowledge and experiences.
- Developing student-centred strategies, which entail flexible and tailored activities that enable students to ground their learning in something relevant to them as individuals.
- Connecting with students' lives, through subject matter that is relevant to students' immediate lives and/or their imagined roles and identities as professionals.
- Being culturally aware, which includes using culturally relevant examples, anecdotes and stories to aid learning, as well as a non-academic frame of reference for teaching (i.e. teaching beyond the academic culture).

(p. 748)

We have incorporated case studies throughout the book that address all three of these broad conceptions of transition across the student lifecycle, and seek to place these within pedagogies that engage students and value their contribution.

References

Aljohani, O. (2016) A comprehensive review of the major studies and theoretical models of student retention in higher education. *Higher Education Studies*, 6(2). Available from: http://dx.doi.org/10.5539/hes.v6n2p1.

Barnett, R. (2014) *Conditions of flexibility: securing a more responsive higher education system*. Higher Education Academy. Available from: www.heacademy.ac.uk/system/files/conditions_of_flexibility_securing_a_more_responsive_higher_education_system.pdf [Accessed 8 September 2017].

Bennett, D., Richardson, S. & MacKinnon, P. (2016) *Enacting strategies for graduate employability: how universities can best support students to develop generic skills – Part A*. Canberra, ACT, Australian Government, Office for Learning and Teaching, Department of Education and Training. Available from: www.olt.gov.au/project-how-universities-can-best-support-students-develop-generic-skills-enacting-strategies-gradua [Accessed 18 July 2017].

Bridges, W. & Bridges, S. (2017) *Managing transitions, 25th anniversary edition: making the most of change*. 4th ed. London, Nicholas Brealey.

Burnett, L. (2007) Juggling first-year student experience and institutional change: an Australian example. In: National Resource Center for the First-Year Experience and Students in Transition. *20th International Conference on the First-Year Experience. July 9–12.* Hawaii's Big Island, Hawaii, p.19. Available from: https://research-repository.griffith.edu.au/bitstream/handle/10072/32622/51648_1.pdf;jsessionid=B3AB089192AD00A21077E92F2DC03411?sequence=1 [Accessed 27 September 2017].

Calderon, A. (2012) Massification continues to transform higher education. *University World News*, 237, 2 September. Available from: www.universityworldnews.com/article.php?story=20120831155341147 [Accessed 17 July 2017].

Chalmers, D. & Partridge, L. (2013) Teaching graduate attributes and academic skills. In: Hunt, L. & Chalmers, D. (eds.), *University teaching in focus: a learning-centred approach.* London, Routledge, pp. 56–73.

Committee on Higher Education (1963) *The Robbins Report.* Available from: www.educationengland.org.uk/documents/robbins/robbins1963.html [Accessed 27 September 2017].

Department for Business, Innovation and Skills (2011) *Supporting graduate employability: HEI practice in other countries.* BIS research paper number 40. Available from: www.gov.uk/government/uploads/system/uploads/attachment_data/file/32421/11-913-supporting-graduate-employability-other-countries.pdf [Accessed 30 September 2017].

Gale, T. & Parker, S. (2013) *Widening participation in Australian higher education: report to the Higher Education Funding Council for England (HEFCE) and Office of Fair Access (OFFA), England.* Leicester, UK, CFE (Research and Consulting), and Lancashire, UK, Edge Hill University.

Gale, T. & Parker, S. (2014) Navigating change: a typology of student transition in higher education. *Studies in Higher Education*, 39(5), 734–753.

Heussi, A. (2012) Postgraduate student perceptions of the transition into postgraduate study. *Student Engagement and Experience Journal*, 1(3). Available from: http://dx.doi.org/10.7190/seej.v1i3.52.

Hockings, C., Cooke, S. & Bowl, M. (2010) Learning and teaching in two universities within the context of increasing student diversity: complexity, contradictions and challenges. In: David, A.M., Bathmaker, G., Crozier, P., Davis, H., Ertl, A., Fuller, G., et al. (eds.), *Improving learning by widening participation in higher education.* London, Routledge, pp. 95–108.

Hunt, L. & Chalmers, D. (2013) *University teaching in focus: a learning-centred approach.* London, Routledge.

King, R. (2004) *The university in the global age.* Basingstoke, Palgrave Macmillan.

Krause, K.-L. & Coates, H. (2008) Students' engagement in first-year university. *Assessment and Evaluation in Higher Education*, 33(5), 493–505.

Lizzio, A. (2011) *The student lifecycle: an integrative framework for guiding practice.* Available from: www.griffith.edu.au/learning-teaching/student-success/first-year-experience/student-lifecycle-transition-orientation [Accessed 17 July 2017].

Matheson, R. & Sutcliffe, M. (2017) Belonging and transition: an exploration of international business students' postgraduate experience. *Innovations in Education and Teaching International*, 1–9. Available from: http://dx.doi.org/10.1080/14703297.2017.1279558.

Menzies, J.L. & Baron, R. (2014) International postgraduate student transition experiences: the importance of student societies and friends. *Innovations in Education and Teaching International*, 51(1), 84–94.

Morgan, M. (ed.) (2012) *Improving the student experience: a practical guide for universities and colleges*. London, Routledge.

National Committee of Inquiry into Higher Education (1997) *Higher education in the learning society: Report of the National Committee of Inquiry into Higher Education (The Dearing Report)*. HMSO.

Sheader, E.A. & Richardson, H.C. (2006) Homestart: a support for students in non-university accommodation. In: Cook, A., Macintosh, K.A. & Rushton, B.S. (eds.), *Supporting students: early induction* [a publication from the STAR Project]. Coleraine, University of Ulster, pp. 51–72.

Thomas, L. (2012) *Building student engagement and belonging at a time of change: final report for the What Works? student retention and success programme*. Higher Education Academy. Available from: www.heacademy.ac.uk/system/files/what_works_summary_report_1.pdf [Accessed 17 July 2017].

Tobbell, J. & O'Donnell, V.L. (2013) Transition to postgraduate study: postgraduate ecological systems and identity. *Cambridge Journal of Education*, 43(1), 123–138.

Tobbell, J., O'Donnell, V.L. & Zammit, M. (2008) *Exploring practice and participation in transition to post-graduate social science study: an ethnographic study*. Higher Education Academy.

United Nations Educational, Scientific and Cultural Organization (2016) *Global Education Monitoring Report 2016 – Education for people and planet: creating sustainable futures for all*. 2nd ed. United Nations Educational, Scientific and Cultural Organization. Available from: http://en.unesco.org/gem-report/ [Accessed 27 September 2017].

West, A. (2012) Formative evaluation of the transition to postgraduate study for counselling and psychotherapy training: student perceptions of assignments and academic writing. *Counselling and Psychotherapy Research: Linking Research with Practice*, 12(2), 128–135.

Whittaker, R. (2007) *Quality enhancement theme first year experience, supporting transition to and during the first year project*. Quality Assurance Agency. Final Report.

Yorke, M. (1999) *Leaving early: undergraduate non-completion in higher education*. London, Routledge.

Yorke, M. & Longden, B. (2004) *Retention and student success in higher education*. Maidenhead, Society for Research into Higher Education and Open University Press.

Yorke, M. & Longden, B. (2008) *The first-year experience in higher education in the UK: final report*. The Higher Education Academy.

Chapter 2

Identifying student need

Sally Brown

Introduction to the chapter

What do students want? How can we satisfy their multiple, diverse and sometimes competing needs? This chapter will explore the nature of the student population and the challenges that they face and bring to the higher education environment, together with exploring some popular misconceptions staff have about students, and vice versa. It will highlight any additional needs faced by international students and discuss ways in which we can challenge preconceptions.

Current trends

Any sentence beginning 'Students nowadays . . .' is likely to degenerate into bland and outdated generalisations very quickly. Here, I aim to identify and provide a personal list of some current trends that characterise the UK and global higher education context.

Trend 1: students viewing themselves as consumers

Commentators in the UK, Australia and other nations where fees have been introduced in the last two decades comment on the changed nature of the transaction between students and universities. As Callender and Jackson (2008) have argued: "The [parliamentary] White Paper, 'the future of higher education' (Department for Education and Skills, 2003) framed the issue of student choice in very narrow terms, reflecting the notion of higher education as a market and students as consumers" (p. 407). They indicate that the establishment of a quasi-market has been linked to governmental desires to see student choice as an increasingly important driver of teaching quality. As students choose 'good-quality courses', the metrics of what such courses look like has inevitably become a hotly contested topic. The White Paper argued that "student choice can only drive quality up successfully if it is underpinned by robust information" (Department for Education and Skills, 2003: 47, para. 4.1). One such measure introduced in the UK in 2017 is the Teaching Excellence Framework (TEF).

Based on publicly available benchmarked measures of student satisfaction, retention and graduate-level employability, together with a contextual statement produced by the institution, the outcomes of the TEF categorised participating higher education institutions into gold, silver and bronze ratings to somewhat mixed responses. Although participation was voluntary, at the time of writing some institutions are appealing the outcomes on the grounds that the measures were not fit for purpose in measuring teaching excellence. Future plans for subject-level TEF appear to be no less complex and controversial.

Indubitably, nevertheless, colleagues report students being more litigious, demanding and having higher expectations about all aspects of the student experience, including comfortable learning environments, extensive student support, ready access to web and library resources, and high-quality living accommodation.

In universities in many nations, student opinion is sought through surveys. In the UK, we have the National Student Survey (NSS), the US has a National Survey of Student Engagement, and Australia a Student Experience Survey. In the UK, the NSS feeds into quality assurance judgments and the TEF, and this has considerably strengthened the impact of the student voice in universities. In 2017, the NSS survey was lengthened with new questions on 'learning opportunities', 'learning community' and 'student voice' that further emphasise to universities the importance of gaining positive evaluations by students, which necessarily change institutional attitudes and behaviours.

Implications for those supporting transition include needing to clarify expectations pre- and post-admission about what the university is able to offer in each of these areas, as well as guidance on how to seek appropriate help when needed, and how to manage problems and make complaints.

Trend 2: some loss of confidence in the concept of graduate premium

The rationale behind the imposition of fees in the UK was largely based on assurances that graduates benefit in financial terms and in other ways throughout their whole careers, but this is increasingly being questioned. The added value of having a degree depends, it seems, to some extent on whether you studied at an elite organisation, the subject you studied and other factors, including your race and your gender. It is hard to differentiate, for example, between the career advantage you have from graduating and the advantages you often already had in terms of social and cultural capital that helped you get into an elite university at the outset.

Data for 2016 intakes in UK universities showed a significant drop in domiciled students studying part-time for a first degree, from 196,395 in 2008–2009 to 169,915 in 2015–2016 (Higher Education Statistics Agency, 2017), while overall recruitment rose. This change has been partly put down to the changes in part-time degree funding and reflects the changing perceptions of the value of a degree versus the financial cost. Employers too are starting to question the importance of simply having a degree compared to demonstrated skills in "logical thinking, ability to understand the root cause of a problem, rapid comprehension of new concepts, self-motivation, a confidence-inspiring and professional manner and a strong work ethic," as suggested by Dominic Franiel, head of student recruitment at accountancy firm EY (cited in Matthews, 2017: 34).

Matthews (2017) argues that behavioural and cognitive abilities as measured by bespoke tests can be a better predictor of recruits' performance than top degree classifications, citing a decision made by Penguin Random House UK to dispense with a graduate-only recruitment policy, as they have found no link between having a degree and workplace performance.

Such loss of confidence by potential students and employers in the value of a degree per se, coupled with considerable political movements in the UK away from a consensus that high fees are necessary, draw into question the whole proposition that higher education is a private rather than a public good.

Trend 3: different demographics among the student cohort

Internationally, the proportion of a nation's population who can expect to go to university has increased over recent decades. In the UK, after the Second World War, rather than just a tiny elite going to university largely from private schools, the growth of grammar schools meant that more like 10 per cent went into higher education in the 1960s, and nowadays almost half of the age cohort now study at this level. We see similarly changing expectations about who can study at university in many nations in the twenty-first century, particularly, for example, in India and China, where growth in student numbers has recently been exponential.

We have also seen different kinds of students having raised expectations of tertiary education through a range of widening participation initiatives, including 'Aimhigher' (reviewed by Morris & Golden, 2005). We saw in the 1980s and 1990s more 'non-traditional' students entering higher education: more mature students, more part-time students, more women, and more students from black and minority ethnic backgrounds (Bowl, 2003). In recent years in the UK, however, these trends have started to slow down, particularly for part-time students. This has been as a consequence of substantial student fees, extensive discussion about the reality of a 'graduate premium', particularly in arts and humanities, and the value placed on new apprenticeships.

In the past seven years, the UK higher education sector has seen a marked increase in participation of applicants entering first degree study with alternatives to A levels/Baccalaureate entry requirements, such as the Business and Technology Education Council Level 3 Extended Diploma (BTEC), access courses (professionally orientated pathways), recognition of prior learning, and other qualifications. Entrance from these non-traditional pathways has risen in the UK to an all-time high of 68,000 in 2014–2015, while participation in part-time study has declined significantly, especially after the introduction of the £9,000 per year fees (Higher Education Funding Council for England, 2016).

This has hit universities that have traditionally specialised in second-chance and part-time study modes, including particularly in the UK the Open University and Birkbeck College, with inevitable damage to concepts of 'education for all' and widening participation beyond traditional post-school entry.

BTEC students are less likely to progress to higher-tariff universities and Russell Group institutions compared with those undertaking A levels. For example, in 2013, for every 100 A level students accepted into high-tariff institutions, three BTEC students were accepted. In lower-tariff institutions, the figure was 49 BTEC students for every 100 A level students (Universities and Colleges Admissions Service, 2014). These students tend to come from disadvantaged backgrounds and neighbourhoods with substantially less university participation, are more likely to be first-generation students who will have no family knowledge of studying at university, and are more likely to come from an ethnic minority background (Richards, 2016; Rouncefield-Swales, 2014). They have a higher non-retention rate in higher education than A level students, and non-completion rates are higher for those from the lower socio-economic groups. In 2012–2013, 68 per cent of BTEC entry students graduated, compared with 93 per cent of traditional A level entrants (Rouncefield-Swales, 2014).

Mature students are more likely to leave after year 1 of their degree than younger students and are twice as likely to drop out during their degree programme. The rates in 2013–2014 were 12 per cent for mature students and 6 per cent for young students (Higher Education Funding Council for England, 2016). Mature students are more likely to be commuter students (Thomas & Jones, 2017), which means they are less likely to be able to fully participate in extracurricular activities than students who can live on or near campus. In the UK, around 25 per cent of students currently remain in their family home, and this is set to rise in the UK to 50 per cent by 2020 (Pokorny, Holley & Kane, 2017). Students who through circumstance need to remain at home have less choice of university. This impacts on the subsequent diversity of many universities' intakes.

In the UK, following the Brexit referendum and with a government at the time of writing committed to radically reducing the number of immigrants coming to study in British higher education institutions (HEIs) (since student numbers are not omitted from immigration figures), there is huge uncertainty about the proportions of international students who can be recruited by HEIs, offering opportunities in Australasia and elsewhere to capitalise on the UK government's short-sightedness. Universities globally tend to rely on international student recruitment to cross-subsidise their programmes, and in particular to make niche Masters programmes viable, so the future in this area is highly unpredictable.

Trend 4: changes in perceptions about teaching and learning

Medieval models of university teaching typically comprised a lecturer relying on a text (sometimes chained to the lectern) from which he read/dictated, with students transcribing/making notes, the principal objective being to transmit knowledge from an acknowledged source to the students behaving in the mode of (relatively) passive recipients (and indeed such approaches are not unknown in twenty-first-century universities in many nations). When photocopying (and later electronic transmission) superseded the need for note-taking as a form of replication, many started to question the transmission mode of teaching, and some moved to more interactive approaches, including a reversion to Socratic modes of learning through discursive dialogue and active problem-solving.

Maieutic models of learning (Brown, 2015), whereby curriculum *delivery* is seen as being undertaken by facilitators (acting more like a midwife than a postman) who can help, advise and intervene when things go wrong, with only the labouring student able to bring forth learning, have become more common. However, there has sometimes been a gap between student and academic expectations about what learning actually involves. Many academics talk nowadays of learning being a partnership activity (e.g. Bryson, 2016) involving co-construction of learning, but service-orientated students often want something a little more packaged and readily consumable, with more of the work done for them (e.g. an accessible set of notes on a topic).

But there are significant changes in the way in which both academics and students regard knowledge: with ready access to factual content, opinion and data via the internet, learning material off by heart seems much less relevant than being able to locate, quickly scrutinise, quality-assure and prioritise information that might be useful in tackling problems. In subject areas where content rapidly becomes out of date, memorising and mimesis is much less important than evaluation and analysis. A core problematic area for students transitioning into higher education from learning contexts (like many schools) where they are fed predigested gobbets of information for regurgitation in exams is learning how to develop and use autonomous academic skills and sound academic conduct.

Arguments rage about the extent to which plagiarism is growing in an age when it is more readily doable than in former times (for an informed response, see Carroll, 2009), but it remains the case that for some students, *ownership* of knowledge is as alien a concept as *ownership* of music, images or news, since all are freely available electronically. For some entering higher education, discussions about acknowledging sources and using accurate referencing seem ridiculously old-school, and this can be problematic.

Trend 5: changing expectations of the skill sets students have on entry to university, need during their study, and must evidence on graduation

It is unhelpful to assume that students arrive at university fully prepared to make the most of their studies, to be autonomous learners, work as partners with peers, think critically, work through setbacks, and make the most of explicit as well as implicit learning opportunities. While academics can make some baseline assumptions about prior levels of achievement, language capability and the ability to work to targets, students' relative abilities are likely to be hugely variable depending on whether they have:

- come straight from school or have industrial, professional or other experience;
- followed academic or vocational pathways (such as BTEC);
- studied a narrow range of subjects (such as UK A levels, where students are likely to have specialised in three subjects) or a broader foundation programme;
- studied domestically or abroad;
- had experience of self-directed study or largely had their learning pathways closely managed; and
- experienced a relatively small range of assessment methods such as exams, essays and multiple choice questions, or whether they have experienced more diverse approaches such as portfolios, group assignments and reflective diaries.

Capabilities, sometimes termed 'literacies', that enable students to get the most from university include academic literacy, information and digital literacies, assessment literacy, and social and interpersonal literacies, which together are necessary to help students achieve their best (Brown, 2015: 88–105). Students are expected to understand complex university organisational structures and navigate university systems, including virtual learning environments, a range of search engines, databases and information management systems, presentation and word processing systems, as well as getting on top of content knowledge in the subject(s) they have chosen to study. It can be immensely challenging for some to find their way around vast and sometimes multisite campuses, negotiating complex school and faculty structures and learning what teams such as Registry, Residential Services, Information Services, Quality Management, Student Support, Learning Development and others can do to support their learning journeys, especially where, as is sometimes the case, such knowledge is siloed and closely defended.

Assessment literacy implies not just understanding terminology such as criteria, weighting, peer assessment, deferrals, condonements, interlocation and aegrotat degrees, but also developing the capacity to develop their own internalised set of standards and to monitor and supervise their own learning: "Students are able to realise complex and sophisticated outcomes when they have the opportunities to learn about, internalise and apply the relevant standards. This can be achieved through observation, modelling, discussion, reflection and practice" (Higher Education Academy, 2012: 22). Students who understand how assessment works and can use feedback to continuously improve their performance tend to perform better than students for whom it is all a mystery.

The kinds of skills we expect graduates to demonstrate entering employment vary from subject to subject, but some generic skills are frequently described as graduate capabilities ('know-how' as well as 'knowledge of'; Hart, Bowden & Watters, 1999). For example, Kember and Leung (2005) identify these as critical thinking, creative thinking, the ability to pursue lifelong learning, adaptability, problem-solving, career relevance, discipline knowledge, communication skills and interpersonal skills. Others might include reflection, resilience and self-belief, and those described by Franiel (cited in Matthews, 2017; trend 2).

The implications for those concerned about transition in, through and beyond university is that we need to ask ourselves what we are doing to foster, enhance and recognise the skills that will help those we teach to be successful students, as employees and as citizens, and this has substantial implications for curriculum design, and particularly assessment. We need to use authentic assessment approaches that, for example, require students to be able to "investigate realistic or ill-structured problems, identifying potential solutions and opportunities within them . . . develop strategic thinking in response to problem solving and management . . . working within constraints . . . applying their academic learning to designing and delivering solutions" (Brown, 2016).

International students in transition

International students often have expectations as varied as the many nations from which they originate, so generalisation and blanket advice needs to be treated cautiously. The best source of information about students' expectations and needs is usually the students themselves, but there are some pedagogic discontinuities around approaches to teaching and learning, which the next section attempts to unravel.

Perceptions about *how students are expected to learn at university* is variable: in some nations, accurately demonstrating the learning by heart of tutor-delivered content is most highly prized, whereas elsewhere use of that information in context is the prime expectation. As Beetham (2010) proposes:

> When the focus is on accuracy of reproduction, learners will be given opportunities to practise the required concept or skill until they can reproduce it exactly as taught. When the focus is on internalisation, learners will be given opportunities to integrate a concept or skill with their existing beliefs and capabilities, to reflect on what it means to them, and to make sense of it in a variety of ways.
>
> (p. 33)

Interpersonal issues can be problematic too. For some students, *argument and debate* may be unfamiliar and profoundly uncomfortable if they are used to contexts where consensus is key, and indeed asking them to take a personal (and perhaps controversial) position on an issue can be very frightening if their home nation is one where dissent is highly unpopular or dangerous. Students from countries where the collective voice is predominant, or there is a culture of non-verbalised debate and unspoken thought sometimes find Western classroom debates alienating. Expectations on whether a correct answer is sought can be highly variable (Ryan, 2000), and there can be issues around students who are not prepared to ask questions in class or seek support, for fear of 'losing face', or causing the teacher to 'lose face', so requests for them to do so can result in silence, then follow-ups outside class time.

Levels of formality can vary, for example, in how lecturers dress and how they expect to be addressed ('Sally' or 'Professor Brown'?) (Carroll & Ryan, 2005). The differences in status gap (e.g. as shown by physical position) between students and tutors from nation to nation can be disconcerting for students in new environments.

Levels of student support available or considered appropriate vary from nation to nation, with students expecting almost parental levels of commitment in some nations (expecting perhaps detailed advice on pre-submission drafts), while others are sometimes surprised that any help is given at all beyond lectures.

Methodologies and approaches to assessment vary considerably from nation to nation (Sambell, Brown & Graham, 2017): in Northern Europe/Scandinavia, there is wider use of oral exams than in many other nations, and there are substantial variations in the amount of computer-supported assessment across nations.

For some students from nations where 1,000-word assignments are required, or where computer-based multiple-choice questions are the norm, being expected to write 3,000- to 5,000-word assignments comprising continuous prose can be an unwelcome shock. Encountering group or peer assessment for the first time can be alienating for students who cannot conceive how their peers can contribute in any way to their learning, which is why it is important that induction activities include risk-free rehearsals, with opportunities for discussion and clarification of requirements.

Students entering higher education from a different country can be completely thrown by the assessment discourse in use, for example around marks necessary to pass an exam or assignment, which are by no means standardised (anywhere from 35 to 80 per cent is not unusual, and some programmes require 100 per cent correct solutions). The expected word count of assignments and duration of exams is highly variable, and successful transition into a new nation's assessment culture requires clarification of such issues at an early stage.

Similarly, it may be necessary to induct students into your local practices in terms of *feedback*:

- What is the purpose of feedback (corrections, comments on effort, advice for improvement, pointers towards helpful resources)?
- How much help can they expect (just ticks, or detailed and extensive developmental comments)?

- What are they expected to do with it?
- How will it be delivered (oral, written, in person, face-to-face)?
- Who can they talk to about it (it is worth noting that this isn't an issue that applies to international students alone)?

If we are effectively to support student transitions, particularly at entry, it is well then to challenge easy assumptions that staff and students can make, and instead work with sound information to shape our practices. The next section looks at some erroneous assumptions and some of the implications for positive transition contained within them.

Avoid making assumptions

Five assumptions it is easy for university staff to make

1 All students nowadays are fully comfortable using digital technologies

We assume that students have highly developed competencies in using computers and personal devices. However, many of our cohorts include mature students who may not have had regular access to technological support and training, students from nations where technology is advanced but regular access is restricted by the discontinuous supply of electricity, students who don't own expensive kit as they are financially constrained, and students who have disabilities that impair their abilities to use technologies fully. *Implications*: We can't assume that all students will be comfortable with using all the technologies that are integral to our programmes.

2 Students all tend to be looking for the easiest way to get through their studies

While some students are focused on what Entwistle (1998) and others call strategic approaches to learning, others have a genuine love of the subjects they study and are interested in going beyond the basic requirements to achieve well in assessment tasks, to achieve deeper understanding of their chosen disciplines. *Implications*: It really helps to clarify for students what we typically expect from them in terms of workload and study behaviours.

3 Students are out to cheat and plagiarise as much as they can

Carroll (2009) argues that any university that claims to have negligible plagiarism is deluding itself, but that there are strategies we can adopt that can ensure that it is held in check, including importantly making the 'rules of the game' known to students and building a community of learning in which plagiarism is not seen by students as acceptable. *Implications*: Programme leaders need to include clarification of what plagiarism comprises within induction and reinduction, and why it is poor academic conduct, as well as explaining the processes by which universities track it and what sanctions are used when it is discovered.

4 Students will read all the feedback we give them on assignments avidly in the expectation that it will help them to improve their next piece of work

This is certainly not the case unless we make strenuous efforts to help students recognise that the prime function of assessment is to help them improve on future performance (Gibbs & Simpson, 2005). *Implications*: Programme leaders and assessors need to build information about how feedback will be given into early assignment briefings and enable practice in reading and interpreting feedback.

5 Students are waiting with bated breath to listen to every word you have to share with them in your lectures/labs/seminars and other contact sessions

Students have many competing calls on their time, including part-time work, domestic commitments and activities that maintain their wellbeing, including sport and exercise. As 'customers', they may expect backup resources to be provided routinely for those who don't or can't make it to taught sessions. *Implications*: While it is good practice to provide support resources, we must open dialogues with students about how these will be provided, how they should be used before and after classes, and how important it is that they become part of a cohort, in class or virtually, to build a learning community.

Five assumptions it is easy for students to make erroneously

1 The induction period is a time to make merry/stay at home

Many of the induction activities we carefully plan to help students orientate themselves towards productive study can be lost on students who see this period as time to have lots of parties or to save the bus fare by not coming in for sessions. If freshers' weeks are badly organised or badged inappropriately, students would be justified in having either of these views. *Implications*: It is important that we design induction to be a purposeful series of activities, not just an event, and that we consider the diversity of students experiencing induction. For example, for some students re-entering higher education after a break from study due to family circumstances, ill health, mental health episodes or other reasons, we need to recognise that we need to use sensitivity in our approaches.

2 Everyone is cleverer than me here

If a student has been among the brightest in their class/school before they attend university, it can be a huge shock to encounter lots of peers who are of equal or greater intelligence than them, and it may take a while for this enhanced peer pressure to feel comfortable. *Implications*: Students may find their self-efficacy is not as robust as they might have thought (see Dweck, 2000), and may need support in recognising what they can do, what they can't do, and how to seek the kind of help they might need.

3 It's only me who is making heavy weather of this; everyone else is settling in

It's easy to assume that the air of confidence that others exude is genuine, but actually most students take a while to accommodate to the changed environment of university study, especially if they have had lots of personal support at school/college, or if they have been out of education for a while and have rusty study strategies. *Implications*: No one wants to be marked out as someone who needs 'equalisation support', so it's important that help with developing academic literacies is mainstreamed rather than being seen as targeted only at the people who are struggling.

4 Attending the timetabled sessions and doing the course assignments is all I have to do at university; the rest of the time is my own

In the UK, as in many other nations, we are struggling with what 'teaching intensity' means, since politicians and others are questioning what value for money is provided by courses with little attendance requirements. These are sometimes seen as soft options by students, whereas a course that maybe has no more than eight hours' required attendance may expect that students read half a dozen lengthy volumes a week or do three times as many hours of independent study. *Implications*: It's important to clarify what our expectations are in regard to attendance and engagement if students are to achieve the best they can. Some universities provide videos of a previous generation of students talking about what they wished they had known before they started study. Hearing messages from students about how important time management is, roughly how many hours a week successful students commit to independent work, how important it is to pace workload rather than leave everything to the last minute, and how invaluable the face-to-face live or virtual cohort wide sessions are can be much more effective than hearing them from academic staff.

5 All I have to do to achieve highly in assignments is to listen well in lectures, take good notes, learn it all off by heart, and repeat it in exams and essays

Students who have used such an approach need to know that this is never likely to be sufficient for high achievement, since higher education study implies much more in the way of critical thinking and thoughtful analysis for excellent outcomes, together with independence of thought on many programmes.

Implications: As educators, we must ensure that our curriculum design is fit for purpose and our assessment is authentic, so that students are left in no doubt that mere memorisation and regurgitation is not enough. If, for example, we persist in using assessment only through time-constrained unseen exams, students could be forgiven for persisting in their misapprehensions.

These kinds of illusions can be quite widely held, so it's therefore really important that erroneous assumptions by students and those who teach/support them are dispelled.

A way forward

Identifying student support needs is easiest to achieve in contexts where the staff and students work well together to provide a nurturing learning community for students right at the start of their academic lives, and this will be discussed in Chapter 4. The trends and commonly held beliefs already highlighted demonstrate a complex change agenda that involves not just induction and transition support, but a broader approach to changing curriculum design, delivery and assessment that includes all aspects of a higher education environment. This cannot be achieved by fiat or dictat, instead relying on advocacy based on evidenced/informed scholarly practice (Brown, 2011). Good leadership from the upper echelons of a university on the implementation of a sensible and rational change initiative is necessary but insufficient on its own; to effect change requires take-up by those charged with implementation on the ground. Inter alia course leaders, personal tutors, classroom and virtual teachers, learning support staff, placement supervisors, technicians, IT staff, administrators, quality assurance and enhancement colleagues, and staff such as car park supervisors and cleaners can all have an impact on struggling students.

Similarly, if managers want high take-up of a plan for change, evidence-based practice is vital in convincing staff of the need for change (see Chapter 9); for example, how good feedback can improve students' achievement levels (Nicol & Macfarlane-Dick, 2006) and the importance of induction in promoting retention and success (Thomas, 2012).

Conclusions

We have myriad reasons for wanting students to succeed, including ensuring the high reputation of our institutions and programmes, the uses made of associated metrics in quality judgments in many nations, and financial imperatives to support retention, but more important than these is our moral duty to do the best we can by students transitioning into, through and beyond university. At its best, higher education can be positively transformative and life-enhancing for our alumni, and soul-destroying for those who fail or underperform. Paying attention to transition through the stages is critical to student success.

References

Beetham, H. (2010) Active learning in technology-rich contexts. In: Beetham, H. & Sharpe, R. (eds.), *Rethinking pedagogy for a digital age: designing for 21st century learning.* 3rd ed. London, Routledge, pp. 31–48.

Bowl, M. (2003) *Non-traditional entrants to higher education: "They talk about people like me".* Herndon, VA, Stylus.

Brown, S. (2011) Bringing about positive change in higher education: a case study. *Quality Assurance in Education,* 19(3), 195–207.

Brown, S. (2015) *Learning, teaching and assessment in higher education: global perspectives.* London, Palgrave.

Brown, S. (2016) *Twenty-first century assessment in higher education.* [Presentation] Enterprise Academy, University of Sheffield, 28 April. Available from: www.sheffield.ac.uk/polopoly_fs/1.573576!/file/Sally_Brown_slides.pptx [Accessed 4 January 2018].

Bryson, C. (2016) Engagement through partnership: students as partners in learning and teaching in higher education. *International Journal for Academic Development,* 21(1), 84–86.

Callender, C. & Jackson, J. (2008) Does the fear of debt constrain choice of university and subject of study? *Studies in Higher Education,* 33(4), 405–429. Available from: http://dx.doi.org/10.1080/03075070802211802.

Carroll, J. (2009) Plagiarism as a threat to learning: an educational response. In: Joughin, G. (ed.), *Assessment, learning and judgement in higher education.* Dordrecht, Springer, pp. 1–17.

Carroll, J. & Ryan, J. (2005) *Teaching international students: improving learning for all.* London, Routledge.

Department for Education and Skills (2003) *The future of higher education CM5735.* London, The Stationery Office.

Dweck, C.S. (2000) *Self theories: their role in motivation, personality and development.* Lillington, NC, Taylor & Francis.

Entwistle, N. (1988) Motivational factors in students' approaches to learning. In: Schmeck, R.R. (ed.), *Learning strategies and learning styles.* New York, Springer, pp. 21–51.

Gibbs, G. & Simpson, C. (2005) Conditions under which assessment supports students' learning. *Learning and Teaching in Higher Education,* 1, 3–31.

Hart, G., Bowden, J. & Watters, J. (1999) Graduate capabilities: a framework for assessing course quality. *Higher Education in Europe,* 24(2), 301–308.

Higher Education Academy (2012) *A marked improvement: transforming assessment in higher education.* York, Higher Education Academy. Available from: www.heacademy.ac.uk/system/files/a_marked_improvement.pdf [Accessed 18 September 2017].

Higher Education Funding Council for England (2016) *Higher education in England 2016: key facts.* Higher Education Funding Council for England.

Higher Education Statistics Agency (2017) *Changes in undergraduate student numbers between 2008/09 and 2015/16.* Available from: www.hesa.ac.uk/news/07-08-2017/undergraduate-student-numbers [Accessed 18 September 2017].

Kember, D. & Leung, D.Y. (2005) The influence of active learning experiences on the development of graduate capabilities. *Studies in Higher Education,* 30(2), 155–170.

Matthews, D. (2017) Do critical thinking skills give graduates the edge? *Times Higher Education,* 3–9 August, p. 34.

Morris, M. & Golden, S. (2005) *Evaluation of Aimhigher: excellence challenge interim report*. Department for Education and Skills. Research report number 648.

Nicol, D.J. & Macfarlane-Dick, D. (2006) Formative assessment and self-regulated learning: a model and seven principles of good feedback practice. *Studies in Higher Education*, 31(2), 199–218.

Pokorny, H., Holley, D. & Kane, S. (2017) Commuting, transitions and belonging: the experience of students living at home in their first year at university. *High Education*, 74(3), 543–548.

Richards, B. (2016) *Passports to progress: how do vocational qualifications help young people in building their careers? Part one*. London, Social Market Foundation.

Rouncefield-Swales, A. (2014) *Vocational progression to selecting universities: comparisons and trends 2010–13*. Bath, Western Vocational Progression Consortium.

Ryan, J. (2000) *A guide to teaching international students*. Oxford, Oxford Centre for Staff and Learning Development.

Sambell, K., Brown, S. & Graham, L. (2017) *Professionalism in practice: key directions in higher education learning, teaching and assessment*. London, Palgrave Macmillan.

Thomas, L. (2012) *Building student engagement and belonging in higher education at a time of change: a summary of findings and recommendations from the What Works? student retention & success programme*. Available from: www.heacademy.ac.uk/knowledge-hub/building-student-engagement-and-belonging-higher-education-time-change-summary [Accessed 19 September 2017].

Thomas, L. & Jones, R. (2017) *Student engagement in the context of commuter students*. London, Student Engagement Partnership.

Universities and Colleges Admissions Service (2014) *UCAS response to the Ofqual consultation on new A level regulatory requirements*. Universities and Colleges Admissions Service.

Chapter 3

Developing belonging, community and creating professional identity

Ruth Matheson and Mark Sutcliffe

Introduction to the chapter

Gale and Parker (2014), in their typology of student transition in higher education, identify three main conceptions of student transition: transition as induction, transition as development and transition as becoming. Central to this *becoming* is the development of an individual professional and personal identity. This chapter will explore the importance of developing a higher education community, underpinned by trust and belonging that enables transition in, through and out of university towards *becoming*. It will also highlight how embedding flexible pedagogies into curriculum design can promote the development of community, break down social and cultural barriers, and enable students to be ready for a complex and changing world.

Lizzio (2006) identifies five key 'senses' to support successful student transition, challenging higher education programme designers to consider how the curriculum and learning environment facilitate students' development through the student lifecycle. These five senses of success he categorises as a sense of capability, a sense of connectedness, a sense of purpose, a sense of resourcefulness and a sense of academic culture. Throughout the book, we will make reference to these senses. The design of our curriculum needs to facilitate the development of these senses, recognising that one size does not fit all. This demands creativity in the choice of our teaching activities, and in the learning environment that we create, and to be mindful of difference in our interactions with students. The culture and values that we create within the classroom and within our institutions are central to the development of these senses, and ultimately the development of a self and professional identity. This chapter will focus primarily on the "sense of connectedness" (Lizzio, 2006: 2) and the importance of student–student relationships, student–staff relationships, and how students identify themselves and develop the sense of belonging to their course and institution.

Thomas (2012), reporting on the findings of seven projects looking at retention and success, ascertains that having a strong sense of belonging is crucial to student engagement and success. Her findings also indicate that mainstream activities that have an overt academic purpose and involve all students are the best means of nurturing this belonging.

Belonging

So why is it so important to feel that we belong? First, belonging is an important part of identity. As early as 1943, Maslow identified the importance of belonging in his hierarchy of needs, with only physiological needs (such as food and water) and safety needs being more important. He maintained that people are only able to achieve their full potential once these basic needs have been met. Hagerty et al. (1996) define a sense of belonging as "the experience of personal involvement in a system or environment so that persons feel themselves to be an integral part of the system or environment" (p. 236). According to Baumeister and Leary (1995), such a feeling reflects a basic human instinct, one in which we wish to form and maintain social bonds and be part of something. As such, belonging is significant as it extends to shape our identity, helping to establish important norms and values. As May (2011) states:

> belonging plays a role in connecting individuals to the social. This is important because our sense of self is constructed in a relational process in our interactions with other people as well as in relation to more abstract notions of collectively held social norms, values and customs.
>
> (p. 368)

Belonging also connects with retention and success. Believing they belong on a programme of study is crucial to shaping students' subsequent success on that programme. Meeuwisse, Severiens and Born (2009), in their empirical study of 523 students from across four Dutch higher education institutions, found that "if students feel that they do not fit in, that their social and cultural practices are inappropriate [do not belong], and that their tacit knowledge is undervalued, they may be more inclined to withdraw early" (p. 531). Not only is a lack of belonging linked to withdrawal, but clear links have been made between the extent to which students feel that they belong and their academic self-concept (Ostove, Stewart & Curtin, 2011). Having a strong academic self-concept in turn impacts on the way in which students perceive their own level of competence, and their subsequent commitment to an academic career.

Belonging is also lifelong. The need and ability to develop belonging is important throughout a student's transition within university. However, May (2011) also points out that this ability to achieve belonging is a key skill that students need to be able to master as they negotiate different relationships and environments throughout their lives. How the curriculum and learning environment is structured and organised, and how content is delivered, will greatly shape whether feelings of belonging are generated. The degree to which students feel that they are "personally accepted, respected, included by others" (Goodenow, 1993: 80) plays a large part in determining how connected they feel and whether they feel they belong.

Thomas (2012) identifies four approaches that nurture belonging:

- supportive peer relationships;
- meaningful interaction between staff and students;
- developing knowledge, confidence and identity as successful HE learners; and
- an HE experience relevant to students' interests and future goals.

(p. 7)

To enable these meaningful interactions, there is a need for students to have trust in both staff and fellow students.

The need for trust

Burke et al. (2016) promote the idea that students "feel best in a supportive pedagogical environment in which trust is established" (p. 47). Trust involves a willingness to be vulnerable, where individuals are prepared to take risk, with an understanding that the environment and those around them will ensure their safety. These safety needs, per Maslow (1943), underpin the development of belonging. Therefore, it can be argued that without the development of trust between students, staff and the robustness of institutional processes, it is impossible for belonging to be achieved. Both trust and belonging are dynamic concepts that are constantly changing, being neither fixed nor a given, and are often context-specific. A study by the University of Newcastle, Australia, looking at capability, belonging and equity in university, revealed that many students experienced intensive forms of anxiety throughout their transition into and through university, which Burke et al. (2016) recognised as "connected to their sense of (in)capability and the anxieties attached to being assessed, judged and perceived as incapable by their teachers" (p. 49). Many of these feelings originated from prior educational experiences where they had been shamed. This was particularly the case for students coming to higher education from non-traditional educational backgrounds or entering as first-generation students. Macfarlane (2009) describes the choice to come to university as a "leap of faith," with students trusting that they will benefit from the experience and that it will lead to greater achievements in life (p. 221).

In attempting to define trust, McKnight and Chervany (2001), as cited by Macfarlane (2009), identified four high-level categories of trust:

- benevolence – caring and acting in the interest of others;
- integrity – being honest, truthful and keeping promises;
- competence – able to perform a role; and
- predictability – acting consistently.

(p. 227)

While there has been extensive research on the importance of establishing integration among students, there is a paucity of literature on the ethics of student–teacher relationships in higher education teaching, and yet this is fundamental to good teaching (Macfarlane, 2009). Macfarlane (2009) suggests that qualities such as reliability, responsiveness, assurance and empathy are closely linked to the "personal relationships between the student and the teacher" (p. 224). However, he also recognises that the dual role of teaching and assessment places different power ratios than those previously experienced by most students in elementary school relationships. There is some disagreement in the literature regarding benevolence in terms of student–teacher relationships, with questions being raised as to the nature of the caring and how this relates to the concept of independence (Hagenauer & Volet, 2014). However, the provision of a safe environment, where mutual respect, support and connectedness is fostered, has been found to promote intrinsic motivation, engagement and learning (Fitzmaurice, 2008; Komarraju, Musulkin & Bhattacharya, 2010). This connectedness to both staff and students is closely linked to feelings of belonging.

Macfarlane (2009) also highlights how trust can be undermined by the introduction of innovative teaching and learning methods as this impacts on the predictability of the student experience, with students expressing a preference for conventional methods. This poses challenges and uncertainties for the tutor trying to employ a constructivist approach in an age of consumerism and student satisfaction surveys that underpin university rankings (see Chapter 2). Expectations need to be clear from the outset and a constructivist methodology employed from day 1 to ensure that students know what to expect. This integrity in exposing what is to come and the expectations of higher education inform the design of active induction programmes that place the student at the centre of their learning. Devlin and O'Shea (2012) found that tutors were rated positively when they set high expectations, offering support but not 'coddling' students.

As we can see, trust is a complex, dynamic, shifting concept, resulting from an interplay between values, attitudes, moods and emotions (Jones & George, 1998). Fundamental to the development of trust between students, and between students and tutors, is the students' confidence in the benevolence, integrity, competence and predictability of tutors and fellow students. When these are brought into question, trust erodes, impacting on learning and both social and academic integration. When unconditional trust exists, social relations are likely to extend beyond the formal setting, where students now come to see each other as colleagues and friends. This promotes fundamental changes in relationships between group members, allowing for self-sacrifice (belonging), cooperation (collective learning) and investment in the group's relationship for the future (social capital).

Developing social capital

Pierre Bourdieu, following a systematic analysis of social capital defines the concept of social capital as "the aggregate of the actual or potential resources which are linked to possession of a durable network of more or less institutionalized relationships of mutual acquaintance or recognition" (Bourdieu, 1985: 248). Recognising the benefits of group participation and social networks to individuals, he promotes the idea that through the deliberate construction of sociability, both group cohesion and resource can be created. These social networks are not guaranteed purely through the generation of group participation, but need to be constructed, group relations promoted and embedded, and the benefits to learning realised by students. These benefits can be both social (in gaining a sense of belonging) but also give access to resources from the group members. Social capital is built through both the formal and informal interactions, and can be created both within and outside of the formal curricula.

Nahapiet and Ghoshal (1998) highlight two consequences of social capital: first, it improves the efficiency of action, with information being more easily shared within the network, and with enhanced trust there is a reduced need to monitor this process; second, social capital has been found to encourage creativity, stimulating cooperative behaviour and the development of new forms of association. Therefore, the benefits of creating and developing positive social capital among students is clearly aligned with the development of team-working and networking skills. The generation of opportunities to develop these social networks throughout the student lifecycle, even prior to arrival, is vital to both the creation of belonging (and retention) and for the development of capabilities in networking, so is important in promoting employability.

Belonging through the student lifecycle

Pre-arrival

As previously mentioned, coming to university is a 'leap of faith'; students make a decision based on trust that university will be of benefit to them and their future career prospects. However, Macfarlane (2009) highlights that there is often a gap between the students' "expectations of a university education and their perception of the reality" (p. 224). This gap often centres on the expectation that students will be independent learners, and on staff–student relations and the amount of support given (see Chapter 2).

Induction should begin before the student arrives at university, providing students with opportunities to identify with their new role and the choices that they have made. Lizzio (2011) identifies that students prior to reaching university are starting to gain a "sense of potential student identity," with question such as "how will I fit? what am I able to do? what will this take? what do I want to do?" (p. 8). Therefore, pre-arrival activities need to focus on the creation of this sense of potential identity and belonging. During this stage, it is important to provide students with the opportunity to connect with the university, the course and fellow students. Social media provides an ideal platform for connecting students, enabling connections and friendships to be established prior to face-to-face meeting. Madge et al. (2009) found that students used Facebook to bridge the gap between the old and new, with three main features: to keep in touch with old friends and family, for planning social events and joining university groups, and finally to make social links with others at university.

Students are leaving familiar, safe situations to enter a new world, and often need help in thinking about this transition. Pre-entry activities that encourage a sense of belonging with the chosen course and promote ideas of future aspirations enable students to shift their thinking from the present to look towards future possibilities. For example, documenting their transition through digital stories that capture their preparation for university can enable students to start saying their goodbyes to friendship groups and home, collecting newspaper articles that capture their imagination and are related to their chosen course can aid a sense of belonging to the student's subject area, and if used as early course content can enhance their perception of how their opinion and voice will be valued in this new educational environment. Pre-arrival information that promotes engagement and enables students to identify themselves as students at this early stage is vital in setting the university's values and expectations.

Induction that values belonging

There has been a vast amount of research into student retention, and yet substantial gains are hard to come by, with difficulties remaining in translating what we know with regard to the theory and converting this into practice that makes a difference (Tinto, 2006). What we do know is that student withdrawal has been closely linked to students who encounter poor-quality learning, have little in-class interaction, and who have little opportunity to make friends (Yorke & Longden, 2008). Opportunities for interaction and integration between students and staff are critical in the undergraduate first year (Tinto, 2006; Sheader & Richardson, 2006).

Recent research with postgraduate students showed similar findings (Matheson & Sutcliffe, 2017), echoing the findings of Tobbell, O'Donnell and Zammit (2008). At this early stage, the promotion of both curricular and extracurricular activities that seek to embrace both academic and social dimensions is crucial to promoting the successful movement of the student into higher education and establishing early belonging. Students need to be given the opportunity to make friends, come to terms with the expectations of university, and begin to reshape their self-identity. The importance of establishing trust and building openness and collaboration from day 1 is critical, giving students the opportunity to identify their starting point, motivations and expectations. It is the sharing of these insights that offers opportunities to develop early group coherence. As our own research revealed (Matheson & Sutcliffe, 2016), motivations, hopes, fears and aspirations were found to be broadly similar, irrespective of cultural difference, and students came to recognise that they were not alone or unique, but rather that any trepidation or uncertainty was a collective feeling. Establishing such collective feelings and commonality is vital in shaping more general notions of belonging, and the wider notion of a community of practice.

Induction programmes need to encourage engagement, promote social interaction, support active participation, and explore the individual and group identity of the students (Wilcox, Winn & Fyvie-Gauld, 2005). Experiential activities are particularly useful as they require students to bring prior knowledge to the learning environment and integrate this with new knowledge gained to develop a fresh understanding (Beard, 2010). Activities that value the sharing of different cultural, educational and social backgrounds serve to widen student understanding, promoting opportunities to develop global citizenship. Within this book, there are numerous case studies that encourage students to share and learn from each other.

Staff need to be mindful of the needs of different students. Students with English as a second language may struggle in group activities or when making initial social contact. Activities that remove the need for language could be used to enable students to negotiate this barrier. Time and space for reflection, the opportunity to share experiences, group-based learning, and peer and tutor feedback can all assist in the promotion of social integration and the development of belonging (Matheson & Sutcliffe, 2017). Careful consideration of induction programmes should form a crucial part of curriculum design, and should capture the diversity of education experience, academic requirements and cultural differences of the student group. Induction programmes provide a rich opportunity for students to experience meaningful interaction, in which belonging and trust can be established within the student group and the individual student can be encouraged to reflect and enhance their understanding of self.

From our own research and the research of others, what has become clear is that transition and the creation of belonging does not end at induction, but continues and changes beyond induction, building on early success. Lizzio (2011) defines this as developing a "sense of positive student identity," with students now asking "who do I know? what skills do I have? what needs to be managed? what are my future pathways?" (p. 8).

Transition through, towards, out: enabling belonging, engagement, partnership and identity formation

Induction is just the beginning of the student journey and their engagement with learning, peers and the institution. The importance of belonging remains central to the student experience, characterised by the perceived stability of ongoing interpersonal relationships, regular contact with staff and fellow students, and knowing that they are part of a learning and social community (Baumeister & Leary, 1995). Alongside this connectedness within the institution, Lizzio (2011) highlights the need to make connections with the wider community to enable students to develop a "sense of positive graduate identity" and ultimately a "sense of positive professional identity" (p. 8). This, he says, requires curricular and co-curricular activities that are consistent and reinforce student engagement and partnership. From our research on transition with postgraduate students from 20 different countries (Matheson & Sutcliffe, 2017), the themes to emerge aligned closely with Ryan and Tilbury's (2013) Flexible Pedagogies Framework. Outlined below is how this framework can provide a scaffold for building curricula to aid transition through and out of university by developing belonging, valuing community and promoting the development of self. Like a wheel, learner empowerment provides the hub of the framework from which the spokes of the framework emerge. These spokes they identify as future-facing education, decolonising education, transforming capabilities, crossing boundaries and social learning.

Learner empowerment

We have seen the importance of student–teacher relationships earlier in the chapter, and the nature of these relationships for building trust and belonging. Central to learner empowerment is the development of knowledge, confidence and identity as successful higher education learners (Thomas, 2012). This may require an early focus on the development of academic skills and a sense of capability (Lizzio, 2011). Indeed, Tobbell, O'Donnell and Zammit (2008) highlight the common misconception that postgraduate students enter higher education as *experts*, having the academic capabilities required for both written and verbal academic engagement. Students, at all levels, need to be empowered to succeed, and this often requires the ongoing development and support to develop academic skills and integrate these into their practice (see Chapter 6).

Learner empowerment challenges the traditional hierarchical relationship that exists between educator and learner by placing students in a more active role in taking ownership and becoming co-creators of their learning. This requires the development of a learning environment where students are encouraged to voice opinions, bring experience to the table, and share their values and beliefs. In pedagogies that promote learner empowerment, students become active researchers from the outset, engagement is often expressed as partnership, and student involvement shapes their learning environment. Curricula need to value and acknowledge this change in practice, providing activities that develop students' ways of thinking, independent research skills, and ability to voice their opinions while creating a safe learning environment to develop (see Chapter 7). For many students, especially those coming from non-Western educational backgrounds, this will demand a fundamental shift in behaviour and will require a lot of support. Generating a partnership with students where they feel empowered to contribute to their learning can be challenging for staff, as identified by Healey, Flint and Harrington (2014): "Partnership is essentially a process of engagement, not a product. It is a way of doing things, rather than an outcome in itself. All partnership is student engagement, but not all engagement is partnership" (p. 7). The motivations for entering into such partnerships differ. Staff and students occupy distinct organisational positions that delineate power, identity and responsibilities.

As such, partnerships are not free from difficulties and frequently require new ways of "being, doing and thinking" (Healey, Flint & Harrington, 2014: 9). However, if partnership in learning can be established, then learner empowerment can also be enhanced. These enhancements can include:

1 levels of engagement that enhance motivation and learning beyond that which might be expected;
2 a stronger sense of identity and self-awareness; and
3 the enhancement of the teaching and learning experience for both students and staff.

(Cook-Sather, Bovill & Felten, 2014: 97–132)

Future-facing education

Future-facing education promotes an education that enables "people to think critically and creatively and flexibly about future prospects, to generate alternative visions of future possibilities" (Ryan & Tilbury, 2013: 18). For students to fully participate in future-facing education, there needs to be a level of trust as they expose their ideas to fellow students and educators. This demands a learning environment where new ideas are welcome and students have the freedom to express these with increasing confidence (Matheson & Sutcliffe, 2017).

Lizzio (2011) refers to the nature of transition through university as 'stepping ahead', with students building their resourcefulness and capability to identify their sense of purpose for what lies ahead. This visioning of the future links to the development of students' capabilities to understand different perspectives, challenging social and cultural norms, enabling students to envisage alternative ways of doing and thinking (Tilbury, 2011; Tilbury & Wortman, 2004). For this to happen there needs to be curricula, assessment and teaching practices that enable students to develop these envisioning capabilities. Dunn et al. (2004) promote the use of assessment to encourage visioning, while recognising the high level of skill required and levels of discomfort that this may incur. If students are to move out of their comfort zone, there needs to be a learning environment that supports this. Group work can be used to reduce the pressure on individual students, allowing them to hear other perspectives, providing the opportunity to challenge and have their ideas challenged, leading to the development of collective solutions (Matheson & Sutcliffe, 2017).

Decolonising education

Through decolonising education, students have the opportunity to challenge singular world views and extend their intercultural understanding. With students coming from diverse educational and cultural backgrounds, educators have the ideal opportunity to partner with students to develop a curriculum that values difference, promotes globally sensitive frames and creates a more inclusive learning environment (Ryan & Tilbury, 2013), this in turn promoting a sense of belonging. Through partnership, student engagement is made more authentic with greater opportunities for transformational learning. Partnership in curriculum design and pedagogic consultancy enables the *student voice* to extend beyond the common course evaluation processes. Research has suggested that where this has taken place, it has significantly benefited both students and staff (Healey, Flint & Harrington, 2014).

Activities that allow students to articulate their own cultural backgrounds, expose different values and aspirations among societal or cultural groups, and promote cross-cultural informal socialising provide students with opportunities to deconstruct preconceived ideas. Both extracurricular activities and intra-curricular activities are important in decolonising perspectives. World food days, visual life road maps, sharing of aspirations, and exploring values and ethics all could contribute. Central to transformation, however, is the development of reflective practice and using this to understand 'the self' and others. Frequent opportunities for informal and formal formative feedback also contribute to this self-awareness.

Decolonising education may be more difficult in courses made up of a predominantly homogenous population; however, the use of interdisciplinary teaching, engagement with the wider community and internationalisation of the curriculum all serve to provide students with multiple world views and the sense of belonging to a global community.

Transformative capabilities

Transformative capabilities are important for the development of self (see Chapter 8); having confidence to engage and gain a sense of belonging in different environments enables the individual to act in it. Along with capability comes flexibility to adapt and apply knowledge and understanding to different situations (Ryan & Tilbury, 2013). This transformational learning approach builds on the work of Mezirow (2000). Experiential and active learning approaches underpin the development of these capabilities, demanding flexibility of thinking and application of new and old knowledge in new and challenging circumstances (Matheson & Sutcliffe, 2017). It is the acknowledgment of these transformative capabilities that serve to enable students to develop their own identity.

Crossing boundaries

Crossing boundaries promotes the idea that we need to develop attributes in our students that allow them to go beyond their disciplinary boundaries, work with other disciplines, and apply their knowledge and understanding to complex, real-world scenarios (Ryan & Tilbury, 2013). This involves students sharing perspectives, working in collaboration and developing the 'soft skills' that will enable them to work flexibly with complexity. By incorporating interdisciplinary education into the curriculum, students not only have the opportunity to define their professional identity, but see themselves as 'belonging' to a much wider academic community and real-world community. This is so important in the development of connection and identity (Lizzio, 2011). As students develop their graduate identity, they are looking towards stepping out to the world of work and belonging to a different environment with other ill-defined boundaries. Activities and assessments that require students to engage with employers or students from other programmes, or that highlight the blurred boundaries that exist between disciplines, can foster this cross-disciplinary learning and interaction.

Social learning

Social learning recognises that learning does not happen in isolation, and that both social and cultural contexts have an influence on learning. Social learning theory draws on the work of Vygotsky (1978), Bandura (1977) and Lave and Wenger (1991), among others, who all recognised the importance of the learning environment and the community that it creates. This social learning may be either formal or informal and form part of the formal curriculum (group work, café-style pedagogy, action learning sets or communities of practice) or be extracurricular (through interaction in societies, through Facebook or informal social gatherings).

One way of promoting social learning and in turn creating belonging is through communities of practice. Wenger and Snyder (2000) define a community of practice as a "group of people informally bound together by shared expertise and passion for a joint enterprise" (p. 139). Throughout our lives, we move into, through and out of such communities of practice, at times belonging to many such communities simultaneously. We might be a core member in some, while in others we might only exist on the periphery; "most communities of practice do not have a name and do not issue membership cards" (Wenger, 1998: 7). Through using communities of practice in a university setting, individuals learn how to fit in (belong) and begin to develop their professional self as they see how their contributions benefit the shared outcome.

Students are likely to be members of several communities: a programme of study, a module cohort, a task team, and outside of the more formal higher education communities a sports or social club. Because of this, teaching strategy should, as well as emphasising process and structure, also focus on how to enhance social engagement to these communities. This is addressed in Chapter 7.

The term learning community places a strong emphasis on the interaction between those designated as experts and those designated as learners. In promoting learning communities, educators (experts) are encouraged to forego the expert status and operate within the role of facilitator or mentor, reducing difference and encouraging the participation of all. A strong learning community is one that encourages participation and the sharing of information and ideas, promoting the development of new knowledge and its application. Belonging and trust are key to this process. Belonging and trust become even more crucial when interacting in an online environment. The online learning environment can act as an enabler, promoting participation across campuses, between universities, across nations and prompting new pedagogies (Watling, 2009), both within and outside of the formal curriculum. Learning communities, however, are not without their problems, and the development and maintenance of group relations should be part of the planning process. Groupthink may also be a problem, where ideas tend to converge, leading to uniformity and reduced levels of creativity impacting on outcomes. Such learning communities can be slow to change, being set in their ways and encumbered by tradition.

Transition towards positive professional identity and becoming

Lizzio (2011) refers to this final sense in his framework as a "sense of positive professional identity" (p. 8). Within this, students have a sense of citizenship and leadership (where do I stand?), a sense of proficiency (what is my expertise?), a sense of resilience (how well can I manage change and challenge?), and a sense of contribution and progression (what difference am I making?). During this time, he advocates that senior students, graduates, postgraduates and alumni should be enabled to "step up, out and back" (Lizzio, 2011: 10), through activities that develop capabilities, purposes, resources, connections and identity. Examples may include capstone projects, leadership opportunities, mentoring of others, networking opportunities, invitations to return and bring back industry experience, internships, and open-door registers to connect alumni and promote future opportunities. These activities serve to promote the development of the individual and their professional identity while reinforcing connections to the institution and maintaining belonging. The development of self will be explored further in Chapter 8.

In conclusion

As we have seen, creating belonging, community and professional identity is a complex process that demands curricular and extracurricular activities that lead to 'becoming'. The transitionary student lifecycle should promote active participation, student–educator interactions that value, respect and support students, the development of academic and social integration leading to resilience to enter the next stage, and the development of self.

The subsequent chapters in Part II provide more detailed examples of successful interventions/activities that will assist you in building these pedagogies into your practice.

References

Bandura, A. (1977) *Social learning theory*. New York, General Learning Press.

Baumeister, R.F. & Leary, M.R. (1995) The need to belong: desire for interpersonal attachments as a fundamental human motivation. *Psychological Bulletin*, 117(3), 497–529.

Beard, C. (2010) *The experiential toolkit: blending practice with concepts*. London, Kogan Page.

Bourdieu, P. (1985) The forms of capital. In: Richardson, J.G. (ed.), *Handbook of theory and research for the sociology of education*. New York, Greenwood, pp. 241–258.

Burke, P.J., Bennett, A.K., Burgess, C., Gray, K. & Southgate, E. (2016) *Capability, belonging and equity in higher education: developing inclusive approaches*. Curtin University, Perth, National Centre for Student Equity in Higher Education, pp. 47–49.

Cook-Sather, A., Bovill, C. & Felten, P. (2014). *Engaging students as partners in learning and teaching: a guide to faculty*. San Francisco, CA, Jossey-Bass.

Devlin, M. & O'Shea, H. (2012) Effective university teaching: views of Australian university students from low socio-economic status backgrounds. *Teaching in Higher Education*, 17(4), 385–397.

Dunn, L., O'Reilly, M., Parry, S. & Morgan, C. (2004) *The student assessment handbook: new directions in traditional and online assessment*. London, Routledge.

Fitzmaurice, M. (2008) Voices from within: teaching in higher education as a moral practice. *Teaching in Higher Education*, 13, 341–352.

Gale, T. & Parker, S. (2014) Navigating change: a typology of student transition in higher education. *Studies in Higher Education*, 39(5), 734–753.

Goodenow, C. (1993) The psychological sense of school membership among adolescents: scale development and educational correlates. *Psychology in the Schools*, 30(1), 70–90.

Hagenauer, G. & Volet, S.E. (2014) Teacher–student relationship at university: an important yet under-researched field. *Oxford Review of Education*, 40(3), 370–388.

Hagerty, B., Williams, R., Coyne, J.C. & Early, M. (1996) Sense of belonging and indicators of social and psychological functioning. *Archives of Psychiatric Nursing*, 10(4), 235–244.

Healey, M., Flint, A. & Harrington, K. (2014) *Engagement through partnership: students as partners in learning and teaching in higher education*. Available from: www.heacademy.ac.uk/engagement-through-partnership-students-partners-learning-and-teaching-higher-education [Accessed 30 August 2017].

Jones, G.R. & George, J.M. (1998) The experience and evolution of trust: implications for cooperation and teamwork. *Academy of Management Review*, 23(3), 531–546.

Komarraju, M., Musulkin, S. & Bhattacharya, G. (2010). Role of student–faculty interactions in developing college students' academic self-concept, motivation, and achievement. *Journal of College Student Development*, 51, 332–342.

Lave, J. & Wenger, E. (1991) *Situated learning: legitimate peripheral participation*. Cambridge, Cambridge University Press.

Lizzio, A. (2006) *Designing an orientation and transition strategy for commencing students: a conceptual summary of research and practice*. Available from: www.griffith.edu.au/__data/assets/pdf_file/0008/51875/Alfs-5-Senors-Paper-FYE-Project,-2006.pdf [Accessed 21 October 2017].

Lizzio, A. (2011) *The student lifecycle: an integrative framework for guiding practice*. Available from: www.griffith.edu.au/learning-teaching/student-success/first-year-experience/student-lifecycle-transition-orientation [Accessed 12 July 2017].

Macfarlane, B. (2009) A leap of faith: the role of trust in higher education teaching. *Nagoya Journal of Higher Education*, 9, 221–238.

Madge, C., Meek, J., Wellens, J. & Hooley, T. (2009) Facebook, social integration and informal learning at university: 'It is more for socialising and talking to friends about work that for actually doing work'. *Learning, Media and Technology*, 43(2), 141–155.

Maslow, A. (1943) A theory of human motivation. *Psychological Review*, 50, 370–396.

Matheson, R. & Sutcliffe, M. (2016) Creating belonging and transformation through the adoption of flexible pedagogies in Masters level international business management students. *Teaching in Higher Education*, 22(1), 15–29. Available from: http://dx.doi.org/10.1080/13562517.2016.1221807.

Matheson, R. & Sutcliffe, M. (2017) Belonging and transition: an exploration of international business students' postgraduate experience. *Innovations in Education and Teaching International*, 1–9. Available from: http://dx.doi.org/10.1080/14703297.2017.1279558.

May, V. (2011) Self, belonging and social change. *Sociology*, 45(3), 363–378.

Meeuwisse, M., Severiens, S. & Born, M. (2009) Learning environments, interaction, sense of belonging and study success in ethnically diverse student groups. *Research in Higher Education*, 51, 528–545.

Mezirow, J. (2000) *Learning as transformation: critical perspectives on a theory in progress*. San Francisco, CA, Jossey-Bass.

Nahapiet, J. & Ghoshal, S. (1998) Social capital, intellectual capital, and the organizational advantage. *Academy of Management Review*, 23(2), 242–266.

Ostove, J.M., Stewart, A.J. & Curtin, N.L. (2011) Social class and belonging: implications for graduate students' career aspirations. *Journal of Higher Education*, 82(6), 748–774.

Ryan, A. & Tilbury, D. (2013) *Flexible pedagogies: new pedagogical ideas*. York, Higher Education Academy.

Sheader, E.A. & Richardson, H.C. (2006) Homestart: a support for students in non-university accommodation. In: Cook, A., Macintosh K.A. & Rushton, B.S. (eds.), *Supporting students: early induction* [a publication from the STAR Project]. Coleraine, University of Ulster, pp. 51–72.

Thomas, L. (2012) *Building student engagement and belonging in higher education at a time of change: a summary of findings and recommendations from the What Works? student retention & success programme*. Available from: www.heacademy.ac.uk/system/files/what_works_summary_report_1.pdf [Accessed 4 October 2016].

Tilbury, D. (2011) Are we learning to change? Mapping global progress in education for sustainable development in the lead up to 'Rio Plus 20'. *Global Environmental Research*, 14, 101–107.

Tilbury, D. & Wortman, D. (2004) *Engaging people in sustainability*. Gland, Switzerland, International Union for Conservation of Nature.

Tinto, V. (2006) Research and practice of student retention: what next? *Journal of College Student Retention*, 8(10), 1–19.

Tobbell, J., O'Donnell, V.L. & Zammit, M. (2008) *Exploring practice and participation in transition to post-graduate social science study: an ethnographic study*. York, Higher Education Academy.

Vygotsky, L.S. (1978) *Mind in society: the development of higher psychological processes*. Cambridge, MA, Harvard University Press.

Watling, S. (2009) Technology-enhanced learning: a new digital divide? In: Bell, L., Stevenson, H. & Neary, M. (eds.), *The future of higher education: policy, pedagogy and the student experience*. London, Continuum, pp. 83–96.

Wenger, E. (1998) *Communities of practice: learning, meaning, and identity*. New York, Cambridge University Press.

Wenger, E. & Snyder, W. (2000) Communities of practice: the organizational frontier. *Harvard Business Review*, 1, 139–145.

Wilcox, P., Winn, S. & Fyvie-Gauld, M. (2005) "It was nothing to do with the university, it was just the people": the role of social support in the first-year experience of higher education. *Studies in Higher Education*, 30(6), 702–722.

Yorke, M. & Longden, B. (2008) *The first-year experience in higher education in the UK: final report*. The Higher Education Academy.

Part II

Chapter 4
Managing and setting expectations
Loretta Newman-Ford

Introduction to the chapter

Think back to your own experience of going to university. For most of us, the transition to life as a higher education student was a time of both excitement and apprehension, as we asked ourselves: 'Will I be able to cope with the demands of university?' 'Will I receive the right support?' 'Will I make new friends?' 'Will I enjoy my course?' 'Will I achieve my ambitions?'

Most of us will have entered higher education with a unique set of hopes, fears, aspirations and expectations about what university would be like and who, or what, we would become by the time we were ready to graduate. We may also recall how our expectations changed over the course of our studies, as our skills and competencies developed and as our focus shifted, perhaps towards employment or further study, as we neared graduation. Unfortunately, though, more often than not, there are gaps between applicants' ambitions and hopes for life at university and the reality of being a student (Higher Education Policy Institute and Unite Students, 2017).

This chapter will explore the nature of student expectations, including the divergence between learner expectations and those of higher education institutions, and the ways in which learner expectations shift over time as student populations change, and as learners progress through the different stages of the higher education lifecycle. The chapter will focus on how purposeful activities can be used to understand and manage student expectations as they transition in, through and out of university (Lizzio, 2011).

Why do we need to understand and manage student expectations?

Evidence suggests that many students enter university with unrealistic, and leave with unmet, expectations (Krause & Armitage, 2014). Universities UK (2016) found that poor course organisation is the number-one reason for university not meeting a student's overall expectations, followed by the volume of contact hours, support for independent study and teaching quality. Since there is a deep connection between applicants' expectations of higher education and students' overall satisfaction, we can begin to see the direct impact of learner expectations on a university's reputation, recruitment and financial status. Failing to meet or manage students' expectations can also have severe consequences in relation to retention and success. Yorke and Longden (2008) found that mismatched expectations between learners and higher education institutions can result in engagement and transition issues. As a result, universities have been prompted to make understanding and meeting the needs of students – or at least managing their expectations – a priority.

The literature on student induction and retention highlights the first few weeks and months as a critical period for students, as they become accustomed to university life and higher education study. Many are unprepared for this new way of learning (Ozga & Sukhnandan, 1997; Yorke, 1999), including the level of work, time and effort required to successfully complete their programme of study (Leese, 2010).

A survey of 7,109 full-time first-year undergraduates from across 23 varied institutions by Yorke and Longden (2007) also revealed that one-third of respondents felt that academic work was harder than they had expected, and that over half of those having difficulty coping with academic study had considered withdrawing. The results also showed a limited willingness by learners to 'read around' the subject of study – though the data showed that older students were more motivated than their younger peers in this respect.

Scott (2008) also noted that more and more students are taking up paid employment alongside their studies, which has resulted in greater expectations of flexible forms of educational delivery, and in particular increased use of technology-enhanced learning.

The changing nature of student expectations of higher education

The modern student is more selective and more demanding, expecting a tailored higher education experience according to their individual needs. The Quality Assurance Agency for Higher Education's *Student Expectations and Perceptions of Higher Education* study (Kandiko & Mawer, 2013) found that students from all year groups, institutional types and subjects have developed a consumerist ethos towards higher education, with students wanting more 'value for money' in relation to contact hours, support, resources and investment in learning spaces (see Chapter 2). It has been suggested that the single most important driver of value is the extent to which their expectations are met (Neves & Hillman, 2017).

The information learners receive at all stages of the student lifecycle is key to shaping and managing expectations. Kandiko and Mawer (2013) recommend managing student expectations about value for money by explaining to learners:

- the relationship between fees and the quality and value of their degree;
- the subject and teaching qualifications of their programme team, and the process for recruiting academic staff;
- how money is spent on learning and teaching; and
- how teaching is structured and allocated, including the ratio of staff and students, size of tutorials and seminars.

(pp. 7–9)

In addition, contemporary students are more diverse. Some students, such as those from backgrounds in which there is limited or no experience of higher education, often lack the familial support needed to help them come to terms with the expectations of university study (Yorke & Longden, 2007), making university seem like an 'alien place' (Scevak et al., 2015).

Interestingly, a study in the US identified differences in the academic expectations of male and female students, with males believing that a student could miss more teaching sessions and revise for less time than females in order to pass assessments, or achieve a high grade in an exam (Lammers et al., 2005). This suggests that there may be a greater tendency for males to underestimate the time and effort needed for successful higher education study.

Perhaps the most notable divergence in academic perceptions and expectations are between students from different cultural backgrounds, particularly in relation to learning and teaching approaches; there is sometimes a contrast between British expectations of "critical evaluation, originality, academic freedom and independent thinking" (Jin, 1992: 393) and other academic cultures, which are characterised by academic authority. Research indicates that a sense of 'belongingness' within the academic community is a predictor of progression and success among international students (Glass & Westmont, 2014; Hausmann, Schofield & Woods, 2007). Some case studies in the book have endeavoured to bridge this gap (e.g. Case Study 3).

Student expectations can also vary based on their mode of study. In their survey, Forrester and Parkinson (2004) found that the main concern for over half of distance learning students relates to their feeling of isolation, lack of contact and social interaction, and their physical distance from the university.

Sound approaches to managing expectations

Pre-entry activities

Pre-entry activities can be effective in helping students to form realistic expectations, and develop peer networks and links with academic tutors, academic skills, confidence and a sense of belonging (Thomas, 2012). A popular approach is the summer school, designed to provide prospective students with opportunities to experience higher education prior to their arrival. For instance, Case Study 1 describes how at Utrecht University, all pre-entry students are invited to experience a 'typical' day in higher education. As well as being expected to undertake a small amount of independent study in preparation, students experience a lecture, workshop and assessment, as well as peer and tutor feedback. At the end of the day, learners discuss in small groups their experience of higher education and how this compared with their expectations.

Pre-arrival self-reflection surveys can also be a helpful tool for exploring and understanding student expectations about studying at higher education. During induction, students could have the opportunity to discuss their responses with personal tutors and/or within small peer groups to explore commonalities or differences in perceptions and to clarify misconceptions. Students could then be asked to write a short, reflective essay towards the end of the induction period, comparing their expectations with their actual experience of higher education. Other suggestions for pre-entry activities and support include:

- Setting pre-arrival projects, such as the creation of scrapbooks or photo albums that represent each student's hopes, fears and expectations in relation to higher education. Learners could then share their project with fellow students/tutors during induction.
- Providing electronic pre-arrival guides and resources, and 'taster' activities or readings that offer a flavour of higher education.
- Using online communities or discussion boards to encourage pre-arrival students to connect with one another, ask questions and clarify expectations.
- Personal tutors connecting with their tutees to discuss why they have chosen the programme, any concerns, and to set expectations for week 1.

Student charters

Student charters, particularly if drafted collaboratively with students, can be a useful way of communicating what students can generally expect from their provider, as well as what the university expects of them. It could comprise expectations about learning, teaching and assessment, support services and learning environment (e.g. University of Nottingham, 2017), and contact and study hours expected (e.g. University of Newcastle, 2017).

A charter could be purposefully introduced during induction activities and revisited during significant stages of student transition. The University of Reading (2017) has created activities designed to encourage active engagement with the charter, develop a sense of belonging, and unpick the rights and responsibilities outlined within the document. For instance, the 'Words in Context' activity requires students to explore different expectations and working relationships between staff and students. Groups are asked to identify key words within the charter, then discuss what the words mean in context (such as whether the same meaning applies to staff and students, and if not, why not). Groups then explore the different perceptions and expectations among members by discussing, for instance, what each student thinks 'timely' means.

Other early induction ideas include:

- The use of structured timetables (as in Case Study 2), which provides a breakdown of workload, time frames, group work and independent study that indicate the time and effort learners are expected to invest in their studies.
- The use of personal response systems that allow students to respond anonymously to questions relating to their academic expectations, confidence and skills. Discussion follows, and collective responses and concerns or misconceptions are addressed.
- Ask each student to draw a 'successful learner'. In small groups, students discuss what a successful learner looks like, what attributes and skills they have, and what behaviours they exhibit. Groups then compile a list of the most important factors for successful higher education study, and rank them in order of importance.
- Build in orientation activities, such as treasure hunts, during induction week that encourage new students to visit and find out about the range of professional services available to them, including academic skills and library support.

Peer learning

Peer interaction that enables students from different groups or backgrounds to share and assimilate their knowledge, experience and expectations with those of others is key to understanding and challenging learners' perceptions of higher education. Anglia Ruskin University (cited in Thomas, 2012) found that peer mentors help new students to develop accurate academic expectations by helping them 'learn how to learn' at a higher level. Through guiding and advising, experienced students promote independent learning in new students, and as a result of ongoing support and friendship, improve the overall student experience.

Personal tutoring and personal development planning

Kandiko and Mawer (2013) identified that students, first and foremost, expect courses to be personally and vocationally relevant. If their chosen programme of study does not fit with their personal interests, aspirations and expectations, then they are likely to become dissatisfied or drop out. Embedding personal development planning (PDP) and personal tutoring can help to ensure that students have frequent opportunities to discuss their future aspirations and career goals, identify relevant developmental opportunities (both within and outside the curriculum), and seek guidance on module choices that are relevant to their individual needs (also see Chapter 8).

For distance students, the use of technology can provide learners with online spaces in which to communicate, share, support one another and form virtual learning communities. Developing group tasks online and encouraging students to partake in online forums or asynchronous and synchronous dialogue can help learners to feel part of a wider group (Forrester et al., 2004).

Other ideas include using web conferencing tools to encourage peer learning; for example, Royal Roads University, British Columbia, created 'Virtual Experience Labs', where students are split into virtual breakout rooms and each required to give a presentation to their peers on a specialist topic of their choice. Peers and tutors provide each presenter with feedback (Burgess, 2012, cited in Oblinger, 2012).

Subsequent years

Most of the research on student expectations and transitions has focused on the first-year experience; however, it is important to remember that students will experience step changes in both the pace and demands of academic study (Scott & Cashmore, 2012) as they progress. Richardson (2004) found that many students embark on their second year with a false sense of security, later finding that the transition is significantly more difficult than they had expected.

Similarly, O'Donnell et al. (2009) argue that the transition needs of postgraduate students have been largely ignored by higher education institutions due to the assumption that these students are fully prepared for, and know what to expect from, postgraduate study, since it involves "more of the same" or simply "taking things to the next level" (p. 27). The reality is that postgraduate students often find that they do not have the necessary study skills or digital literacy that are integral to contemporary higher education (Masterman & Shuyska, 2012). Students' expectations may be shaped by a previous institution, and they may find themselves at odds with the new university's culture, processes, practices and discourses.

Expectations should therefore be revisited at key progression points throughout the student lifecycle. Reinduction at all levels can help continuing learners to transition into higher levels of study, and this is addressed through some of the case studies in this book. For example, Case Study 5 uses storytelling, including autobiographical accounts and those depicting successful and problematic transitions, to help students identify the strategies, skills and competencies needed for a smooth transition. Many students also benefit from induction programmes that incorporate activities, training and support designed to equip them with appropriate academic skills (e.g. Case Study 4).

Supporting transition out of university and into employment

Across all discipline areas, the main purpose for students entering higher education is to improve their career prospects or enhance their career pathway

(Kandiko & Mawer, 2013). Students therefore expect institutions to not only support and enable them to achieve an academic qualification, but to develop their employability and equip them for future employment. However, the reality is that for many new graduates, the transition into the world of work can be a difficult one as they face a steep learning curve establishing themselves in the workplace. This is often referred to as 'transition shock' or 'reality shock', and describes how graduates engaging in a professional practice role for the first time are confronted with a broad range of physical, intellectual, emotional, developmental and sociocultural changes that can lead to them experiencing feelings of anxiety, insecurity, inadequacy and instability.

Kandiko and Mawer (2013) found that students were rarely satisfied with centralised careers services as a means of preparing learners for, and managing their expectations about, the transition into graduate employment. Instead, students report that embedded learning activities within the curriculum such as tutorials, presentations, work placements and practical sessions that enable them to engage in participatory, authentic learning experiences are most effective (Wharton & Horrocks, 2015). Additional suggestions include:

- designing authentic learning activities that involve real-life problems and/or working with employers, such as 'live projects' (e.g. Case Study 7);
- moving away from traditional assessment methods, including written essays, towards more authentic outputs, such as presentations, 'elevator pitches', journal papers, etc. (e.g. Case Study 31);
- using problem-based or scenario-based learning and teaching methods (e.g. Case Study 12);
- embedding PDP within curricula (e.g. Case Study 8); and
- e-portfolio-based learning to encourage students to continually reflect on and learn from their experiences (e.g. Case Study 10).

Despite student employability being firmly entrenched in higher education's strategic agenda globally, Jackson and Wilton (2016) note that there is consensus that higher education is not providing students with the necessary strategies or capabilities to realise employer expectations (McKeown & Lindorff, 2011; Ng & Burke, 2006; Pegg et al., 2012). To address mismatches in graduate and recruiter expectations, universities may consider:

- co-designing programme curricula with employers to ensure currency and relevancy (including opportunities to engage in modification and periodic review processes);
- involving work placement mentors in the assessment process; and
- working with employers to identify relevant graduate attributes and integrate opportunities for students to develop and demonstrate these within their programme of study.

References

Forrester, G. & Parkinson, G. (2004) *Mind the gap: students' expectations and perceptions of induction to distance learning in higher education*. Presented at British Educational Research Association (BERA) Annual Conference, UMIST, Manchester, UK, 16–18 September 2004.

Forrester, G., Motteram, G., Parkinson, G. & Slaouti, D. (2004). *Going the distance: students' experiences of induction to distance learning in higher education*. Presented at British Educational Research Association (BERA) Annual Conference, UMIST, Manchester, UK, 16–18 September 2004.

Glass, C.R. & Westmont, C.M. (2014) Comparative effects of belongingness on the academic success and cross-cultural interactions of domestic and international students. *International Journal of Intercultural Relations*, 38, 106–119.

Hausmann, L.R.M., Schofield, J.W. & Woods, R.L. (2007). Sense of belonging as a predictor of intentions to persist among African American and white first-year college students. *Research in Higher Education*, 48(7), 803–839.

Higher Education Policy Institute and Unite Students (2017) *Reality check: a report on university applicants' attitudes and perceptions*. Available from: www.hepi.ac.uk/wp-content/uploads/2017/07/Reality-Check-Report-Online1.pdf [Accessed 22 October 2017].

Jackson, D. & Wilton, N. (2016) Developing career management competencies among undergraduates and the role of work-integrated learning. *Teaching in Higher Education*, 21(3), 266–286.

Jin, L. (1992) *Academic cultural expectation and second language use: Chinese postgraduate students in the UK – a cultural synergy model*. PhD thesis, University of Leicester.

Kandiko, C.B. & Mawer, M. (2013) *Student expectations and perceptions of higher education: Quality Assurance Agency report*. London, Learning Institute.

Krause, K.L. & Armitage, L. (2014) *Australian student engagement, belonging, retention and success: a synthesis of the literature*. York, Higher Education Academy.

Lammers, H., Kiesler, T., Curren, M., Cours, D. & Connett, B. (2005) How hard do I have to work? Student and faculty expectations regarding university work. *Journal of Education for Business*, 80(4), 210–213.

Leese, M. (2010) Bridging the gap: supporting student transitions into higher education. *Journal of Further and Higher Education*, 34(2), 239–251.

Lizzio, A. (2011) *The student lifecycle: an integrative framework for guiding practice*. Available from: www.griffith.edu.au/learning-teaching/student-success/first-year-experience/student-lifecycle-transition-orientation [Accessed 17 July 2017].

Masterman, E. & Shuyska, J.A. (2012) Digitally mastered? Technology and transition in the experience of taught postgraduate students. *Learning, Media and Technology*, 37(4), 335–354.

McKeown, T. & Lindorff, M. (2011) The graduate job search process: a lesson in persistence rather than good career management? *Education and Training*, 53(4), 310–320.

Neves, J. & Hillman, N. (2017) *The 2017 student academic experience survey*. Oxford, Higher Education Policy Institute/Higher Education Academy.

Ng, E. & Burke, R. (2006) The next generation at work: business students' views, values, and job search strategy. *Education and Training*, 48(2), 478–492.

Oblinger, D.G. (ed.) (2012) *Game changers: education and information technologies*. Washington, DC, Educause.

O'Donnell, V.L., Tobbell, J., Lawthom, R. & Zammit, M. (2009) Transition to postgraduate study: practice, participation, and the widening participation agenda. *Active Learning in Higher Education*, 10(1), 26–40.

Ozga, J. & Sukhnandan, L. (1997) *Undergraduate non-completion in higher education in England*. Report 2. Bristol, Higher Education Funding Council for England.

Pegg, A., Waldock, J., Hendy-Isaac, S. & Lawton, R. (2012) *Pedagogy for employability*. York, Higher Education Academy.

Richardson, D. (2004) *The transition to degree level study*. York, Higher Education Academy.

Scevak, J., Southgate, E., Rubin, M., Macqueen, S., Douglas, H. & Williams, P. (2015) *Equity groups and predictors of academic success in higher education*. A 2014 Student Equity in Higher Education Research Grants Project. Report submitted to the National Centre for Student Equity in Higher Education. Perth, Curtin University.

Scott, G. (2008) *University student engagement and satisfaction with learning and teaching: review of Australian higher education*. Canberra, Department of Education, Employment and Workplace Relations.

Scott, J. & Cashmore, A. (2012) *Fragmented transitions: moving to the 2nd year*. HEA STEM Annual Conference 2012: Proceedings. Available from: www.heacademy. ac.uk/resources/detail/disciplines/stem/Conf_12_Scott [Accessed 23 October 2017].

Thomas, L. (2012) *Building student engagement and belonging in higher education at a time of change: final report from the What Works? student retention and success programme*. London, Paul Hamlyn Foundation.

Universities UK (2016) *Student experience: measuring expectations and outcomes*. Available from: www.universitiesuk.ac.uk/policy-and-analysis/reports/Documents/2016/student-experience-measuring-expectations-and-outcomes.pdf [Accessed 19 October 2017].

University of Newcastle (2017) *Student charter*. Available from: www.ncl.ac.uk/students/progress/assets/documents/StudentCharter2016-17Final.pdf [Accessed 17 October 2017].

University of Nottingham (2017) *Student charter*. Available from: www.nottingham.ac.uk/currentstudents/student-charter/student-charter.aspx [Accessed 17 October 2017].

University of Reading (2017) *Student charter activities*. Available from: www.reading.ac.uk/web/files/personaltutor/Student_Charter_Activities_2017-18.pdf [Accessed 17 October 2017].

Wharton, Y.C. & Horrocks, J. (2015) *Students' perceptions of employability within their degree programme: highlighting the disparity between what academics believe is included and the student experience*. Enhancement and Innovation in Higher Education, QAA, Scotland (Conference Paper). Available from: www.enhancementthemes.ac.uk/pages/docdetail/docs/paper/students-perceptions-of-employability-within-their-degree-programme-highlighting-the-disparity-between-what-academics-believe-is-included-and-the-stu dent-experience [Accessed 23 October 2017].

Yorke, M. (1999) *Leaving early: undergraduate non-completion in higher education*. London, Routledge.

Yorke, M. & Longden, B. (2007) *The first year experience in higher education in the UK: report on phase 1 of a project funded by the Higher Education Academy*. York, Higher Education Academy.

Yorke, M. & Longden, B. (2008) *The first year experience in higher education in the UK: final report*. York, Higher Education Academy.

Introduction to the case studies

The cases in this chapter explore approaches to understanding, managing and bridging student expectations throughout the various stages of transitions outlined by Lizzio (2011). Across the case studies, the themes of active engagement, learning community and student support are evident. Case studies include:

- a pre-arrival orientation programme that explores the nature of students' chosen courses and their expectations in order to increase retention and success;
- an intervention that uses a structured timetable to manage first-year students' expectations and understanding of independent learning;
- an interactive game-style approach to orientation that is used to disseminate information regarding available support services and to explore student expectations;
- a series of interactive workshops that prepare students for Masters study, promoting social integration and equipping students with key academic skills;
- the use of pedagogic storytelling to prepare students for the next level of academic study, which recognises the skills and competencies required for advancement;
- a programme of varied activities that supports students entering university and potentially living away from home for the first time; and
- a project that brings students together with the aim of planning, starting and running their own creative business.

Case Study 1: Pre-arrival orientation programme to increase retention and success

Leoniek Wijngaards-de Meij, Utrecht University, Utrecht, the Netherlands

Key themes: pre-entry, choice, expectations, engagement, study skills/academic skills, feedback

Aim of the learning activity

The pre-arrival orientation programme helps students post-application, but pre-entry, to explore the nature and expectations of their chosen programme of study and level of study. This helps them decide whether their expectations and capabilities fit with their chosen programme of study, and if necessary change their choice.

Learning outcomes for students

- Develop an understanding of the goals and aims of their chosen programme of study.

- Explore the fit between themselves and their chosen programme of study in relation to level, interest and academic approach.
- Increase engagement with their chosen programme of study pre-entry.

Description of the learning activity

Prior to applying for their programme of study at our university, students will have been through a process of identifying a relevant degree programme. This is often based on their interests, capabilities and understanding of how a specific study will benefit them. Nonetheless, a number of students drop out of their study, citing that the study was not what they expected or questioning their ability to meet the demands of the programme.

To help students before they start with their programme of study, every student who has applied participates in a 'matching process'. Post-application, students fill in an online questionnaire that explores their motivations, capabilities, and understanding of the nature and content of the programme of study. Following the questionnaire, students participate in a number of orientation activities to increase their understanding of the expectations and nature of higher education. These include practical orientation days, group activities, feedback and opportunities to discuss their choices further prior to entry. By offering students an early start (before the real start of the study), and an opportunity to meet other students and teachers, it is hoped that the engagement of the student is increased.

Step-by-step guide to running the activity

Step 1

Post-application, students are sent a questionnaire to enable them to identify their interests and capabilities related to their choice of programme of study.

Step 2

After receiving the questionnaire from the student, the student is invited for the 'try-out' day (six to four months before the start of study). They prepare for this by being sent articles to read and an assignment to put together.

Step 3

The teachers prepare for the day by reading the questionnaires and preparing lectures that are similar to, or cover a topic from, the first year of study.

Step 4

During the try-out day, the students attend the different work forms, and talk with other students, teachers and current students. At the end of the day, they will receive feedback and discuss with others the expectations they have from the study and themselves, and the fit between those.

Step 5

After attending the try-out day, students receive a letter with additional feedback, and offering further opportunities to help them in making a final decision.

Ways in which it could be adapted/extended for different disciplines or levels

The current approach has been used by different disciplines (for undergraduate studies). The approach could also be used by graduate or postgraduate studies. Both the questionnaire and the structure of the day could be adjusted, maybe even extended to two or three days.

Case Study 2: Using a structured timetable to manage first-year students' expectations of independent study

Rebecca Turner, Victoria Hurth, Debby Cotton, Sebastian Stevens, Samantha Child, David Morrison and Pauline Kneale, Plymouth University, Plymouth, UK

Key themes: learning approaches, self-regulation, timetabling, student effort, deep learning, reflection

Aim of the learning activity

The rhetoric of students as independent learners is heavily embedded within higher education (Wingate, 2007); however, students are often unclear as to what this means in practice. Explicitly introducing students to independent learning is an aspect of first-year induction that is rarely considered (Leese, 2010). This intervention aims to scaffold students towards independent learning using a structured timetable.

Learning outcomes for students

- Recognise the level of independent learning required for higher education study.
- Develop effective time management skills.
- Engage effectively with the range of teaching, learning and assessment activities associated with a first-year module.

Description of the learning activity

The level of work, time and effort required for higher education level learning is a concern for many first-years (Leese, 2010). This is an issue that is particularly acute for those entering higher education from widening participation backgrounds who may have limited prior experience or knowledge of what it means to be a university student (Reay, 2002). Where staff and student expectations regarding the level of work needed are not aligned, it can be a major factor in student withdrawal (Wingate, 2007).

In this intervention, a structured timetable was designed that aimed to ease the transition of students into their programme of study. The expectation was that providing a more explicit timetable of activities, including independent study time, would help prepare students for the demands of higher education, as well as the level of learning required in order to achieve (Whittaker, 2008). It would also introduce them to the breadth of teaching and learning activities necessary to succeed.

Entry to higher education presents students with new subjects and ways of learning that they need to become aware of, particularly with respect to adjusting existing study habits (Johnston, 2010; Leese, 2010). Fundamentally, mapping out a module would demonstrate the level of self-regulation, commitment and effort required, and at the same time making more salient to academic staff the expectations being made of students.

Step-by-step guide to running the activity

Rationale

Most institutions provide 'personalised timetables'; however, the information contained therein is usually limited to class scheduling. This intervention builds on the principles of personalised timetables, but provides information about group work and independent study, and schedules time in the first four weeks of the 'immersive timetable' to indicate to students the expected time commitment.

As a general guide, a 20-credit module equates to 200 hours of learning in class, independently and through assessments. Students, and sometimes academics, can often underestimate the time needed to complete different tasks (Johnston, 2010). This intervention aims to demonstrate how they may effectively study for a module. The aim is that the structure can be gradually removed as students become able to manage their time independently.

The intervention

Module teams should collectively map out teaching, learning and assessment activities associated with a module. In doing so, they should estimate the time required for reading, group work, session preparation, etc.

This provides students with an indication of the time and effort needed to engage with activities in a way that promotes deep rather than superficial learning, and reduces student concerns that they are not keeping up due to expectation ambiguity (Whittaker, 2008).

The mapping of activities should be presented on a weekly basis to demonstrate the progress students are expected to make and to encourage planning for formative and summative assessments. Including time slots for group work helps overcome logistical issues, as well as anxieties over arranging meetings. Information should also be given about the extracurricular activities and protected time for these so students recognise the value of these to their academic development and social integration (Kuh, 1995).

This mapping activity should be scaled up to the programme level to ensure that where modules run concurrently, there is not bunching of assessment deadlines or overlap with activities such as field courses. Once finalised, these timetables should be included in programme/module handbooks. Supplementary task lists for each module could also be included that are presented on a weekly basis, providing a checklist of tasks that needs to be completed each week. This can allow students to make a quick check on progress.

Introducing students to the structured timetable

During induction, the timetable should be introduced with explanation of the activities and suggested time allocations. This can stimulate debate with students as to whether they wish to follow the timetable, and if not, on what basis they wish to adapt it. Time should be dedicated to discussing the breadth of teaching and learning activities associated with a first-year module. The timetable can create a forum to explore student expectations of university, reflecting on how this is different to prior learning and how they may need to accommodate or adjust their learning practices/study habits.

Students capture their reflections on the structured timetable and the discussion around higher education level study, time management and self-regulation skills as part of the induction activity that introduces the timetable. Towards the end of their first modules, opportunities are provided for students to talk to module teams about whether their expectations of the time taken for tasks is accurate so that adjustments can be made. This could be facilitated through an assessment submission (if relevant), activities such as professional development planning or in meetings with personal tutors.

Ways in which it could be adapted/extended for different disciplines or levels

This intervention can be applied to any discipline, since concerns around managing student expectations are universal. Targeting first-year students places a focus on the need for students to develop skills such as self-regulation, and through dedicated discussions indicates these are skills students will develop. This will challenge the misconception many first-years have that they are expected to *know* how to study. The level of structuring can be varied by level, or even within a single module, but it may be useful to extend its use if students are particularly unfamiliar with higher education practices. Getting the level of structuring right and removing the scaffold at the appropriate time is a crucial aspect of encouraging student development.

References

Johnston, J. (2010) *The first year at university: teaching students in transition.* Maidenhead, Oxford University Press/McGraw-Hill.

Kuh, G.D. (1995) The other curriculum: out of class experiences associated with student learning and personal development. *The Journal of Higher Education,* 66(2), 123–155.

Leese, M. (2010) Bridging the gap: supporting student transitions into higher education. *Journal of Further and Higher Education,* 34(2), 239–251.

Reay, D. (2002) Class, authenticity and the transition to higher education for mature students. *Sociological Review,* 50(3), 398–418.

Whittaker, R. (2008) *First year enhancement theme, project 9 final report: transitions to and during the first year.* Glasgow, Quality Assurance Agency in Higher Education.

Wingate, U. (2007) A framework for transition: supporting learning to learn in higher education. *Higher Education Quarterly,* 61(3), 391–405.

Case Study 3: Promoting student engagement and managing study expectations: *Passport to Success @ SCU*

Sally Ashton-Hay and Robyn Cetinich, Southern Cross University, Lismore, Australia

Key themes: international students, cultural integration, academic confidence, Masters, social integration, academic skills, learning community, critical thinking, reflection, referencing

Aim of the learning activity

The aim of *Passport to Success @ SCU* is to effectively disseminate vital information on the nature and availability of support services and resources to international students, and help new students to actively explore their own and the institution's expectations of higher education using an interactive game-style approach to orientation.

Learning outcomes for students

- Learn about vital student support services in meaningful and engaging ways.
- Gain confidence in navigating the university's online learning environment and learn about study expectations at SCU.
- Connect and form relationships with other students and key staff in a supportive and fun environment at the beginning of and throughout the first study session.

Description of the learning activity

There are many factors that can impact an international student's academic performance and their overall student experience, including cultural and educational background, social networks, living and financial circumstances, adaptability to a new culture and academic environment, and study strategies/practices, just to mention a few. However, orientation programmes designed to assist students to settle into their new living and learning environment can often be overwhelming and ineffective, especially if vital information is delivered using a 'talking heads' approach to a passive student audience.

Passport to Success @ SCU is designed to address the many challenges new international students face when they commence their studies by delivering vital information and resources during orientation in an engaging, supportive and timely manner. The passport itself is a small booklet with a checklist of activities to be completed during orientation week. The order of activities is loosely aligned with Maslow's 'hierarchy of needs', whereby physiological and safety needs are addressed first, followed by activities that build self-esteem and confidence with their new learning environment. Friendships and a sense of belonging gradually build throughout the week as many activities involve group work and peer student ambassador support. Also included are post-orientation activities designed to check on student wellbeing and academic progress. The overarching goal is to help students feel comfortable, supported and confident in their new environment and to build a strong foundation for students to achieve their full potential, both academically and individually.

The *Passport to Success @ SCU* has a rating scale for students to rate their orientation week experience. Students sign and submit their completed passport to SCU International in an orientation wrap-up session, and this is kept on their student file as a record of their attendance.

Step-by-step guide to running the activity

Passport to Success @ SCU involves a series of activity-based sessions for new students to check off progressively. These include the following.

Step 1: settling-in round robin

The first two days of orientation week involve students working through small group settling-in sessions with student ambassador leaders. All sessions involve problem-solving activities as well as a meet-and-greet with support staff and services:

- *Understanding and talking about culture shock*: small group discussions to identify challenges/concerns and brainstorm solutions and/or support.
- *Finding accommodation*: an interactive tour of the university's UniStays website and booking appointments with an accommodation officer as required.
- *Managing your finances*: small group discussion on living and study costs and filling in a budgeting planner in the passport booklet.
- *Finding part-time work and kick-starting your career*: a computer-based lab to assist students with writing a CV/résumé and tips for seeking/applying for part-time work and preparing future careers.
- *Safety, security and the law*: local police, lifeguards and security staff introduce their services and discuss important safety and security tips. In small groups, students discuss safety and security in the home, using public transport, beach, surf and sun safety, bicycle safety, etc. Police, security and lifeguards fill in knowledge gaps and answer questions.
- *Looking after your health*: students navigate their way around the Overseas Student Health Cover (OSHC) website to build confidence in understanding their cover, as well as what resources and services are available to them, how to register online, how to make a claim, etc.

Step 2: introduction to technology, student portals and enrolling at SCU

The third day of orientation week introduces new students to the university's learning environment:

- *IT essentials*: students practise logging into and navigating their way around student portals.
- *Complying with your student visa conditions*: important visa rules are explained and a visa quiz is completed in their passport booklet.
- *Course information and enrolment*: meeting key staff, followed by course information and enrolment in units.

Step 3: getting prepared workshop

The fourth day of orientation week is a three-part workshop designed to prepare students for their first week of classes, familiarise them with the online learning environment and connect them with important academic support services:

- *Focus on study expectation*: information and Q&A session with an academic and student ambassadors from the school to clarify study expectations, including what students are expected to do before, during and after lectures/tutorials.
- *Focus on academic skills*: a web quest session with an academic skills lecturer in a computer lab. Students complete a matching exercise that introduces and explains SCU vocabulary, followed by an introduction to learning sites for enrolled units. Using a web quest activity, learners then navigate unit material, academic skills resources and booking online appointments. The focus is on building confidence with the online learning environment, preparing for classes, and knowing where and how to seek academic support.
- *Focus on research skills*: another web quest with library staff where students actively learn how to use online databases and research facilities by finding a specific journal article or book related to their field of study with the help of staff and student ambassadors.

Step 4: orientation wrap-up

On the final day of orientation, the focus is on reinforcing important information and strengthening friendships. It involves three important activities:

- *Pathway to Success board game*: similar to snakes and ladders, but rather than just rolling the dice, students answer multiple-choice questions about university from a deck of cards. The game is fun and reinforces information learnt throughout the week, and winners receive a prize.
- *Making a Get Connected appointment*: students make individual appointments to 'reconnect' with a student ambassador or international staff member in week 2 or 3 so that progress can be checked and any issues, concerns and/or challenges addressed that may be impacting on their studies.
- *Submitting the SCU Passport to Success*: students hand in their completed and signed SCU passport for the chance to win a prize. Any student who has not completed or submitted their passport is followed up at the Get Connected appointments.

Ways in which it could be adapted/extended for different disciplines or levels

The *Passport to Success @ SCU* could be adapted/extended in the following ways:

- Focus more on undergraduate learning needs such as developing cultural competence or postgraduate learning needs (e.g. postgraduate career aspirations, development and resume skills).

- Link the vocabulary/web quest activities to discipline-specific content or first assignments in core units.
- Extend *Passport to Success @ SCU* into subsequent semesters with further developmental activities appropriate for year level and discipline.
- Extend *Passport to Success @ SCU* activities to pre-enrolment information and activities so new students are more likely to hit the ground running on arrival.
- Follow up *Passport to Success @ SCU* with the SCU alumni organisation to track students, their career development and professional success.

Case Study 4: Masters carousel: an experiential approach to equip transitioning students with key academic skills for level 7

Sam Davis, Katie Peck and Tanefa Apekey, Leeds Beckett University, Leeds, UK

Key themes: interdisciplinary, experiential, postgraduate, social integration, academic skills

Aim of the learning activity

The aim of this activity is to transform the content and process of postgraduate induction into an interdisciplinary, experiential range of activities to inspire students and prepare them for Masters study. In addition, it aims to structure the learning environment to provide learners with opportunities for social integration and participation in key academic skills, thereby fostering relationships that nurture a postgraduate student community.

Learning outcomes for students

- Foster productive learning relationships among a diverse postgraduate student community.
- Actively communicate key concepts and academic skills expected at Masters level in a UK institution.
- Provide an effective transition to Masters study, a new course, to a new academic environment and a new geographical location.

Description of the learning activity

The skills carousel offers five 30-minute interactive workshops on topics thought essential for Masters study. These include critical thinking skills, critical reflection skills, prioritisation, academic integrity and referencing.

The sessions run concurrently and are facilitated by academic staff. Our interdisciplinary, participatory approach is a radical departure from postgraduate student induction programmes.

Within the skills carousel, students rotate through the series of workshops until they have experienced all five sessions. Each facilitator provides an interactive activity that could be completed by a group of eight to ten students within the allotted time, taking into account student diversity and differing levels of academic ability. As an interdisciplinary induction, it is essential that the workshop topics are not subject-specific, but instead have cross-cutting appeal. For example, in the critical thinking skills workshop, a short, topical newspaper article rather than an academic piece is used with students to practise their reflexive skills of critical appraisal, highlighting language issues, bias and political standpoints, among many.

The two underlying theoretical principles that informed our approach were the experiential and reflective learning cycle (Kolb, 1984) and the principles of education and experience (Dewey, 1938).

Kolb's (1984) experiential and reflective learning cycle promoted an interactive learning environment and encouraged reflection on student learning. Dewey's (1938) principles of education and experience encouraged us to focus on issues of quality and creating high-quality tutor relationships. In addition to these theoretical principles, our approach was guided by a pragmatic concern for creating an engaging experience that incorporated the key principles of a transnational curriculum.

Step-by-step guide to running the activity

Step 1

Plan a series of five workshops, as outlined below. The planning time required is approximately one and a half hours per workshop.

Workshop 1: critical thinking skills

- The purpose of the session is to foster critical thinking skills and enable learners to apply these in practice.
- Select a short topical news item that can be easily read within five minutes. Avoid academic literature to enable students to focus easily on recognisable issues of bias, unsubstantiated opinions, lack of credible evidence, and issues of content and style.
- The outcome is to appreciate that these elements are also present in academic literature, not just the tabloid press, but are less obvious. Students should then be able to apply and develop the critical framework to academic articles.

Workshop 2: critical reflection skills

- This activity introduces students to critical reflection skills and how these might be applied as part of a learning cycle to inform practice.
- Select an example of a student's piece of reflective work, a theoretical model (e.g. Gibbs, 1988) and evaluation criteria. Students read the piece and use the model to identify the critically reflective elements. Applying the set criteria, students are encouraged to discuss the unique content and style of reflective work.
- The outcome is to enable students to identify when and where to use critical reflection while appreciating the elements that constitute reflective writing.

Workshop 3: academic integrity

- This session defines what is and is not acceptable academic practice as per the university's regulations, such as intentional and unintentional plagiarism.
- Common problems encountered by students are identified by using a case study approach (e.g. collusion and poor referencing). From a prepared sheet of differing examples, students are encouraged to highlight the instances of poor academic practice. Following this, the group discuss more appropriate strategies to meet the required academic standards.
- The outcome is to raise students' awareness of the importance of academic integrity and to signpost students to resources that will support them with academic writing.

Workshop 4: prioritisation

- The purpose of this activity is to highlight the specific challenges that Masters study presents and to offer some effective strategies to help students prioritise their workload using Covey's matrix, 'eliminate the unimportant'.
- Students are asked to share a list of current tasks they have and using Covey's matrix, which highlights what is most important and urgent, and they are asked to self-evaluate and position their tasks within the matrix.
- Students watch a short clip on prioritisation (big rocks, little rocks) and then action-plan for a week using Covey's principles of the matrix, positioning the 'big' tasks first and then adding the smaller ones within the time available.

Workshop 5: referencing

- This workshop introduces the principles of citation and referencing, and how to use these correctly when writing for academic purposes.
- To make an otherwise dry academic exercise fun and engaging, students are given an excerpt from an academic paper and challenged to find how many errors they can spot. To assist them, a handy 'short guide' to referencing is provided. A wider discussion then follows where students are encouraged to offer corrections that comply with university regulations.
- The outcome of this session is to enable students to identify the correct forms of citation and referencing as per university guidelines.

Step 2

Workshops (five × 30 minutes) are scheduled in such a way as to enable students to rotate through each of the sessions until they have experienced all five.

Ways in which it could be adapted/extended for different disciplines or levels

The skills carousel is adaptable and can be changed to suit a wide variety of audiences, educational levels and settings. Some options for adaptation include:

- Substitute the range of key skills for others that are the most appropriate for the students of particular institutions or learning environments or academic levels.
- Shorten or lengthen the time of the sessions, broaden the range of sessions to have more than five, or introduce choice so students select workshops that meet their needs.
- Repeat the skills carousel later in the academic year to reinforce the learning once students have had an opportunity to apply their learning during the early formative assessment period.

References

Dewey, J. (1938) *Experience & education*. New York, Kappa Delta Pi.
Gibbs, G. (1988) *Learning by doing: a guide to teaching and learning methods*. Further Education Unit. Oxford, Oxford Polytechnic.
Kolb, D.A. (1984) *Experiential learning: experience as the source of learning and development*. Englewood Cliffs, NJ, Prentice Hall.

Case Study 5: Recoding academic expectations: the use of storytelling-as-pedagogy in supporting the transition of level 5 students

David Aldous and David Brown, Cardiff Metropolitan University, Cardiff, UK

Key themes: storytelling, academic expectations, progression, level 5, level 6

Aim of the learning activity

The aim of the activity is to use storytelling-as-pedagogy to support level 5 (second-year undergraduate) students in decoding the academic expectations of level 6 qualifications through enabling the recognition and transformation of the necessary competencies required to develop appropriate forms of pedagogical practice.

Learning outcomes for students

- Engage with the fictional stories presented and critically reflect upon their own learning experience at level 5 and 6 of university degree programmes.
- Recognise the key skills and competencies required for learning within level 6 of university degree programmes.
- Apply identified forms of skills and competencies within their own learning experience at level 6.

Description of the learning activity

The use of storytelling-as-pedagogy has been celebrated as a means by which students within professional services (pre-service teaching, nursing) learn how to reflect on, question and learn from their experience within the situations they prospectively face (Carter & Doyle, 1996; Wood, 2000). This has a number of applications for supporting students to identify changes to the academic expectations of qualification. Our proposed use of it is based on Bernstein's principles of classification and framing.

As noted by Bernstein (1971, cited in Cause, 2010), classification refers to the degree of boundary maintenance between contents. This can include boundaries between subjects, assessments, physical space and the particular skills needed for a different degree-level study. Where the expectations of a degree programme are strongly classified, students from disadvantaged backgrounds are more likely to recognise valued forms of competency and achieve successful transition. In addition, Bernstein's concept of framing refers to relations within boundaries, identifying "the degree of control teacher and pupil poses over the section, organisation, pacing, and timing of knowledge transmitted and received in the pedagogical relationship" (Bernstein, 1971, cited in Cause, 2010: 7).

Drawing upon this principle, storytelling-as-pedagogy weakens the framing of lecturer and student relations, creating possibilities for developing transformative pedagogical practices that demystify the invisible mechanisms of power and control relations that structure students' progression (Morais & Neves, 2010). This enables learners to gain a critical understanding of the context and also the confidence to navigate the classification boundaries between level 5 and 6 of university qualifications.

The storytelling activity takes place towards the end of level 5. Based on academic ability, students are assigned to mixed-ability groups. The time frame of the activity is important in providing level 5 students the space and time to use the scenarios provided to recognise the academic expectations and pedagogical practices of level 6 and to evaluate their current knowledge and competencies. The curricular structure and pedagogical processes of the activity are designed around the principles of collaborative autobiography (see Carter & Doyle, 1996). The use of collaborative autobiography as both curricula and pedagogical structure provides a space where students can engage in pedagogic action (Bourdieu, 1998) through 'reflective conversations' to develop skills such as critical thinking, decision-making and self-evaluation (Brown, Morgan & Aldous, 2017).

Step-by-step guide to running the activity

Step 1

In session 1, level 5 students are provided with fictional stories based on the experiences of current level 6 students. The use of fictional stories inducts students into what Wheelahan (2010) illustrates as "disciplinary systems of meaning" and helps to develop abilities to recognise the vertical and horizontal discourses that change between level 5 and level 6 (p. 60). Students are provided with two types of stories based on existing empirical research (see Aldous, Sparkes & Brown, 2012, 2014). The first depicts an empowered successful transition and the second depicts a marginalised position and problematic transition, with students struggling to cope with pedagogical and cultural expectations of level 6. Focusing on the interplay of pedagogical and cultural elements in the stories enables students to become sensitised to how academic transitions create moments of both crisis and creativity in their own lives (Brown, Morgan & Aldous, 2017). Strong classification around these moments enables students to identify challenges encountered by learners within the stories and cooperatively explore what skills and competencies could be developed to facilitate enhanced transition.

Step 2

Within session 2, students discuss in small groups the purpose of creating autobiographical accounts of their own experience at level 5 and their progression into level 6. Here, the framing of relations is further weakened by allowing them to draw on the stories and their own experiences to encourage students to develop strategies that could enable the development of pedagogical practices that would enable the successful progression into level 6.

Step 3

In session 3, students are required to present their autobiographical accounts to the other groups. This enables students to publicly share and interpret their experiences. By presenting their stories within small groups, the process of realisation and decoding becomes active rather than passive (Morais & Neves, 2010). In doing so, students identify what competencies and skills were evident within the case studies, and translate and contextualise what knowledge and competencies they will need to develop at level 6. Drawing upon the thoughts of McAllister et al. (2009), this also enables students "to identify what a positive experience *feels* like in a subjective and close way, rather than what it *looks* like in an objective and dispassionate way" (p. 157, original emphasis).

Ways in which it could be adapted/extended for different disciplines or levels

The process of weakening or strengthening the framing of relations in educational settings has a number of applications across vocational qualifications, and can be used with students from a variety of socio-economic and disciplinary backgrounds. For students of a higher ability, the framing of relations could be further weakened, thereby enabling students to assume even greater responsibility in realising the key messages from the stories and developing individualised pedagogical actions. The framing of relations could also be strengthened to ensure that students are provided support in the acquisition of specific skills required for transition between levels 5 and 6.

References

Aldous, D., Sparkes, A.C. & Brown, D. (2012) Transition experiences of post-16 sports education: Jack's story. *British Journal of Sociology of Education*, 35(2), 185–203.

Aldous, D., Sparkes, A.C. & Brown, D. (2014) Trajectories towards failure: considerations regarding post-16 transitions within the UK sport-education sector. *Sport, Education and Society*, 21(2), 166–182. Available from: http://dx.doi.org/10.1080/13573322.2014.890929.

Bourdieu, P. (1998) *Practical reason*. Stanford, CA, Stanford University Press.

Brown, D.H.K., Morgan, K. & Aldous, D. (2017) Changing the student teacher habitus: Bourdieu's theory of practice, crisis, creativity and problem based learning in PE teacher socialisation. In: Richards, K.A.R. & Gaudreault, K.L. (eds.), *Teacher socialization in physical education: new perspectives*. New York, Routledge, pp. 194–211.

Carter, K. & Doyle, W. (1996) Personal narrative and life history in learning to teach. In: Sikula, J., Buttery, T.J. & Guyton, E. (eds.), *Handbook of research on teacher education: a project of the Association of Teacher Educators*. 2nd ed. New York, Macmillan Library Reference, pp. 120–142.

Cause, L. (2010) Bernstein's code theory and the educational researcher. *Asian Social Science*, 6(5), 3–9.

McAllister, M., John, T., Gray, M., Williams, L., Barnes, M., Allan, J. & Rowe, J. (2009) Adopting narrative pedagogy to improve the student learning experience in a regional Australian university. *Contemporary Nurse*, 32(1–2), 156–165.

Morais, A. & Neves, I. (2010) Basil Bernstein as an inspiration for educational research: specific methodological approaches. In: Singh, P., Sadovnik, A.R. & Semel, S.F. (eds.), *Toolkits, translation devices and conceptual accounts: essays on Basil Bernstein's sociology of knowledge*. New York, Peter Lang, pp. 11–33.

Wheelahan, L. (2010) *Why knowledge matters in curriculum: a social realist argument*. London, Routledge.

Wood, D.R. (2000) Narrating professional development: teachers' stories as texts for improving practice. *Anthropology & Education Quarterly*, 31(4), 426–448.

Case Study 6: Supporting the student experience from the outset

Wendy Johnston, Liverpool John Moores University, Liverpool, UK

Key themes: learning community, peer mentors, open days, applicant days, pre-arrival, self-sufficiency

Aim of the learning activity

This intervention outlines systems put in place at a large, diverse metropolitan UK university to help students on the BSc Food Development and Nutrition programme, often living away from home for the first time and facing challenges to their senses of self-sufficiency, to settle quickly into university life and to find a balance between the pressures of student life, studying and social activities.

Learning outcomes for students

- Understand the importance of communities of learning through engagement with the programme activities.
- Recognise the importance of managing a responsible, adaptable and flexible approach to study, work and leisure activities.

- Develop new skills for effective learning within a supportive, structured and managed environment.
- Recognise the range of support mechanisms available to them.

Description of the learning activity

Starting university is challenging for students; they are suddenly expected to manage their daily lives as well as their studies, and this can be a daunting and overwhelming experience in an institution such as ours. Our priority as a programme team is to develop and promote a sense of community and provide a safe, supportive learning environment for our students. We really care about student progression and retention, and work hard to get to know our students individually, to treat them as individuals, to develop trust, and to identify their concerns and expectations from the initial application process right through to graduation.

Step-by-step guide to running the activity

Open days and applicant days

These are the beginning of the process of engagement with the programme, providing the first face-to-face contact with students, and importantly allowing opportunities for all concerned to put names to faces. We recognise that first impressions are impossible to reverse; therefore, we ensure that the welcoming process is proactive to set students on a positive trajectory. The programme team, crucially assisted by current students and peer mentors, provides an overview of the programme and runs cohort-wide activities, but more importantly we *listen* to and talk with the applicants and their parents to gain an understanding of what they hope to achieve from the programme and in their future careers. We can then act to help resolve issues and provide reassurance. Our closed Facebook page allows us to continue this engagement and communication process prior to arrival at university and induction. It provides information relating to the programme, the university and the city, Liverpool, alongside current issues in food development and nutrition, thereby helping to build a community of learning.

Induction

Trained programme peer mentors continue the contact with students following applicant days and prior to induction. They meet students at a designated point on the first day of induction, on enrolment day and the first day of the academic semester, so students are welcomed by friendly peers with a welcoming smile, alleviating unnecessary stress for new students. Peer mentors then help provide support, answer questions and share information throughout the course of study.

An interactive induction process, including a 'food walk' around our cosmopolitan city, a campus barbecue, and interactive activities involving the programme team, students from other levels and peer mentors, helps with orientation and encourages interaction and integration, while fostering a sense of community and developing friendships.

Having relatively small cohorts is advantageous, and early icebreaker activities during induction and taught sessions help us and fellow students learn each other's names, which opens channels of communication, develops trust, and enables students to share issues and concerns more easily.

Semester activities

We use interactive and authentic teaching methods and a varied assessment diet, which helps to support the diversity of our students' needs. Field trips to local businesses early in the semester further help students to interact informally and settle in. We involve students in our own research and enterprise work and encourage them to engage in external work.

The support network we provide includes the programme leader, personal tutor, peer mentors and module leaders. Small weekly peer learning groups (PLGs) supported by peer mentors and a peer learning tutor provide space and time for students to discuss their progress, concerns and expectations, and for staff to listen and act on issues raised. We use data analytics proactively to track student progress, presenting the summarised information to both students and staff, which allows student progression to be discussed openly in personal development progress reviews each semester. The programme leader, with an open-door policy, addresses any issues that students don't feel able to discuss as part of their PLGs. The programme is supported by two student engagement officers who can meet with students outside of PLGs to provide additional guidance. In addition, institutional student advice and wellbeing staff offer a free confidential one-to-one service and provide a safe place for students to share concerns and talk about issues with a professionally qualified and registered mental health practitioner. Completion of the mental health first-aid course can help staff identify common symptoms of mental health issues at university. In addition to the PLGs, programme forums are held once a semester, enabling students from all levels to meet and communicate with the programme team in an informal, relaxed setting over a meal.

Ways in which it could be adapted/extended for different disciplines or levels

The intervention could be applied to any discipline.

Case Study 7: 'Mind Your Own Business': enterprise education – going beyond the classroom

Richard Morris, Cardiff Metropolitan University, Cardiff, UK

Key themes: action learning, experiential learning, peer learning, entrepreneurial skills, reflection

Aim of the learning activity

The Cardiff School of Art and Design implemented an ambitious transdisciplinary curriculum five years ago, allowing students from its undergraduate programmes to collaborate and work together on field projects set by academic staff. Within the field module, students choose a project that best meets their interests or personal goals. 'Mind Your Own Business' is one such project that brings together diverse groups of students with the aim of planning, starting and running their own creative business. Through authentic learning experiences, students apply and enhance their entrepreneurial competencies, while developing clear expectations about what it is really like to create a new business venture. Ultimately, the field projects can help to prepare learners for their transition out of university and into the world of work, or self-employment.

Learning outcomes for students

- Increase confidence to negotiate a creative design direction, and associated business plan, and reflect on personal skills and contribution made to the creative collective.
- Review and reflect on the outcomes of the enterprise-focused project and fully understand how individual strengths and skills can be utilised as part of a creative collective set against a clear business plan and associated objectives.
- Develop and enhance subject skills, assigning current expertise with those from other disciplines to promote an enterprising and entrepreneurial range of outcomes, and assimilate new skills and ideas drawn from the 'creative collective' into their own subject discipline.

Description of the learning activity

'Mind Your Own Business' is one of the field projects that forms part of an assessed, credit-bearing level 5 (second-year) module, embedded within all undergraduate programmes in the Cardiff School of Art and Design. The project, which runs for five weeks, encourages students to apply enterprising skills and attributes to a range of different contexts, including setting up new microbusinesses or developing and growing part of an existing venture. Project groups are provided with seed funding (£100) to invest in their own start-up business. Projects typically involve students designing and making new products, working with charities, non-governmental organisations, the public sector and social enterprises.

The project has been designed to enhance and explore the collective potential of specialist creative and applied skills for enterprise engagement, including the skills needed to pitch and launch a business proposition. 'Mind Your Own Business' connects students from unfamiliar disciplines, including specialist programmes of study and other creative subjects. Students are placed in small teams called 'collectives'. The diversity of each collective generates a range of entrepreneurial responses and the creativity within groups drives the development or enhancement of business opportunities. The assignment brief promotes business-orientated opportunities that support and enable learners to develop higher-level negotiation, persuasion and engagement skills, while recognising the responsibilities of the individual as part of the creative collective.

The projects encourage and demonstrate the value of risk-taking, failure and reappraisal as part of the design development and business planning cycle, while ensuring those creative skills and experiences are reflected upon and personal strategies developed to ensure future individual enterprising successes.

To date, all of the student businesses have generated a profitable income, but more importantly have given students the basic formative tools and skills to sponsor further professional enquiry regarding applied business practice. The real-life nature of the projects means that learners can continue to develop and grow their business venture, should they wish to, thereby promoting further enhancement to undergraduates' employability into their final year of study and beyond.

Step-by-step guide to running the activity

Step 1: setting out the brief

Level 5 students are given a copy of the 'Mind Your Own Business' project brief. The brief is very simple. As a creative collective, students are asked to design, make, brand and market a product, artefact, object or service that can be sold for profit, using their seed funding. The only stipulation is that each project collective pays back the seed fund investment, though any profit made can be kept by the collective, and either split between team members or reinvested in the business. Some collectives may be unable to pay back the seed fund at the end of their project. In these cases, if the collective can prove that the learning process and the development of the enterprise initiative has been beneficial in terms of new knowledge that can be assimilated into core programme study, then this will demonstrate the investment has been worthwhile.

Step 2: day 1, task 1

Students are asked to find out as much as possible about their new creative collective colleagues, as learners are expected to develop an understanding of their colleagues' strengths and weaknesses, in order to draw on these when developing an enterprise proposition. Each creative collective is asked to present a short three-minute SWOT presentation about their team to the other teams, illustrating who they are and why they feel they will be an effective team. Groups decide how they wish to present this information.

Step 3: day 1, task 2

In order to develop each collective's core values, and consequently enterprise priorities, group members are asked to first identify their own values. Students use A3 worksheets to record their individual thoughts, which contains possible values/descriptors to help students get started. Students are also reminded that a value is different to a belief, in that a value is something you hold dear to you, while beliefs can and may change over time. Once learners have finished noting down their own values, they are asked to share these with the rest of their collective in order to create a new, single set of agreed values.

Step 4: day 1, task 3

Once creative collectives have agreed on their core values, they are encouraged to start their enterprise proposition. Groups start by deciding on a team name, and considering how this will be used on printed materials and digital platforms such as websites and social media. Teams are then required to design a suitable brand identity and logo.

Collectives are given a list of business-focused headings to discuss in their planning stage. These include:

1 business plan, investment plan and elevator pitch;
2 brand-building;
3 setting goals and longer-term objectives;
4 risk assessment;
5 market research, market opportunities, identifying the gaps and the competitors;
6 marketing plan;
7 time management;

8   cash flow/finance;
9   legal matters and intellectual property, including patents, trademarks, copyright and licensing;
10 problem-solving, staging the pop-up sales event, and making the pitch presentation; and
11 evidence-modelling.

Teams are asked to identify relevant enterprise-related attributes associated with each of the headings, and consider how and whom in their collective is best placed to lead. Individual responsibilities are then assigned to team members. Creative collectives assess their enterprise initiative in terms of how it represents agreed values, with the warning that there will be tension between personal values and the agreed values of the collective. Each member of the collective needs to remain focused on the agreed values.

Step 5: the pop-up sales event

A key outcome of the project, and a marker for the success of the enterprise initiative, is the pop-up sales event that is held in the Cardiff School of Art and Design building on campus. Teams design, brand and market their enterprise initiative at this event in order to make sales that will enable them to repay their seed investment and make further profit. Teams are required to record the event (before, during and after), typically using video, but also via individual reflective blog entries.

Step 6: assessment of project

Summative assessment of the project is carried out.

Ways in which it could be adapted/extended for different disciplines or levels

This project fits into an applied 'action learning' framework, which can be applied within any other discipline, both at undergraduate and postgraduate levels. The development of the framework loosely follows the design development processes used by designers when answering a design problem, allowing students to sequentially move through stages (observation, brainstorming, prototyping and implementation) that describe each stage of entrepreneurial activity.

Chapter 5

Promoting engagement, active learning and student ownership

Sue Tangney

Introduction to the chapter

The student lifecycle (Lizzio, 2011) encapsulates the evolving identities as students choose a university, enter and progress through the undergraduate stages, and leave university for the employment market. Students *become* students, and later in their course they *become* would-be graduates as they look towards the graduate job market. This may sound trite, but recognition of the changing identity involved in this transition can help us unravel our role as teachers in this transition. This chapter is concerned with how active learning and purposeful student engagement can enhance the transition stages as students move from being newcomers to higher education, to establishing themselves as students, and then move towards a graduate identity.

Gale and Parker (2014) suggest that transition is not a passive response to change, but an active, purposeful journey through often-unknown territory. They highlight *agency* as a key aspect of managing change, and this agency is dependent on appropriate capacity-building. From a learning perspective, transition through university requires developing students' skills, knowledge and attitudes to meet what we envisage a graduate might look like in their discipline. As well as a sound knowledge base, we expect students to develop high-level cognitive skills such as critical thinking, problem-solving and creativity. We also expect students to develop attitudes conducive to the labour market and society at large such as adaptability, resilience, interpersonal skills and global citizenship.

Increasing student autonomy, independence and self-regulatory ability are desired outcomes of a university education (Hattie, 2009). These skills and attitudes are not gained passively. We need to actively engage students so they can progressively actively engage themselves.

Transition in learning

Active learning pedagogies have the capacity to develop the skills that students need to manage continued change in the learning process throughout their university years. These pedagogies can be staged to align with developing student identities, noted by Lizzio (2011) as students enter, progress through and graduate from university. While acknowledging that transition interventions can be done at both co-curricular and curricular levels (Kift, 2009), this chapter will be focused on the curriculum.

Many have acknowledged transition stages of learning. There is, for example, a developing literature focused on pedagogy around transition *into* university (e.g. Morgan, 2012) and the first-year experience (e.g. Kift, 2009). Graduate skills and employability have also been a major focus for universities for many years now (Knight, 2004; Macfarlane-Dick & Roy, 2006), and the identification and focus on development of a specific set of graduate attributes are high on universities' agendas.

The greater emphasis on student-centred pedagogies has also resulted in a burgeoning literature starting in the 1970s with Perry's (1970) work on conceptions of knowledge, and Marton and Saljo's subsequent work (1976; see also Marton, Dall'Alba & Beaty, 1993) on conceptions of learning. Both have been hugely influential and form the basis of many conversations I have with academic staff. Perry (1970) highlighted the transition phases of undergraduate students as they moved through increasingly expanding stages in their understanding of knowledge. The stages range from seeing knowledge as absolute, to realising that knowledge is provisional, to using evidence to take a reasoned perspective, and finally to making a commitment to their own critical perspective.

Marton and Saljo's research (1976; extended by Marton, Dall'Alba & Beaty, 1993) unpacked notions of learning, and their conclusions mirrored Perry. Students move through transition phases of seeing learning as acquiring facts and principles, to applying knowledge in practice, to seeking a more integrative understanding of the subject, and finally having a personal perspective.

So, transition in learning has been recognised for some time, and has spawned further literature from the 1990s onwards around teachers' approaches to teaching that encouraged deep approaches to learning (e.g. Trigwell, Prosser & Waterhouse, 1999; Kember & Wong, 2000; Samuelowicz & Bain, 2001; Entwistle & Peterson, 2004). Student-centred pedagogies became mainstream.

So how can this be used when planning teaching? Some suggestions are:

- Use face-to-face time with students more effectively by focusing on developing cognitive skills rather than imparting knowledge, such as using a flipped classroom technique where 'need-to-know' facts and principles are taught through an online environment, for example, and face-to-face time is spent on higher-level skills such as application, synthesis and analysis (e.g. Case Study 5).
- Extend teaching practice to include discursive elements that heighten understanding of alternative perspectives and integration of ideas, such as group projects, role play and debate (e.g. Case Study 18).
- Aim for authentic assessment briefs, which pique interest, develop student ownership and encourage deeper engagement with this subject (e.g. Case Study 31).

Student engagement

While transition stages in learning can be identified, students have to be willing to participate in appropriate activities. The notion of student engagement has received considerable attention in recent years because of its perception that it leads to better grades, better employability, better retention and increased satisfaction (an important metric in the UK because of the National Satisfaction Survey) (Bryson & Hand, 2008; Harrington, Sinfield & Burn, 2016).

Bryson (2014) comprehensively discusses the student engagement literature, and this, alongside his own research, has led him to the conclusion that student engagement is both complex and difficult to measure. Perhaps the most telling comment he makes, drawing on work by Fredricks et al. (2004, cited in Bryson, 2014), is that student engagement is "pattern centred" rather than "variable centred" (i.e. engagement is not confined to one aspect of students' involvement with the university) (p. 8). Bryson (2014) identified the following influences on student engagement: their aspirations on coming to university, and their expectations as they progress; the academic challenge, degree of choice, and enjoyment of the learning; relationships between staff and students, and students and their peers; and students' sense of belonging and opportunities for personal growth. Engagement therefore permeates the whole university experience, and hence recurs again and again in this book, and is reflected in many case studies, such as Case Study 2.

Whether students are engaged in their learning is also tightly linked with attitudes of staff; enthusiastic staff who purposefully engage with students encourage greater student engagement with their programme of study (Bryson & Hand, 2008). While other aspects of this book focus on academic and social integration for engagement, this chapter will discuss the process of learning, and the nature of learning environments as spaces for student engagement.

Active learning and prior learning experiences

Active learning draws on constructivist conceptions of learning, where learners continually try to fit new knowledge into frameworks or schemata they have developed already. Students therefore are continually building on prior knowledge. These schemata accommodate, expand, and are reshaped and redefined, sometimes in very radical ways as students are exposed to new learning (Fry, Ketteridge & Marshall, 2003). It is a process of becoming. Constructing new frameworks can only be done through active engagement; constructivism rejects all notions of the student being an empty vessel to be filled with knowledge that is then regurgitated or copied.

From a practical perspective, this reshaping happens through meaning-making or sense-making activities. Students explore new ideas by weighing them up against what they know or have experienced in the past. They are making a judgment on the *viability* of new knowledge (von Glasersfeld, 1990), and learning is non-linear and recursive.

Cognisance of prior learning experiences and learners' current understanding therefore are cited often as a key starting point for teachers (e.g. von Glasersfeld, 1990; Lueddeke, 1999). It is argued that bringing existing frameworks of understanding to the fore promotes engagement with new ideas and ease of assimilation. Apart from this cognitive perspective, it is also an opportunity to get to know your students, the life and learning experiences they are bringing to the learning environment, and to build an early relationship with the group you are teaching.

How can these ideas be applied to teaching? Some ideas:

- Find out who your students are and what knowledge, skills and attitudes they are coming with so you can direct focus to most needed areas early. This may take the form of exercises to expose hopes and fears of students as they enter the programme of study, diagnostic testing, or classroom techniques such as think, pair, share (McTighe & Lyman, 1988) (e.g. Case Study 8).
- Periodically check for development of cognitive skills through formative processes; for example, short classroom activities such as the minute paper where students are asked about the most important thing they have learnt over a given period and what remains unanswered (Angelo & Cross, 1993), or developing mind maps individually or collectively.
- As above, focus your teaching time on developing higher-level cognitive skills rather than low-level imparting of knowledge.

Reflection

Reflection is a key aspect of constructivist conceptions of learning. Sense-making involves reflection. Reflective activities can focus not only on the learning activity itself, but the learning *process*, thus developing students' metacognitive skills. Engaging students in purposeful reflection activities is therefore worthwhile, and can be done through individual activities such as:

- journal writing;
- writing action plans following feedback and/or engaging students in exercises that develop understanding of assessment processes (e.g. Case Study 16); and
- meaningful application to real-world scenarios.

Reflection is also enhanced through group work:

- debating;
- group discussions face-to-face or online;
- group projects; and
- consultation exercises with industry.

Dialogic activities such as these also enhance student engagement and give students a sense of belonging to a community. Other relevant interactive activities include:

- students' connection with their personal tutor;
- student peer mentoring activities, perhaps with more senior students (e.g. Case Study 21); and
- engaging students in curriculum development activities (Harrington, Sinfield & Burn, 2016).

Focusing on becoming

While interaction enhances reflection, it also shapes "taken as shared" meanings (Fosnot & Perry, 2005: 28) as students verify understanding, and begin to engage in a community of practice, adopt the discourse that is appropriate, and develop a sense of belonging through this development. We are all engaged in various overlapping communities of practice, and it is worth considering the communities we enable students to access. Deliberately extending students' access to the graduate market as they near their degree completion (or earlier if possible) builds students' identification with *who they are becoming*. Students develop a greater sense of their professional identity and can start making judgments on their potential employability (Lizzio, 2011).

As stated earlier, the increasing focus on graduate attributes has attempted to capture this critical transition. Graduate attributes have the potential to direct the focus of learning and the direction of travel, as students progress through university. Though universities adopt their own specific list of attributes, they often include cognitive elements, personal skills such as student independence and resilience, and social skills such as civic engagement. There is recognition through the development of graduate skills frameworks that personal and professional development are greater than the subject or discipline.

Students' ability to make judgments on their approach to tasks and on the quality of their own work is seen as the most critical graduate attribute of all by Nicol (2010), without which students are unable to develop other typical attributes such as lifelong learning, leadership and global citizenship. Some of these attributes, in particular global citizenship and valuing equal opportunity and diversity, necessitate an examination of one's own values; clearly, the responsibility for this lies wholly with the student. Values-based learning can be incredibly transformative and empowering for students; their world view may be altered irreversibly. However, it can also be very troublesome because of the dissonance that can be created, and has led to a wealth of literature around threshold concepts (Meyer & Land, 2006).

Transition for the future

The graduate market is going to continue to change; most of the graduates of today will have several careers and many will work in jobs that have not yet been created (Jackson, 2011). In addition, there is an increasing focus on developing students' capacity to tackle current global problems we face, and to explore and develop new ways of tackling emerging problems. Preparing students for this level of uncertainty will be the project in the coming years; it is challenging to consider what this might mean. Barnett's (2007) focus for this future of uncertainty is to foster students' will to learn, and to harness learning from both curricular and extracurricular opportunities. Jackson (2011) supports this view, suggesting a focus on developing students' capacity for agency to enable them to manage a career of uncertainty and ongoing change. At the heart of this is life-wide education, integrating diverse opportunities for learning, which he suggests provides the opportunities needed for developing the level of agency required.

Others (e.g. Quality Assurance Agency for Higher Education, 2013), focusing on education for sustainable development, have suggested more interdisciplinary engagement for students to develop the knowledge, skills and attributes needed to safeguard the wellbeing of future generations. Ryan and Tilbury (2013) have brought together many of these ideas to identify the graduate capabilities they think necessary for such a future, which include:

- empowering learners through co-creation of curricula, teaching approaches and generated knowledge (see Dunne & Zandstra, 2011; Neary & Winn, 2009);
- future-facing education that explicitly engages students in envisioning alternative solutions in the face of complex yet unknown challenges (e.g. Case Study 28);
- decolonising education, which might include adding international case studies to gain a more global perspective, purposefully developing students' intercultural skills, but ultimately to challenge the Western-centric nature of many of our curricula and teaching practices (e.g. Case Study 13);
- developing transformative capabilities, drawing on Jackson (2011), and taking being and becoming and student agency beyond the sphere of the discipline into students' life-wide experiences, embracing a broad spectrum of spaces they inhabit;
- crossing boundaries using interdisciplinary and other collaborative approaches to develop greater integrative, systems-orientated and holistic understandings of situations; and
- enhancing social learning to capture the co-curricular spaces of learning outside of the formal curriculum (e.g. Case Study 22).

These ideas are challenging, and the project barely started. In the recent audit to gauge engagement with internationalisation at my university using an in-house audit tool (Tangney, 2015), it was evident that most courses included some aspects of internationalisation but a fully integrated approach was less common.

Significant work has been done across the sector to invite students' participation in curriculum design and development through integration into key panels and working groups. The transformative capacity for this could be further realised. The notions of students as partners (Healey, Flint & Harrington, 2014), students as change agents (Dunne & Zandstra, 2011), and students as producers (Neary & Winn, 2009) have the potential to develop ideas of the purpose of university for both students and staff, and to engage students in more purposeful participation in the wider community of practitioners and researchers (e.g. Case Study 29).

Interdisciplinary opportunities can be stifled by institutional cultures of siloed faculties and schools, and timetabling challenges, and are often dependent on individuals who are championing them, and so not sustainable.

Flexible pedagogies ask us as teachers to also envision and imagine, and this needs to be supported by an institutional culture that, for example, permits and supports flexible learning spaces, flexible and personalised learning outcomes, and easy integration of interdisciplinary learning. This is the challenge for transition thinking in the future.

References

Angelo, T.A. & Cross, K.P. (1993) *Classroom assessment techniques: a handbook for college teachers*. 2nd ed. San Francisco, CA, John Wiley & Sons.

Barnett, R. (2007) *A will to learn: being a student in an age of uncertainty*. Maidenhead, Society for Research into Higher Education and Open University Press.

Bryson, C. (2014) Clarifying the concept of student engagement. In: Bryson, C. (ed.), *Understanding and developing student engagement*. London, Routledge, pp. 1–22.

Bryson, C. & Hand, L. (2008) An introduction to student engagement. In: Hand, L. & Bryson, C. (eds.), *Student engagement*. London, SEDA, pp. 7–12.

Dunne, E. & Zandstra, R. (2011) *Students as change agents: new ways of engaging with learning and teaching in higher education*. York, Higher Education Academy.

Entwistle, N. & Peterson, E. (2004) Conceptions of learning and knowledge in higher education: relationships with study behaviours and influences of learning environments. *International Journal of Educational Research*, 41, 407–428.

Fosnot, C. & Perry, R. (2005) Constructivism: a psychological theory of learning. In: Fosnot, C. (ed.), *Constructivism: theory, perspectives and practice*. 2nd ed. New York, Teachers' College Press, pp. 8–38.

Fry, H., Ketteridge, S. & Marshall, S. (2003) *A handbook for teaching and learning in higher education*. London, RoutledgeFalmer.

Gale, T. & Parker, S. (2014) Navigating change: a typology of student transition in higher education. *Studies in Higher Education*, 39(5), 734–753.

Harrington, K., Sinfield, S. & Burn, T. (2016) Student engagement. In: Pokorny, H. & Warren, D. (eds.), *Enhancing teaching practice in higher education*. London, Sage, pp. 106–124.

Hattie, J. (2009) *Visible learning: a synthesis of over 800 meta-analyses relating to achievement*. London, Routledge.

Healey, M., Flint, A. & Harrington, K. (2014) *Engagement through partnership: students as partners in learning and teaching in higher education*. London, Higher Education Academy. Available from: www.heacademy.ac.uk/engagement-through-partnership-students-partners-learning-and-teaching-higher-education [Accessed 30 August 2017].

Jackson, N. (2011) The lifelong and lifewide dimensions of living and learning. In: Jackson, N. (ed.), *Learning for a complex world: a lifewide concept of learning, education and personal development*. Bloomington, IN, AuthorHouse, pp. 1–21.

Kember, D. & Wong, A. (2000) Implications for evaluation from a study of students' perceptions of good and poor teaching. *Higher Education*, 40, 69–97.

Kift, S. (2009) *Articulating a transition pedagogy to scaffold and to enhance the first year student learning experience in Australian higher education: final report for ALTC Senior Fellowship Program*. Strawberry Hills, NSW, Australia, Australian Learning and Teaching Council.

Knight, P. (2004) *Learning, curriculum and employability in higher education*. London, Routledge.

Lizzio, A (2011) *The student lifecycle: an integrative framework for guiding practice*. Available from: www.griffith.edu.au/learning-teaching/student-success/first-year-experience/student-lifecycle-transition-orientation [Accessed 12 September 2016].

Lueddeke, G. (1999) Toward a constructivist framework for guiding change and innovation in higher education. *The Journal of Higher Education*, 70(3), 235–260.

Macfarlane-Dick, D. & Roy, A. (2006) *Enhancing student employability: innovative projects from across the curriculum*. Mansfield, Quality Assurance Agency in Higher Education.

Marton, F. & Saljo, R. (1976) On qualitative differences in learning. I: outcome and process. *British Journal of Educational Psychology*, 46, 4–11.

Marton, F., Dall'Alba, G. & Beaty, E. (1993) Conceptions of learning. *International Journal of Educational Research*, 19, 277–300.

McTighe, J. & Lyman, F. (1988) *Cueing thinking in the classroom: the promise of theory embedded tools*. Available from: www.ascd.org/ASCD/pdf/journals/ed_lead/el_198804_mctighe.pdf [Accessed 21 October 2016].

Meyer, J. & Land, R. (2006) Threshold concepts and troublesome knowledge: an introduction. In: Meyer, J. & Land, R. (eds.), *Overcoming barriers to student understanding: threshold concepts and troublesome knowledge*. London, Routledge, pp. 3–18.

Morgan, M. (ed.) (2012) *Improving the student experience: a practical guide for universities and colleges*. London, Routledge.

Neary, M. & Winn, J. (2009) The student as producer: reinventing the student experience in higher education. In: Bell, L., Stevenson, H. & Neary, M. (eds.), *The future of higher education: policy, pedagogy and the student experience*. London, Continuum, pp. 192–210.

Nicol, D. (2010) *The foundation for graduate attributes: developing self-regulation through self and peer-assessment*. Available from: http://qmwww.enhancementthemes.ac.uk/docs/publications/the-foundation-for-graduate-attributes-developing-self-regulation-through-self-and-peer-assessment.pdf [Accessed 21 October 2016].

Perry, W.G. (1970) *Forms of intellectual and ethical development in the college years: a scheme*. New York, Holt, Rinehart & Winston.

Quality Assurance Agency for Higher Education (2013) *Education for sustainable development: draft guidance for UK higher education providers*. Gloucester, Quality Assurance Agency for Higher Education.

Ryan, A. & Tilbury, D. (2013) *Flexible pedagogies: new pedagogic ideas*. York, Higher Education Academy.

Samuelowicz, K. & Bain, J. (2001) Revisiting academics' beliefs about teaching and learning. *Higher Education*, 41, 299–325.

Tangney, S. (2015) *Internationalisation of the curriculum*. Cardiff, Cardiff Metropolitan University. Available from: www.cardiffmet.ac.uk/about/ltdu/Documents/int_self_eval_tool.pdf [Accessed 7 July 2017].

Trigwell, K., Prosser, M. & Waterhouse, F. (1999) Relations between teachers' approaches to teaching and students' approaches to learning. *Higher Education*, 37, 57–70.

von Glasersfeld, E. (1990) An exposition of constructivism: why some like it radical. *Journal for Research in Mathematics Education*, Monograph, vol. 4, Constructivist views on the teaching and learning of mathematics, 19–29.

Introduction to the case studies

Student engagement permeates this book and is a key aspect of managing transition, and the cases in this chapter focus on active learning pedagogies that promote engagement, ownership and a sense of belonging. It is evident that student agency is critical; however, the capacity for agency needs to be developed and nurtured through progressive and enriching learning activities that develop sense-making skills, independence, and skills of reflection, discernment and creativity. In addition, the willingness to engage with learning also needs nurturing through staff–student relationships, developing students' sense of belonging, and providing a learning environment that acknowledges the skills, attitudes, prior knowledge and cultural perspective that students bring. New pedagogic approaches will need to be further developed to cater for an increasingly complex world.

The case studies include:

- an induction activity that develops academic skills and promotes a sense of belonging in a group of international students;
- using the flipped classroom and a personal response system to engage students in active learning and collaborative activities;
- engaging students in reflective practice through using an action research model;
- using media to engage students in building bridges between theory and practice;
- using problem-based learning in a research methods module; and
- developing the global citizen through purposeful learning activities and assessment practices.

Case Study 8: The transition tube

Mark Sutcliffe, Cardiff Metropolitan University, Cardiff, UK

Key themes: personal development planning, academic skills, reflection, belonging, international students

Aim of the learning activity

The aim of the transition tube is for current students to develop a transition resource for incoming students, and has been used successfully for the past two years with predominantly international students on a Masters level international business management programme. Current students within a personal development planning (PDP) module reflect on their own transition experience throughout the year and provide advice and guidance on many aspects of course engagement to incoming students. Tasks for the tube are staged throughout the year at key transition points in the course. The transition tube they create is then presented as a gift to incoming students on the following year's programme.

Learning outcomes for students

- Appreciate and practise the academic skills required to complete the course.
- Develop a sense of belonging in the university and the city.
- Assist the transition of the subsequent cohort.

Description of the learning activity

The transition tube is a year-long project, and it is launched during the induction period. The tube itself is a recycled Pringles container that students fill with materials at key personal development points as the year progresses.

Over the year, at key points, students are required to reflect on their integration into the programme and their ongoing learning, and add content to the transition tube. The activities that form the basis for the content are primarily reflective and correlate with developmental activities throughout the module; they also enhance learning and engagement across the whole programme.

For example, a task requiring students to reflect upon and devise a questionnaire for working with feedback is set when students have their first marked work returned. The undertaking of a skills audit is undertaken at a later point in the course when students are discussing employability issues and effective job application processes. The tasks enhance current students' reflective skills but also ask them to articulate this for subsequent students. Some tasks assist with integration into a new city and university life, and in developing a sense of belonging to the university community.

The transition tube brief clearly outlines the learning outcomes of the activity. The tasks themselves are determined as the year unfolds, though they are generally similar from year to year. This allows the opportunity to target specific skills or developmental needs depending on the student cohort and their prior learning experience. It also allows students to see and appreciate transition as an emergent process. The tube requires good management so that tasks are completed on time; regular formative feedback is given on the process.

Step-by-step guide to running the activity

The following activities are staged throughout the year.

Tasks 1 and 2: saying hello and transition resource, following the induction period

Students are required to complete two tasks following the induction period. The first is to compose a letter introducing themselves to a stranger, saying who they are and where they come from, and how they have come to be at the university. They are also asked to include something in the letter about their hopes, fears and expectations for the year to come. The second task requires students to identify a resource that will help a new student to navigate the induction period more successfully. This provides an opportunity for students to reflect on how the induction went, and to consider what additional resources might have been useful. In seeking out a resource for the incoming student, they are effectively finding additional resources for themselves and also providing feedback to academic staff on additional resources that might have been useful in the induction period. Some examples that students have included are bus timetables, the location and direction to local shops, and where help and advice might be found within the university.

Task 3: skills development, a few weeks into the skills development programme

Students are asked to devise a skills promotion newsletter, focusing upon either effective note-taking or successful academic writing. These two skills have been identified as the most important for students entering this programme of study. While students are offered support for these, the newsletter provides the opportunity for the student to unpack these skills for themselves, and consider how they might effectively promote to other students the benefits of such skill development and enhancement.

Tasks 4 and 5: out and about and survival strategy, the end of the first term

At the end of the first term, students are set two light-hearted activities aimed at social integration and encouraging group cohesion. Both involve the use of coloured travel labels. In the first, students are asked to identify and present five places in or around Cardiff to visit. This activity acknowledges the cultural transition that most of the students have undertaken in coming to the UK.

The second task requires students to identify and present five things that they do to survive the demands of the academic work placed upon them. As with the other reflective activities, this provides an opportunity for students to consider alternative strategies of engagement. Ideas that they have generated have included better time management, the keeping of a work deadline diary, walks in the park, and regular visits to the gym.

Task 6: learning from feedback, after a point where students have received feedback

For task 6, students are requested to devise and develop a questionnaire focusing upon how students might best learn from feedback. This is to be suitable for other students to use, and to enhance the value they might gain from the feedback they receive. Students are required to reflect upon their own evaluation of feedback and think carefully about what they would like to know, and how they might have benefited from such a questionnaire if they had had to complete it.

This task was designed to coincide with the concurrent research methodology module looking at questionnaire development.

Task 7: mapping skills and attributes, towards the end of a programme of study, or where employability has been discussed

In this task, students are required to undertake a skills and attributes audit. They are required to identify skills and attributes they currently have, and to identify appropriate evidence to support this claim. Students are required to map these skills against the university's graduate attributes framework. Once they have done this, they must produce a short video discussing the importance of such a mapping exercise and how their skills have developed over the year. To pass this message onto new students, all students are required to design a key ring reflecting who they are. The key ring is then produced, and the video they recorded uploaded onto a virtual reality web server. This is then attached to the key ring. When new students scan the key ring with the appropriate software, the student's video message is revealed. For the incoming student, this enhances the feeling of being part of a community of practice stretching across cohorts.

Task 8: good luck letter and decorating the tube, at the end of the year

Students are asked to compose a letter to the new student wishing them luck, and explaining what they thought was the secret to success on the Masters programme, reflecting upon the content of the letter they had composed in task 1. As above, this offers the opportunity for considered reflection on the year, and their own learning pathway. Students are encouraged to offer any tips or words of wisdom to help them on their way. In decorating the tube, students were given the theme of 'journey'.

Resources needed are Pringle containers. Other resources are made available for various task activities, such as coloured travel labels, and resources are provided for students to undertake the final decoration of their tubes prior to its final submission. The resources required for the activities will vary depending upon the tasks specified. The only constraint on any resource is that it must fit within the container.

Ways in which it could be adapted/extended for different disciplines or levels

Although used within a postgraduate award, any programme that operates a PDP module should be able to easily adapt this activity. The tasks included within the tube can be adjusted to level, and the relative skills and competencies of the students. The award that this task is used within recruits a high number of international students, and although they find the initial conceptual idea of the tube difficult to grasp, once the first few activities have been completed the anxiety attached to this task diminishes.

Case Study 9: 'Technologising' the postgraduate classroom

Sara Smith and Martin Khechara, University of Wolverhampton, Wolverhampton, UK

Key themes: collaborative learning, active learning, feedback, flipped classroom, international students

Aim of the learning activity

The aim of this intervention is to increase student engagement in modules through the application of the flipped classroom approach in conjunction with other in-class knowledge review technologies. We have found this particularly useful with a culturally diverse student population.

Learning outcomes for students

- Demonstrate an increased engagement in the given subject area.
- Develop the ability to work as part of a group to complete tasks.
- Appreciate the role of tutor- and peer-led learning using technology.

Description of the learning activity

Our approach focused upon interactions between peers and instructors through activity and feedback. By adopting an active learning approach, we shifted the focus from teaching to learning, aiming to promote a learning environment more amenable to the metacognitive development necessary for students to become engaged, independent and critical thinkers (Bligh, 1998). We hypothesised that the introduction of technology-based tools allowing us to redesign our instructional approach, and the incorporation of active learning and student-centred pedagogy, would improve student attitudes and also their enjoyment of the material.

Freeman et al. (2014) define active learning as an approach that "engages students in the process of learning through activities and/or discussion in class, as opposed to passively listening to an expert. It emphasizes higher-order thinking and often involves group work" (p. 8413). We primarily focused on the use of two different technologies. First, we 'flipped' or 'inverted' the classroom using Panopto (www.panopto.com), a software package that allows lectures to be captured by tutors easily on their desktop or laptop and watched by students outside of contact time. A range of studies have evaluated 'flipping' using different approaches (Bates & Galloway, 2012; Berrett, 2012; Smith et al., 2015).

Second, we used Socrative (www.socrative.com), an online application that enables the use of instantaneous questioning and feedback of students' responses via mobile devices. This activity provides the tutor with an insight into levels of understanding, as well as allowing students to evaluate their own progress. Studies suggest that Socrative affects students' collaborative learning and enhances the student learning experience (Awedh et al., 2014).

Step-by-step guide to running the activity

Flipped classroom content should be recorded and delivered to students at least one week before the face-to-face session. This will give students time to access the content. Experience shows that a late availability of feedforward material such as this results in simple non-engagement with the content. Recordings are best made on a stand-alone recording solution such as Panopto or similar software. These allow an academic to deliver content to a camera that is recorded and uploaded to the web for later viewing. A web link is sent to students to access the content before they attend the actual face-to-face session. Recordings may be through a podcast or vodcast, depending on the preference of the academic. Recordings are best done apart from a busy academic office and at least 50 per cent extra time allocated to allow for editing and retakes that are sometimes required.

Software solutions for learning such as Socrative provide an app-based interface that allows simultaneous questioning and feedback while providing an anonymous platform for students to respond to questions out of the spotlight of the traditional classroom setting. This functionality is essential for the approach described here as traditional question-and-answer sessions do not provide the emotional safety Socrative can give. The question format is best left as simple true or false questions as these have proved to be just as effective as multiple-choice questions and are not seen as 'dumbing down' content by students. These tests are very quick to set up and can be done days or hours before the face-to-face session.

The tests themselves can be delivered at the beginning of the face-to-face session or after a short keynote lecture that reviews the main points of the flipped lecture. Comments from students show there is no real preference, although they do indicate the tests are engaging and allow them to measure progress through the module content.

A range of tasks can also be provided for the group to be performed individually or as smaller groups. Activities done singly are best hands-on, where students explore content through related experience. For example, dissecting fruit and demonstrating the significance of the cut to the appearance of the tissue section is not only enjoyable, but also engages students in the critical aspects of histology. Other appropriate simulacrum cognate with subject area could be used to the same effect.

Group tasks can adopt a 'bring your own device' approach where each group is set a specific task, such as produce a poster or information sheet about a specific topic. Online information can be accessed to support the task, and each group reports back or presents to the class later. A defined time limit of usually 60 minutes is given. These tasks, although essential for building relationships between peers in the classroom, must have a defined structure as students have been seen to struggle with more open-ended tasks. They should also be independent of the flipped content if possible to allow engagement of those who will not have engaged beforehand. These students will access the content following the session and be better prepared next time.

Ways in which it could be adapted/extended for different disciplines or levels

The approach described here can be applied to any course, level or module where engagement with the content is a problem. It is not discipline-specific, and the principle of review, feedback, and peer-to-peer and peer-to-teacher group interaction reinforces relationships and belongingness in the classroom, independent of discipline. It is the peripheral activities that underlie the tasks making up the group working events that must change to accommodate various subject areas. Carefully crafted, these can be the fulcrum around which these sessions turn, and they must be properly considered before delivery.

References

Awedh, M., Mueen, A., Zafar, B. & Manzoor, U. (2014) Using Socrative and smartphones for the support of collaborative learning. *International Journal on Integrating Technology in Education*, 3(4), 17–24.

Bates, S. & Galloway, R. (2012) *The inverted classroom in a large enrolment introductory physics course: a case study.* York, Higher Education Academy.

Berrett, D. (2012) How 'flipping' the classroom can improve the traditional lecture. *The Chronicle of Higher Education*, 19 February. Available from: https://people.ok.ubc.ca/cstother/How_Flipping_the_Classroom_Can_Improve_the_Traditional_Lecture.pdf [Accessed 26 October 2017].

Bligh, D.A. (1998) *What's the use of lectures?* 5th ed. San Francisco, CA, Jossey-Bass.

Freeman, S., Eddy, S., McDonough, M., Smith, M., Okoroafor, N., Jordt, H. & Wenderoth, M. (2014) Active learning increases student performance in science, engineering, and mathematics. *Proceedings of the National Academy of Sciences of the United States of America*, 111(23), 8410–8415.

Smith, S., Brown, D., Purnell, E. & Martin, J. (2015) 'Flipping' the postgraduate classroom: supporting the student experience. In: Layne, P. & Lake, P. (eds.), *Global innovation of teaching and learning in higher education: transgressing boundaries*. Series: Professional Learning and Development in Schools and Higher Education, Vol. 11. New York: Springer International Publishing, pp. 295–316.

Case Study 10: Encouraging reflective practice through action research process models

Stuart English, Northumbria University, Newcastle, UK

Key themes: reflection, action research, personal development planning

Aim of the learning activity

Students tend to focus on the object of their study without necessarily developing their own self-awareness. This intervention aims to support students to triangulate their own perspective on their practice, to evaluate their actions, and to reflect on what they know about themselves, their perception, their drivers and their limitations.

Learning outcomes for students

- Demonstrate an awareness of the practicalities of the planning, action, observation, evaluation and reflection cycle of action research methods in the context of design practice.
- Show an understanding of the process of recording reflective practice project materials to effectively enable evaluation and reflection on action and in action through hindsight and simultaneous review, respectively.
- Create action research and reflective practice models appropriate to the student's own working context and apply these in action.

Description of the learning activity

The intervention is founded on principles of action research (Lewin, 1946, 1952; McNiff, 1988; Carr & Kemmis, 1986) and reflective practice (Schon, 1983, 1987; English, 2009), and enables students to create a structured planning and recording process and apply this in action.

A template is created based on a cyclic action research model; this is typically broken down into planning, action, observation and reflection (and other fields, depending on the student). Copies of the template are used as diary pages to plan and record day-to-day practice. A cycle may take anywhere between an hour and a week to complete.

The planning part of each cycle includes the student's personal aims and objectives, as well as the purpose of the particular task. However, later, as the student develops mastery of the process, insights arising through reflection begin to drive the planning part of the cycle.

The intervention relies on the honest engagement of students with the challenges of their practice on a day-to-day basis. This is facilitated through coaching and collaboration within a community of practice.

Step-by-step guide to running the activity

The intervention is structured in four stages: literature review, interpretation by student, application in practice, and review and reflection. However, it is important to note that students need to take an honest and enquiring approach to get the most out of the intervention.

Students are usually able to interpret the literature and create a cyclic process model for application in practice within one to four weeks. Mastering the method in practice can take a lot longer, and is usually an iterative process spanning several months, if not years. The activity can be broken down as follows:

1 Literature review exploring the field of action research and reflective practice.
2 Students design their own reflective practice process model based on their literature review and interpretation of action research principles. This is usually communicated using a simple diagram based on a cycle of planning, acting, observing and reflecting.
3 This process model is implemented into students' day-to-day practice; this is often achieved through the use of a recording template derived from the cyclic reflective practice model.
4 Having applied this in action, it is often necessary/desirable for the student to alter or develop the model based on their practical experience. This is entirely appropriate, and students are encouraged to record the changes they have made and why they have made them.
5 The students' recording template can be used like a diary page both to plan actions and to record observations, evaluation and reflection. The aim of each cycle is to generate insights that can then be fed back into the planning part of the next cycle.
6 Students generate insights by reflecting on their experience of practice. Insights often result from: (a) surprise, when events do go according to plan; (b) disaster, when things go entirely wrong, sometimes with serious impact; and (c) persistent frustration, which is often overlooked in the early stages of this intervention, and it is often not until several months of evidence has been collected that persistent frustration can be identified.

7   Review of action research method and theory of reflective practice relative to the students' practical experience.
8   Students' review of their own learning and the development of their self-awareness.

Ways in which it could be adapted/extended for different disciplines or levels

The approach is easily transferable to other disciplines since it is process-driven and is applied by the student in their own particular field of practice. The impact of the intervention is very much dependent on the level of engagement the student is prepared to take. This can often be an emotional rollercoaster for students, and can be supported through involvement in a tutor-facilitated community of practice consisting of a cohort of students who are all engaged in their own practical work-based challenges and who are open to both being coached and coaching others.

References

Carr, W. & Kemmis, S. (1986) *Becoming critical: education, knowledge and action research*. Basingstoke, Falmer Press.
English, S.G. (2009) *Enhancing the reflective capabilities of professional design practitioners*. Undisciplined! Design Research Society Conference 2008, Sheffield Hallam University, Sheffield, UK, 16–19 July 2008.
Lewin, K. (1946) Action research and minority problems. *Journal of Social Issues*, 2(4), 34–46.
Lewin, K. (1952) *Field theory in social science: selected theoretical papers*. Edited by Cartwright, D. London, Tavistock.
McNiff, J. (1988) *Action research-principles and practices*. London, Macmillan.
Schon, D. (1983) *The reflective practitioner: how professionals think in action*. New York, Basic Books.
Schon, D. (1987) *Educating the reflective practitioner: toward a new design for teaching and learning*. San Francisco, CA, Jossey-Bass.

Case Study 11: Increasing student engagement in a biomedical science award: peer-supported learning through video

Sara Smith, Liz O'Gara and Martin Khechara, University of Wolverhampton, Wolverhampton, UK

Key themes: collaborative learning, reflection, active learning, employability, using media

Aim of the learning activity

Students on large laboratory-based modules struggle to engage and link tasks to the real world of the work place. This intervention aims to increase engagement, provide employability contextualisation to in-class practical activities, and develop skills and attributes such as problem-solving, adaptability, initiative and self-awareness.

Learning outcomes for students

- Demonstrate greater engagement in large class groups.
- Develop a clearer understanding of the skills required for the workplace.
- Develop the ability to contextualise their learning for the workplace.

Description of the learning activity

As practitioner-researchers, the aim of our intervention was to improve learning experiences of students, enabling them to fully engage with the laboratory session and to support a deep approach to learning. This intervention focuses on using student-produced video to support student learning. Because students work together, it also enhances peer-learning skills.

An action research approach informed the inquiry. Research into how students learn or approach learning is underpinned by the "'constructivist principle that we construct meanings of phenomena from an array of social and personal influences" (Cousin, 2009: 184). Students' learning approaches are not intrinsic characteristics of the student, but rather they are dynamic and are likely to change depending on how students perceive the learning task (Ramsden, 2003: 45).

Studies have identified that instruction that emphasises interaction between tutors and peers supports a shift from teaching to learning (Armbruster et al., 2009). Such an environment supports learning strategies within students that promote independent learning and critical thinking (Biggs, 1996).

Peer-assisted learning has also been widely recognised as an effective strategy for teaching new concepts (Tenney & Houck, 2003). Reports suggest that this approach boosts student engagement and promotes both active learning and subject comprehension.

Videos have been used in different ways for many years to support student learning in all branches of education, enabling the presentation of complex procedures that allow students to visualise the techniques they will be required to perform in class (Shepherd, 2003). Our intervention combines use of videos and peer-assisted learning, and investigates to what extent peer-developed 'skills' videos support the development of laboratory skills and an awareness of the application of these skills in the workplace.

Step-by-step guide to running the activity

Students' role

Students on placement, with support from laboratory training officers, designed and filmed videos to demonstrate:

- tasks in two routine pathology laboratories that represented two different disciplines within pathology; and
- the practitioners' role in each laboratory, and how the procedures/techniques they perform in this role support a diagnosis or decision on patient care.

Placement students were given a two-week time frame to film in the laboratory before returning the completed video for editing. Providing a deadline ensures that there is time for post-production editing and timely publishing of the video. Having previously undertaken the practical classes, placement students were able to contextualise the techniques learnt in class, demonstrate how they related to the 'real world', and how they employed skills learnt at university during their placement year.

Students were given a clear outline of the aim of the videos but were also allowed a degree of artistic freedom that allowed the videos to be more appealing to their peers. Production of the videos by the placement students was on a voluntary basis, but was designed to support their reflection on practice and to provide them with the chance to contextualise their academic studies with their practice in the workplace.

Handheld video cameras were provided that were simple to use, with an anti-shake function and inbuilt microphone. This helped to enhance the quality of the recording. Poor-quality recordings may reduce the likelihood of student engagement, even though they are peer-produced.

Our role

Videos were reviewed by us and laboratory-based training officers supporting the students to ensure that they met their remit, and also that patient confidentiality was not breached and appropriate ethical considerations adhered to.

We edited the videos using video editing software (we used Microsoft Moviemaker) and added introductory slides to the presentation, introducing the video, outlining learning outcomes and highlighting the students' role.

Subsequent students

Videos were made available for viewing on the university virtual learning environment (VLE) at least one week prior to the laboratory session, allowing current level 5 students to have access prior to, during and after their practical sessions. Ensuring students have adequate time to access these is essential to maximise engagement. The module ran over 12 weeks, and students completed practical classes and assessments for the module.

In addition to being able to view the videos outside of the laboratory class, students also had access to the VLE on touchscreen tablet devices in the laboratory during the taught sessions. This enabled them to compare the techniques they were performing with those performed in the clinical setting to greater enhance their understanding of application to practice.

Challenges and further development

The amount of time required to record the videos and then to edit these files cannot be emphasised enough. One video had to be remade due to patient confidentiality issues. As outlined, it is essential to ensure that additional time is planned to make sure that videos are ready well in advance of the intervention.

The development of an instructional video by placement students to support other students to make the links between academic studies and practice in the workplace has now been adopted by several placement tutors as a learning task as part of the placement year.

Ways in which it could be adapted/extended for different disciplines or levels

Students highlighted a range of benefits of the peer videos. They not only felt that they supported understanding of practical tasks, but also increased their engagement and motivation during the module. The videos provided currency for study through engagement in a real-world dialogue with the workplace, albeit a virtual one. Such an approach could be adapted to a range of disciplines, using peers to support the conceptualisation and transfer of knowledge. Students suggested that this approach also provided them with a greater feeling of professional identity. The students making the videos valued reflecting upon their current practice and the links to their academic studies.

References

Armbruster, P., Patel, M., Johnson, E. & Weiss, M. (2009) Active learning and student-centered pedagogy to improve student attitudes and performance in introductory biology CBE. *Life Science Education*, 8, 203–213.

Biggs, J. (1996) Assessing learning quality: reconciling institutional, staff and educational demands. *Assessment Evaluation in Higher Education*, 21(1), 5–15.

Cousin, G. (2009) *Researching learning in higher education*. London, Routledge.

Ramsden, P. (2003) *Learning to teach in higher education*. London, RoutledgeFalmer.

Shepherd, K. (2003) Questioning, promoting and evaluating the use of streaming video to support student learning. *British Journal of Educational Technology*, 34(3), 295–308.

Tenney, A. & Houck, B. (2003) Peer-led team learning in introductory biology and chemistry courses: a parallel approach. *The Journal of Mathematics and Science: Collaborative Explorations*, 6 (Fall), 11–20.

Case Study 12: Deepening engagement through problem-based learning (PBL)

Alastair Tomlinson, Cardiff Metropolitan University, Cardiff, UK

Key themes: problem-based learning, employability, research methods, collaborative learning, active learning

Aim of the learning activity

This problem-based learning intervention aims to promote deeper engagement with research methods in second-year environmental health undergraduates, encouraging active learning to address a 'real-world' problem requiring research investigation. This is done through activating prior knowledge and social learning in the context of a complex real-world scenario. The intent is to give students greater confidence in applying research methods in their academic work and future practice.

Learning outcomes for students

- Determine a research topic relevant to environmental health that is worthy of investigation.
- Work in a team to design and formulate a research proposal.
- Apply principles of project planning and research ethics to a specific proposal.
- Analyse and interpret data relevant to research.

Description of the learning activity

In this situation, the identified problem was students' lack of confidence in applying knowledge of research methods to their own work, with consequent issues in the eventual quality and rigour of their research projects. Research methods teaching was delivered using a traditional lecture approach, and individually assessed by written research proposal. Student feedback was that they found the module 'boring' and struggled to see the relevance to environmental health practice. A PBL approach was therefore used in this intervention.

PBL is an approach to learning and teaching (and curriculum design) where students learn through facilitated enquiry into a 'problem' and develop a viable solution (Savery, 2015). The problem is typically complex and often based on real-world circumstances, with no single correct answer.

Students work in groups to identify what they need to learn in order to address the problem, engage in self-directed learning, share their findings, and work together to integrate and apply this new knowledge to the problem in order to generate a solution or response (perhaps following further study). PBL has a strong focus on the *process* of acquiring knowledge and understanding, through research, meaning-making, and using discretionary and decision-making skills, rather than simply the acquisition of content.

Reflecting on this, I felt that a more aligned delivery model would involve students actually using research skills and designing research for themselves. Using a PBL approach could enable students to engage with research methods in the context of a real-world situation and promote deeper learning.

PBL can provide intrinsic motivation and long-term retention of knowledge, and enhances skills in critical thinking, analysis of complex situations, identification and use of appropriate resources, team-working, and effective oral and written communication. It can strongly support development of both professional skills and graduate attributes. Problems arouse situational interest that drives learning, and are supported by flexible scaffolding provided by cognitively and socially congruent tutors (Schmidt, Rotgans & Yew, 2011). A well-designed, engaging curriculum such as PBL can encourage more students to reveal academic potential (Gallagher & Gallagher, 2013).

Step-by-step guide to running the activity

The context for this activity was a 10-credit level 5 research methods module in which 75 per cent of the module assessment related to the PBL tasks; the remaining 25 per cent was addressed by an online examination on statistics (teaching delivered separately and not part of the PBL section of the module).

Designing the problem trigger

The problem trigger was fictional but based on a real-world situation (an explosion at a fireworks warehouse). In this instance, a single developing scenario was used to drive all the PBL tasks. The scenario was intended to give a wide scope of potential avenues for investigation (as opposed to a single obvious or 'correct' path to follow). Multimedia (videos, photos, eyewitness accounts) were drawn from the original real-world situation to encourage richer and deeper engagement with the scenario. The University of Adelaide's *Leap into . . . Problem-Based Learning* resource

(Kiley et al., 2000) was particularly helpful in the development stages of the intervention.

PBL process

The PBL assessment tasks were designed to model the process of planning a research project, moving from initial ideas, reviewing the literature through to final research proposal. Tasks were initially formative and then low-stakes in order to enable students to gain familiarity and confidence with the PBL approach to learning.

Week 1: Contact sessions provided an initial induction process into the PBL approach and common issues encountered in group work.

Week 2: The problem trigger was introduced and students completed the first task, in which they identified the key issues to manage the aftermath of this incident and prevent similar future incidents, including priorities for further research investigation (formative groundwork for subsequent summative tasks).

Subsequent tasks were then introduced over the course of the module, including:

Week 4: Literature review task introduced. Students were asked to undertake a brief literature review into one of the priority issues they had identified. What is already known? What are the gaps in knowledge that future research could address? (Low-stakes – 10 per cent).

Week 6: Research proposal tasks introduced. Teams were asked to develop a research proposal to investigate a specific issue arising from this incident (intended to build upon issues identified through literature review).

Week 9: Assessment scheduled via interim presentation where there is opportunity for peer and staff feedback (15 per cent of final mark).

Week 12: Final written submission, worth 50 per cent of module.

In addition to facilitated PBL sessions, students also had access to collaboration facilities via the virtual learning environment (team discussion boards and wikis), as well as an initial set of links and resources on research design and methods.

Summative assessment

Summative assessment was done on a group basis, leading to an overall group mark. This was adjusted to reflect individual contributions following an online peer-assessment process (WebPA, 2014).

Lessons learnt

Evaluation from the initial cycle indicated that while students liked the real-world scenario, they felt underprepared for this new mode of learning, and did not know what was expected of them. To address these concerns, further 'scaffolding' was introduced in the module induction and initial PBL sessions, including:

- providing greater structure to the PBL process – using the Maastricht University seven-step approach, clearly defining the roles of students and facilitators within a PBL group;
- using learning agreement templates to identify learning objectives arising from PBL sessions;
- providing additional support resources (e.g. keynote mini-lectures – 20 minutes – and online resources); and
- tailoring the problem – finessing some issues that were causing unnecessary confusion/distraction while still retaining the muddy nature of a problem with no single correct answer.

Other issues that were identified and tackled were:

- This is the first module where PBL is used in the programme; students have had 18 months of 'traditional' study up until now. Sessions are usually delivered by a single member of staff. It was found that facilitating shorter sessions with only two or three groups at once seemed to work better than a longer session with five or six groups present.
- PBL also challenges staff in getting to grips with facilitation techniques and dilemmas (when and how to intervene or leave alone). Where more than one member of staff has been involved in facilitating the module, this has been a focus for discussion prior to and after sessions – both in terms of the approach taken, and specific issues being raised by groups, and the nature of the support offered.
- As the use of PBL expands within the team (see below), this is being further developed into a formalised tutor development programme, incorporating sessions reviewing problem trigger design, facilitation techniques and assessment.

Ways in which it could be adapted/extended for different disciplines or levels

The approach has been extended and embedded in the new BSc Public Health degree at Cardiff Met. Students encounter PBL from the beginning and throughout the programme, with approximately one-third of the degree being delivered using PBL. This is a hybrid approach – not all modules are delivered by PBL, and PBL is not the only means by which students can engage in deeper learning – but at any point in the programme students study at least one module where PBL is the chief learning and teaching approach.

PBL also provides opportunities for inter-professional education; students from different disciplines may consider different perspectives on a professional problem to develop a holistic response.

References

Gallagher, S. & Gallagher, J. (2013) Using problem-based learning to explore unseen academic potential. *Interdisciplinary Journal of Problem Based Learning*, 7(1), 111–131.

Kiley, M., Mullins, G., Peterson, R. & Rogers, T. (2000) *Leap into . . . problem-based learning*. Available from: http://hdl.handle.net/2440/1220.

Savery, J. (2015). Overview of problem-based learning: definitions and distinctions. In: Walker, A., Leary, H., Hmelo-Silver, C.E. & Ertmer, P.A. (eds.), *Essential readings in problem-based learning: exploring and extending the legacy of Howard S. Barrows*. West Lafayette, IN, Purdue University Press, pp. 5–15.

Schmidt, H., Rotgans, J. & Yew, E. (2011) The process of problem-based learning: what works and why. *Medical Education*, 45(8), 792–806.

WebPA (2014) (Version 2.0.0-11). Available from: http://webpaproject.lboro.ac.uk [Accessed 26 October 2017].

Case Study 13: Assignment design for students on international mobility

Gareth Barham, Cardiff Metropolitan University, Cardiff, UK

Key themes: intercultural, mobility, global citizen, internationalisation

Aim of the learning activity

This case study focuses on the staged learning and assessment design implemented for Cardiff School of Art and Design students on a two-week short-term mobility project involving two universities in South Korea. The assignment was structured around the need for students to develop intercultural capabilities rather than approaching the experience with a 'tourist'-like outlook. While we used it as part of the mobility experience, it could be adapted to use in any home situation.

Learning outcomes for students

- Consider how their discipline is represented and understood within other cultures, widening their frame of reference beyond a Western outlook.
- Raise awareness of their own cultural perspectives and develop their confidence to question their own values and those of others responsibly and ethically.
- Develop an understanding of what it is to be a global citizen, and engage with issues of equity and social justice, sustainability and reduction of prejudice, and stereotyping and discrimination through art and design practice.

Description of the learning activity

In 2016, Cardiff Metropolitan University arranged a transdisciplinary two-week visit for 20 art and design students (and two members of staff) to South Korea. This formed part of an overall five-week project, including preparation, the visit itself and embedding the experience into subsequent practice on their return.

It was recognised that the students needed structure to help them to engage with their environment, develop intercultural capabilities and avoid them becoming 'tourists' in the traditional sense. This structure was provided by the Oxford Brookes' *Internationalisation Kit* (Oxford Brookes University, 2011), and its three levels of immersion and intercultural competencies provided the necessary structure for the assignment design:

- *Global perspectives* required students to research how their discipline is understood in other cultures.
- *Cross-cultural competence* required students to develop awareness of how their own cultural values may differ from those of their South Korean hosts and provided an interesting backdrop for in-country activities.
- *Responsible (global) citizenship* formed the basis for post-trip activities, with students demonstrating engagement with issues of equity and social justice, sustainability and reduction of prejudice, and stereotyping and discrimination through their practical art and design interventions.

The structure for assessing the students' work was provided by the Kitano Model (Kitano, 1997). It presented an excellent framework by which to measure the success of students' intercultural capabilities by describing three different approaches to internationalisation:

- *Exclusive*: Kitano describes as primarily 'income-generating'. This seemed an accurate term for describing students' creative output that only sought to exploit another culture for commercial gain.
- *Inclusive*: Kitano's description was an accurate account for students whose work recognised that other cultural perspectives exist but did not attempt to understand or engage in any meaningful way. This level of intercultural competence she described as that of a 'tourist'.
- *Transformed*: Here, the student understands how their work is understood from the perspective of others and is considered to be 'capable, ethical and sensitive'. Here, Kitano describes the individual as an 'explorer', and creative output reflects this.

Step-by-step guide to running the activity

There were three phases to the overall project:

- two weeks of preparatory briefings and seminars;
- two weeks of in-country activities; and
- one week upon return to Cardiff where students were encouraged to reflect on their experience and delivered an impact statement on how their experience would influence their practical art and design work.

Time was then allocated for students to engage in their practice for the remainder of the term, at which point their practical interventions were assessed by viva voce.

First phase: developing global perspectives (Oxford Brookes University, 2011), weeks 1 and 2

Students attended seminars introducing them to cultural information about South Korea and the two universities they would be visiting. Motivated by a sense of anticipation, discussions ensued about their expectations and prior knowledge of the culture and customs of the country. This was important as it disclosed some of the preconceptions that students had. They were asked to record their preconceptions about Korean culture in a blog. When asked why they wanted to travel to South Korea, the common response from the students was that they wanted to experience a culture that was 'different' and 'alien' to their own.

An assignment was then set for the following week requiring the students to deliver a presentation about how their own subject areas are represented in South Korea. They were also expected to identify museums and galleries that they would like to visit in Seoul. This activity began to align the students' frame of reference beyond a purely Western one, and provided a framework for later consideration of how their in-country experiences compared with their initial pre-departure expectations.

Second phase: cross-cultural competence (Oxford Brookes University, 2011), weeks 3 and 4

This involved the visit to South Korea itself. The first 24 hours included a group evening meal at an authentic Korean restaurant, and a city bus tour that, though a tourist experience, provided geographical and historical context for their visit and exposure to aspects of culture and life in Seoul.

During the following three days, students attended morning lectures and workshops at Kookmin University. They had to make their own way there, and so included planning of travel routes, engaging with city infrastructure and developing the confidence to explore Seoul by themselves. The afternoons were free for students to organise visits to their chosen museums and galleries.

A group seminar was held in the evening at the end of the first week. Students were asked to compare their experiences to date against their pre-departure preconceptions, and all students recognised that their initial ideas about the people of South Korea were based on stereotypes and misconceptions.

The weekend's activities involved a visit to the demilitarised zone between South and North Korea. The purpose was to highlight the political context of daily life in South Korea, and some of the students found this an emotional experience.

At the beginning of the second week, the group travelled to the southern city of Busan to participate in a collaborative design project with students at Dong-A University. This two-day group assignment required the local students to showcase their home city and became one of the highlights of the two-week visit. Friendships were made and trust and understanding developed between the students.

Back in Seoul for the final two days of the trip, students were asked to prepare individual presentations reflecting on how their attitudes to South Korean culture had developed over the two-week visit. The following bullet points were provided as a framework for their presentation:

- Include your pre-departure observations and reflect on which of those may have been influenced by stereotypes.
- Consider some of the differences you have observed about life and art and design in South Korea.
- Reflect upon why things may be different from your point of view. Include your understanding of what the South Koreans may think of you, your own culture, emotions and ethical values.
- Does this reflection cause you to question your own understanding of cultural identity, emotion, and moral and ethical values?
- Include images of your trip to support your claims.

Students delivered their presentations at Kookmin University to their peers, South Korean students with whom they engaged during the first week's activities, and academic staff from Cardiff Metropolitan University and Kookmin University. Feedforward advice was provided that set tasks of further reflection and research to prepare students for their summative assessment back in the UK.

Third phase: responsible citizenship (Oxford Brookes University, 2011), week 5

Back in the UK, students were encouraged to reflect on how their experience of another culture had altered understanding of their own cultural values and to think about how this might motivate them to operate in the future. The assessment asked students to evidence sensitivity to other cultures through a creative project by posing the following question:

> Begin to think about ACTION – So what? Present a narrative on your blog about how your understanding of global issues is influencing your work. How does your developing inter-cultural competencies influence your art and design practice? How are you thinking globally and acting locally?

Assessment

The students' work was assessed using the Kitano Model (Kitano, 1997) as above. Some student projects were considered to be *exclusive*, recognising that international markets existed but did not attempt to explore any further. Most of the students' projects responded in a way that was regarded as being *culturally inclusive*, demonstrating awareness of other cultural perspectives. A few of the students' works were recognised as being a *transformed* response, with students demonstrating sensitivity to the perspective of 'cultural others'. An example of a response at this level was a thought-provoking study by one student of how the South Korean K-pop and hip-hop music genres are depicted in the media compared to similar music styles in North American media. The student's project concluded with a series of illustrations painted in a manner reflecting and celebrating contemporary Korean style but depicting hip-hop dance moves emanating from the North American hip-hop scene.

It is remarkable that when asked at the end of the 11-week project what surprised the students so much about their trip to South Korea, their unanimous response was that they never thought that they would have so much in common with the people there, a marked shift from the students' initial thoughts.

Ways in which it could be adapted/extended for different disciplines or levels

Published methods for creating an internationalised curriculum by the Centre for Curriculum Internationalisation at Oxford Brookes University and Kitano's methods to measure internationalisation can be applied to any discipline. They are also frameworks for use not just with mobility students, but in any home in-class activity aimed at developing students' intercultural capacity.

References

Kitano, M.K. (1997) What a course will look like after multicultural change. In: Morey, A.J. & Kitano, M. (eds.), *Multicultural course transformation in higher education: a broader truth*. Boston, MA, Allyn & Bacon, pp. 18–30.

Oxford Brookes University (2011) *Internationalising the curriculum resource kit*. Oxford, Oxford Brookes University, Centre for Curriculum Internationalisation. Available from: www.brookes.ac.uk/services/cci/resourcekit.html [Accessed 12 October 2017].

Chapter 6

Developing academic integration

Chris Dennis, Jake Bailey and Stuart Abbott

Introduction to the chapter

This chapter will focus on the importance of academic integration into and through higher education. Broadly speaking, we aim to cover a range of ideas and practices that are important when considering when and how students begin to feel 'academic' and the means by which we, as practitioners, are able to foster this sense of belonging. We first provide brief comment on the increasing diversity of the student body; following Broughan and Hunt (2013), we argue that this has important consequences for pedagogical approaches in higher education. Next, we examine academic integration and position it as a conceptual tool that can be used to engage a diverse population of learners more meaningfully, helping them to establish a stronger connection to their educational experience. In the following section, we argue that the development of academic skills as part of wider academic practice is a fundamental building block of learner engagement and integration within higher education. Here, we present a range of practical examples to illustrate some of the different ways that learning and assessment can be designed to build students' skills and confidence, and importantly help them 'understand the rules' of academia. The final section addresses a fundamental question: How do you know if a student is academically integrated?

Increasing diversity of students

The idea of academic integration has gained traction as a consequence of the changing demographics of higher education; students are entering higher education with increasingly varied educational and life experiences. Such diversity has been acknowledged by Broughan and Hunt (2013); these authors have also highlighted its impact on the pedagogical approaches utilised in higher education. Students arrive with different levels of understandings of higher education, wildly contrasting confidence in their ability to meet its demands, and varying degrees of academic skills. Those with limited understanding of expected practices, low confidence in their ability to meet them, or poorly developed academic skills are likely to find integration particularly challenging. As Tinto and Cullen

(1973) identified, such students are more likely to withdraw. It is important to recognise that this can be equally true for both undergraduate and postgraduate students, and so in this chapter we will consider a range of important touchpoints within the student lifecycle (Lizzio, 2011). Importantly, as Tinto (2009) noted, institutions and staff have the power to increase academic integration and foster student success by creating experiences that help students understand academic expectations and make them feel involved with their learning. Understood in this way, supporting students to become academically integrated is crucial if student performance and retention is to be improved.

What is academic integration?

'Academic integration' is a term gaining increasing currency in pedagogical literature, incorporating topics such as student retention, inclusivity and the notion of 'graduateness'. The idea evolved out of a conceptual model devised by Tinto and Cullen (1973) relating to the number of students failing to complete programmes of study at higher education institutions in the United States. Subsequent research has highlighted the complexity of academic integration, in that it is dependent on many more factors than just academic success. Recent studies have suggested that integration can be supported by experiences that promote understanding of academic expectations and by encouraging metacognitive processes that empower students to become drivers of their own learning development (Tinto, 2009; Bovill, Cook-Sather & Felten, 2011; Elkington, 2014; Healey, Flint & Harrington, 2014). Essentially, an academically integrated student may be usefully defined as one who can effectively participate and perform within an academic community. An important component of integration is the ability of a student to develop academic identities; these identities, which are dynamic in nature, can be cultivated – indeed integrated – through pedagogic practices. Academic integration, therefore, is not something that is either achieved or not; rather, it is more properly seen as a developmental process, one that is intimately linked to the learning experience and its outcomes.

In this light, another concept that is relevant to this discussion is the student lifecycle. In higher education, lifecycles are structured around what can be termed instrumental 'touchpoints' (such as induction or movement between years), with the power to shape and impact both students' learning experiences and their developing academic identity (Lizzio, 2011). As discussed in Chapter 1, the importance of the lifecycle model has had the effect of foregrounding transitional identities and their development in the facilitation of academic integration. The role of the pedagogical practitioner throughout the student lifecycle is to create social learning conditions characterised by reciprocal trust and collaboration (Lizzio, 2011; Elkington, 2014), thereby providing opportunities to facilitate and provoke learner identity negotiation. This is achieved through partnership between teacher and student in developing collaborative, inclusive and reflective learning and assessment experiences (Healey, Flint & Harrington, 2014). From the perspective of the individual learner, such experiences must occur together with opportunities to make the learning experience relevant, meaningful, and above all authentic, if they are to have an integrative influence on the learning experience (Entwistle, 2000; Healey, Flint & Harrington, 2014). This culminates in the integration of students as represented by the exercise of greater agency in personal academic development.

Developing academic integration through reflection

Academic integration may be fostered through pedagogies that place the student at the centre of the learning experience. Engaging students in the development of their own learning in this way not only encourages them to assume greater responsibility for their academic development; it also helps to build confidence. Consequently, students may begin to feel a greater sense of belonging within an academic community (Bovill, Cook-Sather & Felten, 2011; Healey, Flint & Harrington, 2014; Healey, Bovill & Jenkins, 2015). Student-centred learning is also inclusive, in that it does not discriminate according to prior learning experiences. Indeed, the effectiveness of student-centred learning can often be attributed to the diversity in the experiences of the students involved.

Empowering students through student-centred approaches to learning can also have the effect of promoting greater self-awareness. Reflective exercises, or tasks that require participation in metacognitive processes, can play a key role in building confidence and promoting a greater sense of belonging (Healey, Flint & Harrington, 2014). Such exercises might take a variety of forms, including written assignments requiring students to reflect on their learning journey over the course of a module or an academic year (e.g. Case Study 14), or photo or video diaries compiled in groups, that achieve the same purpose. While these tasks have value in themselves and can therefore stand alone, in some cases it is appropriate for them to be embedded within assessment. A reflective element fits quite neatly into a patchwork assessment (Winter, 2003), for it allows the students to consider their own academic development through participation in a more tangible process (e.g. Case Study 17). Whatever form the reflective exercise takes, its value lies in its contribution to the process of identity formation. By making students more aware of their own academic development as it occurs, a greater sense of belonging to the academic community is experienced; in other words, in very real terms, they are beginning to take on a socially constructed academic identity.

Reflective exercises promote integration by building confidence through self-awareness and by allowing students to share experiences where such exercises are undertaken in a social learning setting. The development of skills associated with academic practice, such as evaluation and contestation of knowledge, academic writing and referencing, achieves a similar goal. Provision of this sort promotes among students a greater sense of feeling properly equipped to participate in academic activities as a legitimate member of an academic community (Gourlay, 2009; Healey, Bovill & Jenkins, 2015).

Developing academic literacy

Skills development is at its most effective when it is delivered in an embedded and contextualised way (Wingate, 2006). Exposing students to bite-sized skills instruction, perhaps at the beginning or end of a session, two or three times a week, can have a profound impact on the overall quality of work submitted for assessment. For example, an extract of academic writing can be used as the basis for discussing the key features of such writing, paragraph structure, common writing errors, and referencing; if used frequently, students will become very familiar with the literacies and behaviours associated with an academic identity. Bespoke sessions, looking at more specialised skills, such as information literacy, also play an important role in this respect. In the case of information literacy, an academic librarian will be able to guide students through a variety of subject-specific resources available through powerful, federated search engines. Information literacy sessions can play a key role in fostering a sense of integration, as identifying, accessing and then using academic sources is one of the most important skills required by students as they transition into an academic identity and join the academic community. Skills development reaches its full potential in this regard when it is combined with assessment. Assessment tasks focused on the development of academic skills and assessment literacy may be formative or summative. For example, students might be asked to write a short paragraph, in an academic style, summarising a journal article; alternatively, specific skills, such as referencing, might be assessed through an online quiz; an exercise that prompts the creation or application assessment criteria in peer- or self-assessment settings might be utilised ahead of individual summative exercises. Such tasks, which are usually low-stakes, can easily boost confidence, since they provide students with assessment scenarios in which achieving a high score is not only attainable, but the modes of academic practice by which this can occur are made explicit. Furthermore, since these tasks are likely to focus on specific academic 'literacies', the sense of accomplishment experienced by those students who score highly will have a hugely positive effect on their confidence.

Developing academic integration through assessment

Assessment, when considered more broadly, has the potential to play a critical role in fostering academic integration among students as both recipients *and* as co-creators of learning (Healey, Flint & Harrington, 2014; Healey, Bovill & Jenkins, 2015), not least because it captures and builds on many of the elements of a student-centred approach to learning discussed above. Effective assessment tasks form an integral part of learning design; if an assessment exercise is to promote academic integration, it needs to be aligned with appropriately designed academic learning outcomes and activities (Biggs, 1996). Utilising assessment in this way begins with opening the assessment process in order to make what might be described as tacit knowledge – or an appreciation of the requirements of assessment that a tutor might assume a student possesses – as clear as possible (Gourlay, 2009).

Some specific activities are particularly effective in breaking down any perceived barriers between assessor (or tutor) and those being assessed (e.g. Case Study 16). Formative assessment, if supported by effective feedback, might also be used for this purpose (e.g. Case Study 19); the impact of such tasks is greatly enhanced by the incorporation of reflective elements (e.g. Case Studies 14 and 17).

By way of an example of formative assessment design, one of the authors of this chapter led a module where formative student presentations were placed at the end of learning blocks spaced equally throughout. Each presentation was linked to an element of the written assessment task to ensure that students could see the link between classroom activities and the summative assessment (i.e. that it was constructively aligned). Importantly, these tasks created opportunities for students to receive formative feedback from both tutors and peers as they progressed through the module (Irons, 2007). This approach was designed to test learners through presenting their ideas to and discussing them with others, necessarily stimulating reflection on the strengths and limitations in their knowledge and interpretations. Overall, the formative assessment design contributed to the effort to create a collaborative learning community, promoting an openness to sharing ideas and being challenged, while also providing an opportunity to see how the students' learning was progressing.

Summative assessment might also be used to promote assessment literacy among students. However, assessment that contributes towards a student's final mark for a module will inevitably carry higher stakes; it is therefore perhaps less useful in this context than formative tasks. A final point relating to assessment is timing. Formative assessment that requires students to reflect on learning experiences is most effective when implemented at the beginning and end of an academic year (e.g. Case Study 14). By using key moments in the student lifecycle for the purposes of assessment, it is possible to capitalise on points of transition in which students are keenly engaged in negotiating the assumption of different identities.

Partnership in learning

Underpinning much of what has been discussed above is the notion of partnership between tutor and students. Empowering students to drive learning forward enables them to play an active role as co-creators of learning and as agents for change, working in partnership with tutors as well as with peers. From a practitioner's perspective, this means developing an appreciation of the notion of partnership as a process, one that is made up of such elements as authenticity, inclusivity, reciprocity, trust (between tutor and student) and community, as well as empowerment (Healey, Flint & Harrington, 2014). By addressing such contentious factors in the learning experience, partnerships in learning between tutor and students offer an effective way of facilitating academic integration by embracing the very elements within the learning experience that might hinder its development.

How do we know students are integrated?

Superficial indications of the extent of academic integration among students may be found in patterns of attendance, retention statistics relating to individual programmes of study, and overall scores in measures such as the UK National Student Survey (NSS). More precise measures that might complement the broader impression provided by statistics include any means of gathering qualitative feedback, such as module evaluation surveys, or the explanatory comments added as part of the NSS. However, while these tools might provide a snapshot of student sentiment hinting at the extent to which a greater sense of belonging to an academic community has taken hold, such measures reveal little of the quality of any integration that might have occurred. Similarly, academic skills sessions, particularly any provision of this type that is linked to formative or summative assessment, do not necessarily in themselves constitute any sort of marker as to the extent of integration. The learning activities and tasks that underpin such provision, especially those linked to assessment, may highlight an individual student's adeptness at producing work tailored to a set of specific marking criteria, but it is difficult for a practitioner to appreciate from these outcomes, that student's perception of their position within an academic community.

More nuanced approaches to capturing meaningful feedback are required (e.g. Case Study 19). There is a need for approaches that open up the data collected by shining a light on the relationships built between practitioners and students, on the one hand, and between individual students and their peers, on the other. Such approaches should focus on three key areas: the nature and quality of the interactions taking place within these relationships; the mindset of students as they evolve during a programme of study, but particularly when tackling assessment; and the level of understanding among students of the applicability of the skills and experiences acquired during their studies to the professional contexts where they might seek employment. With these considerations in mind, it is more appropriate to build into teaching ways of gathering evidence that are reflective of the learning experience within individual modules or programmes of study. This idea takes us back to the importance of learning design and the need to employ approaches to teaching that incorporate – or even privilege – elements that allow for the recording of the student perspective. Reflective exercises, particularly diaristic ones, are potentially very useful here, for they allow the student to perceive the process of academic development, while the tutor, simultaneously, is able to gauge the effectiveness of teaching in working towards integration.

Feedback collected during or at the end of an individual teaching session will also speak of the quality of the interactions that have taken place. Such data may be used to assess the extent of integration, for feedback does not have to be negative in order to reflect a lack of integration. Indeed, minimal feedback may more obviously point to a student who is less engaged than others. This type of evidence is perhaps most effective when it is used in conjunction with more traditional ways of measuring academic success, such as written assessments. Assessment literacy, in this way, plays a key role in measuring integration, for in order to perform well, a student is required to demonstrate adeptness in using the skills or attributes traditionally interpreted as hallmarks of academic success, such as academic writing, referencing, and the application of criticality. Regardless of the professional or vocational relevance of some of these skills, a student's ability to meet specific criteria provides a powerful marker of the level of their academic integration. In order to heighten the efficacy of assessment as a more meaningful measure of academic integration, it may be necessary to adapt the form in which it is employed so that it more properly caters for different learning styles. Furthermore, effective assessment also encourages students to engage more meaningfully in the type of learning that builds confidence and promotes integration. Such learning usually has elements of working in partnership with tutors or social learning at its core.

Conclusion

The notion of 'academic integration' references a range of relevant experiential concepts that contribute to the very heart of the student experience – these include the development of learner practice and identity from that of the academic novice towards that of the academic graduate. Such progression occurs within both individual and social learning contexts. For the learner, the experience of the process of academic integration will often be one of dynamic and complex change. This transitory experience will at times be one of uncertainty and challenge, while at other points characterised by a flowering of understanding and aptitude exemplified by the advance of learner confidence and the blossoming of graduate identities. For the teacher, such dynamism offers an extant momentum with which student-centred learning and teaching practice can be aligned to the benefit of both academic disciplinary learning as well as the broader student experience. For the academic lecturer, recognition and understanding of the process of academic integration offers an opportunity, indeed a structural mechanism, to positively harness the transformation occurring within learners towards that of the integrated academic practitioner.

References

Biggs, J. (1996) Enhancing teaching through constructive alignment. *Higher Education*, 32(3), 347–364.
Bovill, C., Cook-Sather, A. & Felten, P. (2011) Students as co-creators of teaching approaches, course design and curricula: implications for academic developers. *International Journal for Academic Development*, 16(2), 133–145.

Broughan, C. & Hunt, L. (2013) Inclusive teaching. In: Hunt, L. & Chalmers, D. (eds.), *University teaching in focus: a learning-centred approach*. London, Routledge, pp. 182–198.

Elkington, S. (2014) Academic engagement. In: Bryson, C. (ed.), *Understanding and developing student engagement*. London, Routledge, pp. 176–190.

Entwistle, N. (2000) Promoting deep learning through teaching and assessment: conceptual frameworks and educational contexts. In: *TLRP 1st Annual Conference, Teaching and Learning Research Programme*. Leicester, UK, 9–10 November 2000. Available from: www.etl.tla.ed.ac.uk/docs/entwistle2000.pdf [Accessed 27 April 2011].

Gourlay, L. (2009) Threshold practices: becoming a student through academic literacies. *London Review of Education*, 7(2), 181–192.

Healey, M., Bovill, C. & Jenkins, A. (2015) Students as partners in learning. In: Lea, J. (ed.), *Enhancing learning and teaching in higher education: engaging with the dimensions of practice*. Milton Keynes, Open University Press, pp. 141–172.

Healey, M., Flint, A. & Harrington, K. (2014) *Engagement through partnership: students as partners in learning and teaching in higher education*. Available from: www.heacademy.ac.uk/system/files/resources/engagement_through_partnership.pdf [Accessed 6 September 2017].

Irons, A. (2007) *Enhancing learning through formative assessment and feedback*. London, Routledge.

Lizzio, A. (2011) *The student lifecycle: an integrative framework for guiding practice*. Available from: www.griffith.edu.au/learning-teaching/student-success/first-year-experience/student-lifecycle-transition-orientation [Accessed 28 September 2017].

Tinto, V. (2009) *Taking student retention seriously: rethinking the first year of university*. [Lecture] Queensland University of Technology, Brisbane, 5 February.

Tinto, V. & Cullen, J. (1973) *Dropout in higher education: a review and theoretical synthesis of recent research*. New York, Columbia University.

Wingate, U. (2006) Doing away with 'study skills'. *Teaching in Higher Education*, 11(4), 457–469.

Winter, R. (2003) Contextualizing the patchwork text: addressing problems of coursework assessment in higher education. *Innovations in Education and Teaching International*, 40(2), 112–122.

Introduction to the case studies

The process of academically integrating students requires their engagement in academic communities *through* academic activity. Such engagement can take many forms, but the case studies highlighted here all seek to promote a greater informed awareness of academic practices and processes among learners in order that they can then apply such understanding to their own learning and assessment practices. The cases included are presented here with a view to their adaptation within various learning contexts, or indeed as a means of stimulating new ideas altogether.

The case studies include:

- a learning activity that seeks to integrate learners from diverse backgrounds into academic communities by reflectively highlighting the value of existing knowledge, skills and aptitudes;
- provision of a student-led online platform that offers opportunity for new and prospective international students to actively engage in the learning environment of their new institution prior to arrival;
- an example of a 'playful learning' approach being used to engage students in discussion of assessment literacy, particularly the subjective nature of assessment;
- a patchwork assessment that supports learners in developing a metacognitive understanding of learning topics and their own personal approaches to their learning;
- a hands-on learning activity designed to develop analytical, reflective, problem-solving and verbal communication aptitudes; and
- increasing student engagement with feedback and feedforward using screen and audio recording software.

Case Study 14: Supporting the transition of mature learners into higher education

John Butcher, The Open University, Milton Keynes, UK

Key themes: transition, reflection, transferable skills, aspirations

Aim of the learning activity

The Open University retains a commitment to open entry and does not set mandatory entry requirements. Activities have to be designed that support students from groups traditionally under-represented in higher education. Barriers to the success of such students include lack of educational confidence, low (or no) prior qualifications, lack of learner resilience, and 'imposter syndrome'. This case study will describe the embedding of reflective assessment activities and the development of studentship skills in Open University entry modules. It is not discipline-dependent and is readily adaptable to other institutions.

Learning outcomes for students

- Demonstrate clear, effective and appropriate communication.
- Formulate a learning plan that begins to develop study and career goals.
- Reflect on own learning and progress.

Description of the learning activity

Students are introduced to two complementary assessment tasks, engaging with the activities at the beginning and end of the entry module. The underlying principles are drawn from the pedagogic literature around supporting non-traditional students to transition successfully into higher education. These include: the value of scaffolding learner-reflection on prior educational experience around personal and work achievements in order to identify relevant/transferable skills already possessed; aligning personal and learning goals with a transparent understanding of the trajectory of higher education skills development; and embedding skills development in module content.

Step-by-step guide to running the activity

Activity 1

This requires learners to reflect on their educational journey (for some students, this may have negative connotations), and why they have chosen to engage with higher education at this time in their lives, and to indicate (however tentatively) their personal/employability aspirations as part of a learning plan. This is appended to the first assessment of content and carries an assessment weighting. This activity is assessed by tutors, and feedback should contextualise the life experiences they bring to their learning. The aim is to build trust between student and tutor in order to overcome barriers associated with mature student identity, and to clarify precisely what the student hopes to gain from the module – this can be supported or gently redirected by the tutor's feedback.

Timescale: Within the first four to six weeks of the entry module. Feedback should be provided within a three-week turnaround to ensure impact on subsequent learning.

Resource: Teaching/student support would need to refocus in the run-up to the assessment to ensure students understood the nature and importance of reflection as a critical skill in becoming a successful learner (perhaps sharing anonymous examples and critiquing them). The learning plan could either consist of a series of prompt questions or a pro forma. Feedback would focus on the depth of reflection and the practicability of the learning plan. Tutors may need some professional development to share good practice in this aspect.

Activity 2

This requires learners to reflect on what they identified in their first activity (above) and review the extent to which their transition to a successful higher education learner has been as they expected or has been affected by one or more critical points in their learning journey. It is appended to the final assessment task on the module, is weighted, and could be formative or summative. Often, students will identify different aspects of the subject matter they enjoyed compared to what they expected to enjoy, or articulate how they were able to use skills (e.g. time management) from their pre-higher education selves, or report how crucial individuals (e.g. peers, a tutor) encouraged them to persist. Tutor feedback should focus on feeding forward into a longer-term learning plan.

Timescale: Embedded as part of the final assessment task on the module, students engage with a reflective activity to review their original learning plan and their response to tutor feedback. Tutors would feedforward to support progress into year 2 and the development of a more sustainable and longer-term learning plan.

Resource: Tutor/student support time ahead of the assessment point would need to demonstrate the importance of engaging in the activity and model the kind of response that would gain a high mark. Evidence from this review could be embedded into an institution's PDP strategy – mature learners in particular could be encouraged to capture learning in this medium, but it is relevant to all learners.

Ways in which it could be adapted/extended for different disciplines or levels

The activities described were designed with entry-level learners in mind as a core part of a first undergraduate module. It is currently used across the curriculum through three cross-disciplinary modules (arts and languages; people, work and society; science, technology and maths). It is effective across all three and would require little or no adaptation for different subjects. It could be easily adapted for different levels and would support transition into subsequent years. The reflective prompts would simply need to target progress in learning from the previous year.

Case Study 15: Aiding active learning through pre-arrival, student-led resource for international students (student pre-arrival induction for continuing education [SPICE])

Monika Foster, Queen Margaret University (formerly Edinburgh Napier University), Edinburgh, UK

Key themes: pre-arrival, international, online, academic and social integration

Aim of the learning activity

The aim of this activity is to provide a student-led online platform to actively engage new and prospective international students in the learning and teaching environment of the host university prior to the start of their course. This suite of activities is aimed at enabling students to integrate more successfully within their new environment and achieve better study results while making the transition to the university a much more enjoyable experience. The outcomes of online activities enable the programme leader and support tutors to identify the student's strengths and weaknesses prior to the start of the programme.

Learning outcomes for students

- Recognise expectations and actively engage in the new learning and teaching environment of the host university prior to arrival.
- Engage with pre-arrival activities designed by students for students that address 'real' issues and student struggles, and enable appropriate peer support.
- Develop skills to aid integration into the new learning and teaching environment in order to achieve better academic results.

Description of the learning activity

International students when transitioning to a new learning and teaching environment encounter a number of challenges related to the differences in academic cultures, the expectations of students at higher education level in the UK, integrating socially, and living and studying in a new country. On arrival, induction to university life often happens too late for these students unable to address the breadth of the new skills and awareness needed in time to succeed. Standard inductions often cover areas identified as necessary from an academic staff perspective. Previous research (Foster, 2010, 2011a, 2011b; Foster & Anderson, 2015) suggests that students, even before their arrival to study in the UK, form relationships with same-nationality students and use their peers' advice to prepare for and begin their study in UK higher education. This peer advice can be misleading and can lead to new students following the same, potentially not very well-developed pathway.

To break this cycle and take advantage of peer support offered, an interactive student-led platform – designed by working with a mixed-nationality group of over 200 students from different subject areas – was developed that utilises peer advice in a coordinated and appropriate way. A link to the site of SPICE International can be found at http://open.napier.ac.uk/.

Step-by-step guide to running the activity

Before arrival to the UK, but after a conditional offer is issued, all international students are introduced to an interactive, pre-arrival resource, 'SPICE International'. This resource includes a selection of tasks and student voices recorded from the students who have completed their study at the university (no long documents or students being told what is the right thing to do).

The students complete the tasks and move up to the next level. There are 10 units or levels, and students must complete the unit before moving on to the next one.

The units include the following areas:

Unit 1: Studying at a UK university

Unit 2: Your learning style

Unit 3: Time management during your studies

Unit 4: Lectures

Unit 5: Tutorials: group work and presentations

Unit 6: Writing essays and reports

Unit 7: Academic language

Unit 8: Using resources for your research: referencing and avoiding plagiarism

Unit 9: Assessment

Unit 10: Study support

Students receive a certificate on completion, and their record of completing SPICE goes to the designated programme leader and support tutor. The record shows what areas students struggled with and had to take a few times before getting it right. It also shows some of the open-ended answers students have given, which gives a good indication of the students' English language skills and their general orientation with the new learning and teaching environment. Based on this record, the support tutor can prepare a programme of workshops for a student and offer them at the time of induction. Often the needs of international students are assessed way after the start of the programme, and by the time adequate support is offered it may be too late before the first assessments are due.

Students are also introduced to a buddy scheme with a fellow student currently studying in the university who can offer help and advice (the buddy student volunteers are briefed and prepared how to support new international students and what help is on offer, so the cycle of 'peer help' within the same national groups and potentially repeating the same mistakes is broken, and students are offered peer support in a more structured way). When the new international students arrive on campus, they meet their buddy students, and the relationship can continue or stops depending on both students' preference.

Ways in which it could be adapted/extended for different disciplines or levels

The way SPICE International can be used can vary a lot. It can be used as a fully online resource, but with many partners in areas where online access for students is limited, the approach can be more classroom-based. This involves working with a partner college or university to design a bridging programme that utilizes SPICE International materials as a classroom-based activity. The buddy scheme is supported by the local college; for example, Skype sessions with the UK-based buddies are organised in the college. The support from the local tutors is crucial in that they can highlight the benefits of an early induction and encourage students to take part in the SPICE programme and the buddy programme.

Upon arrival to the UK, the use of SPICE and the buddy scheme can be extended beyond induction and continue into the academic year. It is a great platform to ensure students receive necessary advice in a structured way.

References

Foster, M. (2010) *Online study skills resource SPICE project*. Available from: www.heacademy.ac.uk/knowledge-hub/monika-talks-about-student-pre-arrival-induction-continuing-education-spice-project-0 [Accessed 30 October 2017].

Foster, M. (2011a) Engaging students in enhanced academic transitions. In: Foster, M. (ed.), *Working with cultural diversity in higher education*. Special 28. London, Staff and Educational Development Association (SEDA).

Foster, M. (2011b) Engaging students in enhanced academic transitions: a case on online study skills resource SPICE. *Journal of Learning Development in Higher Education*, 3. Available from: www.aldinhe.ac.uk/ojs/index.php?journal=jldhe&page=article&op=view&path%5B%5D=71&path%5B%5D=80 [Accessed 30 October 2017].

Foster, M. & Anderson, L. (eds.) (2015) Exploring internationalisation of the curriculum to enhance the student experience. *Journal of Perspectives in Applied Academic Practice*, 3(3). Available from: https://jpaap.napier.ac.uk/index.php/JPAAP/issue/view/12 [Accessed 30 October 2017].

Case Study 16: The biscuit game

Sally Brown, independent consultant, UK

Key themes: evaluation, assessment, feedback, integration

Aim of the learning activity

This light-hearted game was devised for use with students, staff new to assessing, and experienced staff as part of a long-term project at Anglia Ruskin University to transform assessment and feedback. It raises some very serious issues about the complexities and imprecision of assessment.

Learning outcomes for students

- Informally discuss with fellow learners and staff some of the tacit assumptions we make about assessment.
- Generate productive discussions about how criteria are applied in practice and how they link to the marks given.
- Demonstrate and apply a greater sense of assessment literacy.

Description of the learning activity

This game involves 'playful learning', undertaking a supposedly silly task but using it for serious purposes, with decisions about biscuits being used metaphorically for the ways in which we make judgments against criteria in assignments. It makes use of ideas developed as part of the HEA project *A Marked Improvement*, subsequently taken forward at ARU (HEA, 2012). The task demonstrates that assessment is a complex, nuanced task with some grey areas, and just as agreed definitions of biscuits are not always readily achievable, assignments benefit from dialogue before, during and afterwards to clarify expectations. It acknowledges that assessment can often be an imprecise and inexact activity, and it is helpful to recognise that absolute certainty about grades is not always achievable, especially if more than one person is involved.

It can be helpful for students, new staff and experienced staff to bring to the surface the fact that although criteria may be considered to be explicit, the way people are graded according to agreed criteria can differ substantially. Category definitions can sometimes be complicated when setting assignments. This task models for novices how important it is to have conversations about what criteria really mean. Generic discussion about assessment and how we grade can be extremely valuable in developing assessment literacy, and the game shows how it can often be useful to start from individual perspectives at the outset of an assignment and clarify preconceptions, and to agree definitions of what is, for example, a portfolio.

Step-by-step guide to running the activity

For each table of up to 10 people, you will need a selection of 'biscuits', including, for example, a Jaffa cake, a rich tea biscuit, a budget ginger biscuit, an expensive 'high-quality' biscuit and a Hobnob, plus a cream cracker, a high-bake water biscuit, a piece of Scottish shortbread, a piece of flapjack, and a large coffee shop cookie. These should be on a plate and should be covered with foil or a napkin so they are not visible until stage 3. The facilitator should then give the following instructions:

1 As an individual, in 180 characters describe what a biscuit is, either on paper or as a tweet. If the latter, these can be shared on the hashtag #biscuitcriteria.
2 With colleagues at your table, compare your definitions and aim to achieve consensus about what biscuits are.
3 Unwrap the biscuit plate in the middle of the table and collectively try to decide, using your agreed definitions, whether the items on the plate are biscuits. Do not at this stage eat the biscuits.
4 At your table, discuss what the criteria are for good biscuits. Aim to have criteria across five grades: outstanding biscuits, good biscuits, adequate biscuits, poor biscuits and completely unacceptable biscuits.
5 Collectively choose from your plate five items that you agree are biscuits and collectively rate them on the scale of 1 to 5.
6 Discuss how difficult it has been for you to achieve consensus on the ratings for your biscuits.
7 Discuss in small groups or in plenary the assessment issues that have arisen during the biscuit exercise, and explore how the same issues are reflected in confusion by both students and academic markers about what criteria really mean in practice, how these might be differentially weighted, and how clarity on consensus can be achieved prior to use on a real assessed task.
8 If the biscuits have not been over-handled, you may invite your participants to eat them.

There are potentially cultural dimensions to the game and the problem of producing precise biscuit definitions, since in many nations the concept 'biscuit' is not widely understood or frequently used. Rich discussions often emerge because precise distinctions between biscuits, cookies and crackers are difficult to achieve. Contested criteria include whether they have to be sweet and crisp, the extent to which they can be dunked, and whether a very large biscuit should technically be called a cookie. Many would suggest that the difference between a biscuit and a cake (according to UK legislation relating to VAT payable on Jaffa cakes) is that biscuits go soft when stale whereas cake goes hard.

This game is made available by ARU as an Open Educational Resource.

Ways in which it could be adapted/extended for different disciplines or levels

The game is designed to be interdisciplinary, and can be used with staff and students in a wide variety of subject areas, but it doesn't really work in the many nations where biscuits are not widely eaten. Efforts to find substitute commodities such as chocolate, beer or sweets/candy have not been successful to date, and carry their own cultural problems. Maybe it's just best to play the biscuit game!

Reference

HEA (2012) *A marked improvement: transforming assessment in higher education*. York, Higher Education Academy.

Case Study 17: In praise of patchwork assessment: creating a more flexible process that effectively supports the learning of part-time and in-work students

Stella Jones-Devitt, Sheffield Hallam University, Sheffield, UK

Key themes: assessment, patchwork text, work-based learning, integrated learning

Aim of the learning activity

Patchwork assessment engages students in developing an integrated cognitive understanding of relevant topics while facilitating ongoing reflection and justification for their decision-making and subsequent reasoning. It develops the skills of retrospective synthesis and continuous critical thinking concurrently, while being driven by pivotal learning moments identified by the students themselves.

Learning outcomes for students

- Identify the integrated nature of learning.
- Develop informed and incremental critical responses to learning across each level of study through continuous synthesis of theory and practice.
- Recognise and analyse the incremental, personalised and relevant nature of the learning process through a series of self-managed assessment tasks that bring together learning from across modules to develop relevant academic and reflective skills.

Description of the learning activity

This case study relates to a part-time undergraduate programme, BA (Hons) Health and Social Care Leadership and Management. Students are usually sponsored by their employers (primarily the National Health Service Trusts), and the emphasis is upon workplace impact in addition to personal and professional development. Students have supervisory or leadership experience and enter the programme at level 5 by demonstrating a wide range of experiential learning, which the programme privileges as a key starting point for course pedagogy, practical design and delivery. The programme has been redesigned to reflect a more radical stance when using assessment for learning with part-time, in-work students. In developing this process to replace the traditional end-loaded undergraduate dissertation, the course team drew upon the conviction that within the field of health and social care education, more attention to putting a complex theory into practice – or praxis – should be given, especially in relation to the ways in which the process of learner development is assessed.

In considering more user-friendly and emancipatory approaches to assessment for part-time, in-work students, two Critical Thinking Leadership modules (at level 5 the Critically Thinking Leader for Personal Effectiveness, and at level 6 the Critically Thinking Leader for Organisational Improvement) were created as practical mechanisms for developing innovative assessment for learning processes. Each Critical Thinking module draws upon assessment processes from all other programme modules by using patchwork principles in which objects or concepts emergent from every assessed module are identified by students and 'stitched' together in 'patches' to form overarching, justificatory and individualised narratives (in many ways as 'meta' patchworks) that become personal and professional development tools for the learner and their organisation. These replace the end-point summative traditional dissertation.

Step-by-step guide to running the activity

Each Critical Thinking module draws upon assessment processes from all other programme modules by using patchwork assessment principles in which objects or concepts emergent from every assessed module are identified by students and stitched together – or on occasion unravelled – in patches to form overarching, justificatory and individualised narratives that become personal and professional development tools for the learner and their organisation.

With peer and tutor support, students choose and justify pivotal learning moments throughout each module across a whole course. These 'moments' could comprise an object, concept, conversation or critical incident.

Students produce a three-part patchwork assessment (7,000 words for level 5 and 7,500 for level 6) of emerging leadership themes gained from critical scrutiny of formative and summative assessment processes of all programme modules, along with peer and self-review. These processes are crystallised into either a personal leadership effectiveness and improvement plan using all relevant programme outcomes at level 5, or a personal organisational leadership effectiveness and improvement plan at level 6. Both processes draw upon all learning outcomes at the relevant level.

Part 1 of the assessment involves production of an overarching diagram detailing key themes and rationales for the pivotal learning throughout the programme as both student and leader.

Part 2 considers identification and generation of appropriate evidence that can be used to demonstrate workplace impact as an effective leader.

Part 3 (level 5) involves production of an individually justified personal leadership development and improvement plan, while part 3 (level 6) involves production of an individually justified organisational development and improvement plan.

Overall marks for these modules relate to how well students have addressed all learning outcomes and demonstrated attainment of generic academic outcomes within the process. Developing and critiquing appropriate evidence – and examining the kinds of activities that might produce such evidence – forms a considerable part of the patchwork process as a group of peer learners.

As this more personalised learning progresses across the course, students develop confidence and a sense of identity as learners, rather than solely as workers. Consequently, conceptual gaps between the patches become more complex, closely aligned, sophisticated and increasingly robust as students develop confidence in their skills of both synthesis and reflection at the same time. For staff, this provides an opportunity to consider more engaged ways of working with students in partnership and in co-designing an emerging pedagogical approach.

Ways in which it could be adapted/extended for different disciplines or levels

Scoggins and Winter (1999) first posited their notions of patchwork assessment underpinned by the assumption that this form of assessment would relate to modules and sessions in which individual pivotal learning moments would be documented and stitched together over a period of weeks. While this approach still prevails, there are many other examples in which patchwork assessment processes have been scaled up across programmes, devised across many subject and disciplinary areas and academic levels, and delivered over substantial periods of academic study to become meta-patchwork assessment processes. For a range of approaches, see www.heacademy.ac.uk/resource/patchwork-assessment-practice-guide.

Reference

Scoggins, J. & Winter, R. (1999) The patchwork text: a coursework format for education as critical understanding. *Teaching in Higher Education*, 4(4), 485–499. Available from: http://dx.doi.org/10.1080/1356251990040405.

Case Study 18: Learning to think outside the square

Liz Ditzel and Josie Crawley, Otago Polytechnic, Dunedin, New Zealand

Key themes: reflection, evaluation, creativity, problem-solving

Aim of the learning activity

This hands-on learning activity helps students to develop problem-solving, reflective thinking and verbal communication skills. It utilises a combination of a sealed box and a children's story to enhance observational and problem-solving skills. Learners use prior experience and theoretical knowledge to challenge the status quo by asking questions such as: 'why?', 'why not?' and 'what if?'.

Learning outcomes for students

- Understand the problem-solving process and develop reflective thinking skills.
- Be open to considering new ideas and possibilities, and be able to share ideas and categories, and assess alternative sources of information.
- Be able to apply theoretical knowledge to a practical situation.

Description of the learning activity

Problem-solving can be challenging, especially in a group situation where students may feel uncomfortable in expressing ideas in front of others. In this activity, a safe classroom environment and the teaching tools interplay to help students evaluate evidence. The apparently simple task of judging the contents of the box follows a predetermined sequence of 'looking' (observation, description, thinking) before 'doing' (gaining additional information by touch and sound). This teaches students self-control and to think before doing.

Reading a children's storybook in an adult classroom takes students by surprise and becomes a way of opening up thinking to new possibilities that could be outside their personal experience. A good story captures attention, and invites listeners to sit back, listen and use their imagination. Picture books are particularly useful, as illustrations often take the place of words and are open to multiple interpretations designed to capture attention. In this activity, the story gives students permission to 'think outside of the square' and imagine a range of different possibilities that don't conform to conventional thinking. Adding alternatives generated after the book has been read to the list of probable contents allows students to challenge the status quo and ask new questions such as 'why not?'. Working in small groups encourages students to share personal experiences. Placing information on Post-it notes is an effective and impersonal way of displaying information for all students to see and evaluate.

Step-by-step guide to running the activity

Resources needed

1. A set of small, sealed boxes (hard cardboard or wood) of the same shape and size. Each box contains a movable object and cannot be opened (use different objects and create simple partitions or dividers inside the box if possible).
2. A children's picture storybook called *The Box* by Martha Lightfoot (alternative books can be found).
3. Post-it notes (two different colours), whiteboard.

Procedure and timescale

1. Set up the room with a box on a desk surrounded by five or six seats, invite students to enter the room, and instruct them to *look at* but not touch their allocated box (5 minutes).
2. Ask each student to write a description of what they see before them. Select one student from each group to read aloud their description (10 minutes).
3. Give each student three yellow Post-it notes, ask them to brainstorm the box's possible contents, and record each idea on a Post-it note (5 minutes).
4. Ask students to sort the Post-it notes into categories, and come up in their groups and stick notes on the whiteboard for all to see (10 minutes).
5. Read the children's story aloud to the class, showing the book's illustrations (5 minutes).

6   Ask students to reconsider the contents of the box, given the reading, and record their new ideas on different coloured Post-it notes. Add new notes (and categories) to the display on the board (10 minutes).
7   Invite students to touch and manipulate the box and use this new information to reconsider the box's contents (10 minutes).
8   Ask each group to draw a picture on the whiteboard of what they think is in the box (5 minutes).
9   Debrief the activity (10–30 minutes).

Rationale and principles

Steps 1–4: Use observational and problem-solving skills. Ideas are usually constrained to objects that would fit insides the box, such as a marble, toy, etc. *Ask students to explain why their thinking fits this pattern.*

Step 2: Points out similarities and differences in individual descriptions and highlights the need for accuracy in recording information.

Step 4: Encourages discussion and debate about how to sort and organise information. Relate this to researching an essay and deciding what avenues to further explore (i.e. are there any common arguments for or against a topic?).

Step 5: Reading the book opens up thinking to new and imaginary possibilities, including living creatures, spirits, inanimate objects, etc. being inside the box. *Ask what value this might have.*

Step 6: New ideas and categories are posted. Point out that these may come from alternative sources and are also worth considering.

Step 7: Touching and listening provides additional information. Explore how this helps to solve the problem.

Step 8: Drawing a picture helps to visualise each box's contents. Note contents are different and the boxes are never opened!

Summary: key teaching/learning points

- Make explicit the sequence of observing before touching and listening.
- Emphasise the length of time taken to look and think before taking action. Explore possible reasons for this, such as personal (e.g. a dangerous or poisonous object, microbe or gas) and cultural safety (e.g. privacy, religious beliefs).
- Explore students' reactions to the children's story and discuss new ideas generated by the reading.

- Draw attention to the process students used to categorise their Post-it note information.
- Discuss how the problem-solving and reflective skills developed here could be used in other situations, such as performing a health assessment or conducting research.
- Explore reasons why the boxes are not opened, relating this to problems that cannot be solved or human conditions that cannot be diagnosed.

Ways in which it could be adapted/extended for different disciplines or levels

This activity can be used for range of problem-solving activities, such as researching an essay topic, conducting a literature review, learning to think creatively, and exploring and valuing difference. It can be used in a range of disciplines, such as health, social work and design, that require students to use problem-solving skills based on a sequence of observation, description, assessment and evaluation of alternatives. Students can be challenged to think of ways that evaluating the contents of a small wooden box could be applied to other situations and/or invited to contribute other helpful stories or narratives.

Case Study 19: Use of screen recording software to promote engagement with assignment feedback and feedforward in undergraduate studies

Henry Dawson, Cardiff Metropolitan University, Cardiff, UK

Key themes: feedback, assessment, screencast, online marking

Aim of the learning activity

Higher education suffers from a lack of undergraduate engagement with assignment feedback. This gives rise to repetition of mistakes and poor practice, inhibiting the development of subject-specific and more general academic skills and knowledge. This activity, focused on using screencast feedback, enables the marker to provide more directed feedback to the student, to direct students to additional material, and to reduce marking time.

Learning outcomes for students

- Gain a greater understanding of the expectations of the student through more detailed feedback.
- Benefit from improved understanding of their feedback through the use of visual aids and the tone of their teacher's voice.
- Engage more fully in using feedback to enhance future assessment performance.

Description of the learning activity

Good-quality feedback is a key part of student learning and poor-quality feedback can even harm that learning (Voerman, Meijer & Korthagen, 2012). Assignment feedback should be reflected on and internalised by students. However, the trouble comes with making this happen.

Providing thorough feedback is important to student engagement and their general satisfaction. Thorough feedback can be given in a written format; however, the more modern tools of recorded audio and video allow feedback to be provided more efficiently (Vincelette & Bostic, 2013; Bilbro, Iluzda & Clark, 2013). A great deal more information can be disseminated to the student in the same time that the marker would take to make basic text comments on the work by hand. The feedback can be more detailed and contextualized, and there is the ability to employ tone (Silva, 2012; Vincelette & Bostic, 2013; Bilbro, Iluzada & Clark, 2013).

The use of screen recording software allows students to be presented with a personalised video of their assignment, overlaid by an audio commentary on their efforts. Providing student feedback in this novel and enhanced form, combined with a structure to compel the students to access and interact with that feedback, will lead to higher levels of engagement with feedback and reflection by the students on their work.

Step-by-step guide to running the activity

Participants and setting

The screencast assessment was undertaken on sequential module assessments at levels 4 and 5 for the housing component of an undergraduate programme in Environmental Health. The assignments consisted of reports, including diagrams/photos and tables, focusing on property construction and the use of a housing health assessment tool. Screen recording software was used with assessments at both levels.

Software notes

Camtasia Studio was used to record the feedback. There are other similar packages available.

Prior to assignment submission

At the time students were writing their assignment, they were played three screencasts during lectures. These screencasts showed feedback from an assignment with a very low mark, one with a mid-level mark and one with a high mark. The students were able to see how the assignments were set out and make notes on what the lecturer mentioned in their feedback on each. Permission was obtained to use real student assignments with a medium and a high grade. The assignment with a low grade was mocked up by the lecturer.

Following assignment submission

Students submitted their assignments as both a paper copy and an electronic version of their assignments, using the Moodle online learning platform. Assignments were read and prompts were made in the margins of the paper copies of the assignment, to be used by the lecturer to structure their recorded feedback. These would have been quite cryptic for the student, forcing them to rely on the screencast feedback. The submitted copy of the assignment was placed on the screen and the screen recorded while the lecturer manipulated the text, brought up relevant lecture overheads and web resources, and talked into a microphone headset. Feedback files were 5–15 minutes long.

Feedback required a basic notebook laptop. The Camtasia file initially generated was exported as an MP4 (as this is widely playable) then uploaded onto the online learning platform. In Moodle, you can enable the option to give feedback files and upload the file to the student's assignment feedback area. Files are too large to email.

Students were asked to watch the feedback and then write an email to the lecturer summarising something from that feedback that could be used to improve their grade in future assignments. They were also required to guess their grade. Once the lecturer had received their email, the grade would be sent by return of that email. In addition, students were encouraged to compare their screencast feedback to that from other assignments to look for common factors.

Once a basic grasp of the software has been obtained, grading/feedback time per assignment remained commensurate with written marking and feedback times.

Ways in which it could be adapted/extended for different disciplines or levels

In addition to topic-specific feedback improvements, significant success was gained from encouraging reflection and metacognition from students with respect to their general study skills. This intervention would lend itself to study skills elements of programmes. It is also uniquely suited for assignment formats involving video, diagrams and poster formats.

Screen recording software is ideal for recording 'mini-guides' on tricky or essential concepts, to provide a series of two- to five-minute revision aids for posting online.

The software provides another tool for educators that can be turned to many creative uses, and requires little technical know-how and computing power to use.

References

Bilbro, J., Iluzda, C. & Clark, D.E. (2013) Responding effectively to composition students: comparing student perceptions of written and audio feedback. *Journal on Excellence of College Teaching*, 24(1): 47–83.

Silva, M.L. (2012) Camtasia in the classroom: student attitudes and preferences for video commentary or Microsoft Word comments during the revision process. *Computers and Composition*, 29: 1–22.

Vincelette, E.J. & Bostic, T. (2013) Show and tell: student and instructor perceptions of screencast assessment. *Assessing Writing*, 18: 257–277.

Voerman, L., Meijer, P.C. & Korthagen, R.J.S. (2012) Types and frequencies of feedback interventions in classroom interaction in secondary education. *Teaching and Teacher Education*, 28: 1107–1115.

Chapter 7

Developing social integration

Mark Sutcliffe and Ruth Matheson

Introduction to the chapter

The need for students to integrate socially as well as academically is fundamental to student success. Lizzio's (2011) Student Lifecycle Framework highlights social integration as starting before students arrive at university, as students develop their "sense of inclusion" and ask the question "how will I fit?" (p. 8). This sense influences their choice of institution, and having made that choice the beginning of their social and professional identity with that institution. As students step into and through their chosen programme of study, their focus is around making and maintaining friendships and a "sense of connection" (p. 8), as they consider who they know and how to facilitate these developing relationships. Lizzio (2011) states that students moving out of university begin to develop a "sense of professional community" with questions such as "who are my future colleagues?" and finally, when transitioning as alumni or returning students, their "sense of citizenship and leadership" comes to the forefront as they develop a "sense of positive professional identity", questioning "where do I stand?" (p. 8).

In this chapter, we are going to focus upon the social dimensions of integration and its significance on student retention, transition and wellbeing. We will also explore whose responsibility it is to ensure that students successfully find their *social feet*, and question whether it is the responsibility of staff and the institution, or whether the responsibility lies more squarely with the individual student. We will highlight the cultural dimension of social integration that comes with an increasingly diverse international student population, and how effective cultural integration might be promoted. Finally, we will consider the psychological needs of students.

The case studies to support this chapter will address a wide range of issues. They will highlight activities that promote social and cultural integration, including the role of outward-bound field trips, peer learning networks, and the use of audio magazines to engage a geographically dispersed learner population. Cases will also consider the issues facing students returning to study following a period of absence, and identifying activities that help staff address mental health issues in students.

Defining social integration

Harvey, Drew and Smith (2006) define social integration as "those experiences that help to connect students to the college environment, that aid in their psychosocial development, and that contribute to their overall satisfaction in college" (p. 32). These experiences are largely drawn from students' academic experience, and include both the impact of teaching and learning and the wider set of relationships between staff and students that underpin this interaction. Although the academic sphere is important, research suggests (Wilcox, Winn & Fyvie-Gauld, 2005; Thomas, 2002) that as much emphasis should be placed upon the social sphere as the academic sphere to positively shape students' engagement and retention, and that the two go hand in hand. The nature of social integration is therefore both multidimensional and complex, consisting of both academic and social relationships that are constantly changing and evolving. Brooman and Darwent (2014), in their quantitative study to measure social integration in students, identified three dimensions fundamental to developing positive social integration: the development of a sense of belonging, relationships with staff, and maintaining old friendships.

The habits and practices that are produced through the process of social interaction create what Reay, David and Ball (2001 cited by Thomas, 2012) refer to as an "institutional habitus," a set of expectations and standards that new students are expected to attain and conform to on entry (p. 13). Such expectations and standards are deeply embedded within the fabric of the organisation and are considered by Bourdieu and Passeron (1977) to be socially and culturally biased. Those students that fail to match up to these expectations may well feel that they do not fit and very quickly experience isolation and marginalisation, and typically consider early withdrawal from study. Therefore, those institutions that through their learning and teaching practices actively promote inclusivity, provide opportunities within the academic curriculum for the development of social integration and belonging, and provide opportunities to develop positive staff–student and peer relationships will help to mitigate these feelings of social isolation (Thomas, 2012). This positive institutional habitus will in turn help to promote student confidence and positive self-belief.

Why is it so important?

In 2017, the UK Higher Education Statistics Agency (HESA) announced that the non-continuation rate of full-time students after first year from UK higher education institutions increased for the second year in a row. In 2014–2015, 6.2 per cent of those who enrolled in higher education did not continue their studies beyond their first year, with the drop-out rate for those classified as being from disadvantaged backgrounds slightly higher at 8.8 per cent (Higher Education Statistics Agency, 2017). Although these rates were regarded as not being high by international standards (although this is hard to prove due to differences in definition and data collection practices), they still represent significant numbers of students withdrawing from higher education. However, the reality of those considering leaving higher education is significantly higher. In her study, Thomas (2012) reports shocking statistics that although only between 6 and 8 per cent of students leave, between 37 and 42 per cent seriously consider it. So why do such large numbers of students start but then fail to complete their time in higher education, and an even bigger group contemplate leaving? A wide range of variables have been found to impact upon and explain student retention. These include factors that focus upon academic performance and a general dissatisfaction with the university experience, as well as those criteria that focus more on social dimensions, such as feelings of isolation and not fitting in. Although the academic experience is important in making students feel part of the university community, it is not everything. For Thomas (2012), a "strong sense of belonging in higher education" was critical to promoting retention (p. 13) (see Chapter 3).

The development of peer networks and friendship (Rubin, 2012a), membership and participation in university clubs and societies, and links with staff all play a significant part in helping to retain students and promote engagement. Hamshire, Willgoss and Wibberley (2013), in a review of retention among nursing students in the north-west of England, found that student decisions to leave were often complex, involved a multiple set of academic and social issues, and often impacted upon the student over an extended time frame. It was the accumulation of these multiple factors that was often most significant. A study by Wilcox, Winn and Fyvie-Gauld (2005) found that students who withdrew from study identified between four and nine different reasons for their decision. As well as academic and social factors, material factors were also considered such as finances, although these were the least frequently cited motivations for withdrawal.

Who suffers from a lack of social integration?

The student population today is more socially and culturally diverse than ever. It is necessary that higher education institutions seek to recognise that the student population today will have a wide range of social, cultural and educational experience, and that inclusive teaching and learning models must draw on and use this diversity in order to improve retention rates.

Typically, it has been found (Rubin, 2012a; Rubin & Wright, 2015a; Christie, Barron & D'Annunzio-Green, 2013; Brooman & Darwent, 2014; Patiniotis & Holdsworth, 2005) that those that feel most academically isolated tend to be socially on the fringes, finding it difficult to make friends and fully integrate. Extensive work, such as that by Rubin (2012b; Rubin & Wright, 2015b) in Australia, discovered that retention rates are often poorest among groups of students from the lower socio-economic groups. Such students have been found to participate less in both formal and informal social situations. Rubin and Wright (2015b) suggest that working-class students tend to be older than their middle-class counterparts, and as such tend to have less time to engage in social activities due to work and childcare commitments, reducing the time spent on campus and their ability to form friendships. Additionally, they suggest that finances preclude much extra-curricular or informal social interaction, which often costs money.

Other non-traditional student groups such as direct entrants, many of whom are foreign students completing the final year of their degree, also find social integration difficult. Work by Christie, Barron and D'Annunzio-Green (2013) looking at direct entrants entering a post-1992 university in Scotland considered how students struggle to become "legitimate members" by "coming to know and understand" how to operate in a new community of practice (p. 626). Feelings of loneliness, the remoteness of staff and a general lack of knowledge as to how university operated produced feelings of isolation within this student group. Those direct entrant students that were most successful in integrating tended to be more academically prepared and ready for higher education, having the necessary skills, attributes and very often confidence to be successful within this environment (Thomas, 2012). Being academically ready, and the success that comes from that, should not be underestimated in offsetting the impact of feelings of social isolation (Khawaja & Stallman, 2011).

Many students who find social integration difficult are often part-time, or like many students these days live at home and travel into the university campus. A number of studies (Brooman & Darwent, 2014; Patiniotis & Holdsworth, 2005) have suggested that living off campus significantly reduces the opportunity for students to make friends and engage socially. Although, in a positive light, it has been suggested that living at home might in fact mitigate not only some of the financial insecurity and risk of university (a widely cited reason for withdrawal), but might also, as suggested by Giddens (cited in Patiniotis & Holdsworth, 2005) provide "ontological security," the security derived from the familiar, such as family and community (p. 85).

Whose responsibility is social integration?

Effective social integration is the responsibility of many groups. Students have a responsibility to be open to making new friends and engaging with those opportunities for social engagement that are presented to them. Staff have a responsibility to ensure that students are respected and that opportunities for social engagement are built into the curriculum, learning and teaching methodologies, and the wider academic sphere. At a wider institutional level, the higher education institution has a responsibility to engage students from pre-entry, in, through and out of university to ensure that students can make the most of their university experience and utilise the opportunities and support needed to succeed. This includes institutional enhancement projects, support for clubs, societies and groups, support services that students might draw upon to facilitate more effective engagement, close working relations with the student union, and listening to the voices of both students and staff.

The role of the student

Supportive peer relations and the development of peer networks and friendships should be encouraged even prior to the students' arrival. The use of social media makes this increasingly possible. Pre-arrival activities that allow students to introduce themselves provide opportunities to develop programme cohesion prior to face-to-face contact. Students' induction programmes should place significant emphasis on facilitating peer relations (e.g. Case Study 23) and networks, as the role of peers in helping to act against the uncertainties and anxieties of starting university is important. Peer support helps to reduce dropout rates and establishes a more positive higher education experience. Thomas (2012) identifies the following benefits resulting from friendship and peer relations:

- the promotion of academic integration and belonging;
- the development of student confidence as learners in higher education;
- improvements in student motivation and success;
- a source of academic help and study support;
- an opportunity to share knowledge and assessment preparation;
- the provision of emotional support;
- practical support; and
- allows students to compare their performance against others and seek reassurance in this.

(p. 49)

Although the benefits from peer relations, networks and friendship groups is significant, many students fail to fully appreciate the educational significance that arises from having supportive peer relations. Part-time students, mature students, and students that live locally and commute to university (a growing number) are often groups that express reluctance to enter into new friendships, seeing them as unnecessary. Distant learners present more of a challenge in the development of group coherence and meaningful social relations (e.g. Case Study 21). However, with clear academic benefits arising from strong peer relations, staff and institutions must seek to find ways to embed such opportunities into the academic endeavours of students, facilitating peer relations at the same time. Student group or project work might be the simplest expression of this.

The role of staff

Research suggests (Thomas, 2012) that students who have poor relations with staff, or who feel that staff do not know them, are more likely to consider leaving university and dropping out. Where relationships are strong, and students feel valued, this acts as a positive motivating factor, encouraging greater effort from the student. Good relations, according to Thomas (2012), exhibit the following characteristics:

- staff know students;
- staff appear interested in students and their progress;
- staff are available and respond to students in a timely way;
- staff value student input, and respect the diversity and difference they contribute; and
- students are able to approach staff for support.

(p. 33)

One of the main ways by which staff can establish such a positive relationship with students is via the personal tutoring system. The role of the personal tutor is a significant one, especially for 'at-risk students' (Hagenauer & Volet, 2014), supporting both the students' academic development and underpinning their social integration. Personal tutors fulfil many roles for the student; they act as a point of first contact, help the student to connect with their subject or discipline, and provide both academic and social support, as well as linking to the wider support system provided by the university (discussed further in Chapter 8). Turner et al. (2017) suggest the adoption of an immersive induction programme (see Case Study 2) that facilitates the development of peer networks, robust relationships with staff, active engagement of students with the discipline, and that lead to enhanced course engagement. Turner et al. (2017) recommend that when designing 'immersive student inductions', social as well as academic activities are developed as part of the student experience, ensuring that all students can benefit from the social integration underpinning academic success.

In seeking case studies for this book, what became apparent was the difficulty of finding examples of practice that integrate students after a period of absence into cohorts that already have their own social identity (e.g. Case Study 25). Returning students or direct-entry students often come with additional health, psychological or language needs, and therefore the ways in which to integrate these students need careful consideration.

The role of the institution

Students who feel that they belong to a programme, or more generally to a university, feel valued, and as such are more likely to exhibit higher levels of satisfaction with their study. Given the importance of student satisfaction surveys and similar metrics in determining university rankings and their subsequent impact on attracting new students, such a positive response has significant academic and financial implications. Universities and university departments can go a long way in supporting belonging and the staff that seek to promote it. Resource support for field trips and residential activities and the provision of appropriate social spaces can have a significant bearing on the student experience (e.g. Case Study 23).

The provision and support of clubs, societies and social events should not be overlooked. Students that are more involved in clubs and societies are more likely to exhibit a greater sense of belonging (Thomas, 2012). As part of the university's social engagement provision, various professional services, such as financial advice, counsellors, careers and disability services, can all play significant roles in supporting social integration. Many students are often ignorant that such services are provided, and even when in need they fail to access them. Greater awareness, communication and ease of accessibility should all be considered to more successfully support students in taking up the services provided. Tinto (2006) states that successful education is "the job of the faculty," and that conversation should focus on enhancing student education rather than purely retention (p. 9).

Social integration: when and how?

Although students might drop out at any point in their study, there are particular times when the pressure to leave is more significant than others. Newly arriving students are particularly vulnerable during induction and over the first few weeks of study as homesickness plays a significant role. During this period, there is a strong need to ensure that students build good relationships with staff and that activities attempt to facilitate the building of social relationships and friendships among peers. The creating of such bonds helps students to navigate this period of uncertainty and the "academic culture shock" (Quinn et al., 2005: 21) it entails. The T-shirt induction activity included within this chapter acts as an effective and fun icebreaker, using visual imagery and extracurricular interests and pastimes to break down social barriers (see Case Study 18).

Throughout the year, social engagement through the academic sphere can be provided by group-based learning and teaching, an effective personal tutoring system to support this (as mentioned earlier), and an assessment and feedback system within which students have clarity and confidence. Such a system helps to support the student's academic growth and development, providing an understanding as to what they must do in order to improve and progress. Removing anxiety and building up student confidence helps to promote a deeper sense of belonging.

Social integration through the academic sphere is also supported by the social connection made via clubs, societies and social events, and most significantly through where students live and student accommodation. Students experiencing feelings of marginalisation are most likely not to living in student accommodation, but commuting into the university. Mature students, with caring commitments, may also experience difficulties in engaging in extracurricular activities and clubs. Wilcox, Winn and Fyvie-Gauld (2005) recognise that the relations formed through accommodation ties were most likely to be those that provided the student with emotional support during the early stage, hence those students choosing to live at home often miss out on this vital support network. One way to promote this remote socialisation is through the use of social media.

The growth and development over recent years of social media and the use of online forums and communities such as Facebook have transformed the opportunities for students to engage and establish a social network of friends and gain academic peer support, especially at a distance. Such networks are suggested by Gray et al. (2013) to encourage connection and interaction between students, particularly for students from a diversity of backgrounds, with different language skills, or distance learners where social integration might be problematic.

From social to cultural integration

The need to understand each other's cultural habitus is crucial in aiding transition and social integration for both students and staff (Matheson & Sutcliffe, 2016). Having opportunities for students to share their cultural backgrounds and utilise these within social learning and group activities provides an environment that not only values their cultural heritage, but also individual contributions. This is vital in integrating students from more passive educational traditions into active pedagogies. Gale and Parker (2014) describe these as "curriculum that reflect and affirm marginalised student histories and subjectivities," leading to transition as "becoming" (p. 738). Ryan and Tilbury (2013) emphasise the need for embedding pedagogies that decolonise education, providing opportunities for students to extend their intercultural understanding and nurturing global perspectives (expanded in Chapter 8).

Social integration and mental health

Universities have a strong moral and pastoral obligation to support students in times of mental difficulty. To assist universities with this, there is also a growing body of guidance available to universities on student mental wellbeing during their time in higher education practice for supporting students. What is lacking is a set of joined-up rules, guidance or support infrastructure specifically governing the transition from a child in education to an emerging adult in higher education.

The sector-wide priority is to continue tackling campus community stigma and discrimination. This is best achieved through a robust whole-university approach to the development of mental health literacy across students and staff. To address this, many universities now train staff and students in mental health first aid and embed mental health awareness training within student induction programs (e.g. Case Study 24).

With increased awareness, staff and students can be proactive in helping peers experiencing mental health difficulties to re-engage in appropriate campus community life and better ensure their early access to formal and or informal academic/wellbeing support services. Above all, students with mental health vulnerabilities need to feel a sense of *inclusiveness*.

Conclusion

It is clear that early social integration is fundamental to student retention and subsequent success, and is the responsibility of staff, the institution and the students themselves. As we have seen, many factors impact on the ability of students to integrate, and that integration needs continue throughout the student lifecycle and beyond into the world of work. The case studies within this chapter provide many ideas for enhancing opportunities for this social integration and easing the pathway to developing the necessary skills to succeed both within higher education and the workplace.

References

Bourdieu, P. & Passeron, J. (1977) *Reproduction in education, society and culture*. London, Sage.

Brooman, S. & Darwent, S. (2014) Measuring the beginning: a quantitative study of the transition to higher education. *Studies in Higher Education*, 39(9), 1523–1541.

Christie, H., Barron, P. & D'Annunzio-Green, N. (2013) Direct entrants in transition: becoming independent learners. *Studies in Higher Education*, 38(4), 623–637.

Gale, T. & Parker, S. (2014) Navigating change: a typology of student transition in higher education. *Studies in Higher Education*, 39(5), 734–753.

Gray, R., Vitak, J., Easton, E.W. & Ellison, N.B. (2013) Examining social adjustment to college in the age of social media: factors influencing successful transitions and persistence. *Computers and Education*, 67, 193–207.

Hagenauer, G. & Volet, S. (2014) Teacher–student relationship at university: an important yet under-researched field. *Oxford Review of Education*, 40(3), 370–388.

Hamshire, C., Willgoss, T.G. & Wibberley, C. (2013) Should I stay or should I go? A study exploring why healthcare students consider leaving their programme. *Nursing Education Today*, 33(8), 889–895.

Harvey, L., Drew, S. & Smith, M. (2006) *The first-year experience: a review of literature for the Higher Education Academy*. York, Higher Education Academy.

Higher Education Statistics Agency (2017) *Non-continuation rates summary: UK performance indicators 2015/16*. Available from: www.hesa.ac.uk/data-and-analysis/perfor mance-indicators/non-continuation-summary [Accessed 2 October 2017].

Khawaja, N. & Stallman, H. (2011). Understanding the coping strategies of international students: a qualitative approach. *Australian Journal of Guidance and Counselling*, 21(2), 203–224.

Lizzio, A. (2011) *The student lifecycle: an integrative framework for guiding practice*. Available from: www.griffith.edu.au/learning-teaching/student-success/first-year-experience/stu dent-lifecycle-transition-orientation [Accessed 12 July 2017].

Matheson, R. & Sutcliffe, M. (2016) Creating belonging and transformation through the adoption of flexible pedagogies in Masters level international business management students. *Teaching in Higher Education*, 15–29. Available from: http://dx.doi.org/10.108 0/13562517.2016.1221807.

Patiniotis, J. & Holdsworth, C. (2005) "Seize that chance!" Leaving home and transition to higher education. *Journal of Youth Studies*, 8(1), 81–95.

Quinn, J., Thomas, L., Slack, K., Casey, L., Thexton, W. & Noble, J. (2005). *From life disaster to lifelong learning: reframing working class 'drop out'*. York, Joseph Rowntree Foundation. Available from: www.jrf.org.uk/report/rethinking-working-class-drop-out-university [Accessed 27 September 2017].

Rubin, M. (2012a) Working-class students need more friends at university: a cautionary note for Australia's higher education equity initiative. *Higher Education Research and*

Development, 31(3), 431–433. Available from: http://dx.doi.org/10.1080/07294360.2012.689246.

Rubin, M. (2012b) Social class difference in social integration among students in higher education: a meta-analysis and recommendations for future research. *Journal of Diversity in Higher Education*, 5(1), 22–38.

Rubin, M. & Wright, C.L. (2015a) Age differences explain social class differences in students' friendship at university: implications for transition and retention. *Higher Education*, 70, 427–439.

Rubin, M. & Wright, C.L. (2015b) Time and money explain social class difference in students' social negation at university. *Studies in Higher Education*, 42(2), 315–330. Available from: http://dx.doi.org/10.1080/03075079.2015.1045481.

Ryan, A. & Tilbury, D. (2013) *Flexible pedagogies: new pedagogic ideas.* York, Higher Education Academy.

Thomas, L. (2002) Student retention in higher education: the role of institutional habitus. *Journal of Education Policy*, 17(4), 423–442.

Thomas, L. (2012) *Building student engagement and belonging in higher education at a time of change: final report from the What Works? student retention & success programme.* York, Higher Education Academy.

Tinto, V. (2006) Research and practice of student retention: what next. *College Student Retention*, 8(1), 1–19.

Turner, R., Morrison, D., Cotton, D., Child, S., Stevens, S., Nash, P. & Kneale, P. (2017) Easing the transition of first year undergraduates through an immersive induction module. *Teaching in Higher Education*, 22(7), 805–821. Available from: http://dx.doi.org/10.1080/13562517.2017.1301906.

Wilcox, P., Winn, S. & Fyvie-Gauld, M. (2005) 'It was nothing to do with the university, it was just the people': the role of social support in the first-year experience of higher education. *Studies in Higher Education*, 30(6), 707–722.

Introduction to the case studies

Social integration of students requires input from both staff and students. The case studies presented below tackle some of the difficulties of socially integrating students throughout the student lifecycle. The cases seek to address many different contexts, including difference in cultural and language backgrounds, to recognise and support those with poor mental health, or integrate students entering already formed social groups or having to make connections at a distance. However, all the case studies can be adapted to any context or student group, demonstrating the creative ways that staff are helping students make meaningful connections and develop life skills.

The case studies include:

- an induction activity that develops social integration and cohesion to enable students to make rapid connections and form groups with like-minded individuals;
- a peer mentorship programme, between different cohorts, to support part-time geographically remote students engaged in predominantly online learning;
- the use of a PodMag to increase student engagement, develop a sense of community and promote inclusion for distance learners;
- an outward-bound experience to promote early social integration, develop team-working and promote personal development;
- mental health first-aid training with students to recognise 'at-risk' students and support peers; and
- induction activities that promote integration at multiple entry points and create community.

Case Study 20: The T-shirt exercise: developing rapid integration and social cohesion among first-year students

Jarka Glassey, Newcastle University, Newcastle, UK

Key themes: social integration, cohesion, belonging, retention, reducing barriers

Aim of the learning activity

The aim of the T-shirt activity is to provide students, many of whom are away from home for the first time or finding their feet in a new country and feeling isolated, with an activity in a safe environment to meet like-minded fellow students. This is particularly important for students who feel more hesitant in forming those first important connections for whatever reason (e.g. through language or cultural barriers). The T-shirt activity enables students to identify like-minded individuals to form first connections both socially and professionally. The connections made are then used to form teams who work together on given tasks during the first semester of their studies. This activity was introduced to facilitate faster integration and social cohesion of students on the Chemical Engineering degree.

Learning outcomes for students

- Identify fellow students within their cohort with similar interest and aspirations to facilitate more rapid and closer social integration.
- Develop peer networks and form learning groups that reflect the diversity of the student group and promote understanding of global issues.
- Develop networking skills.

Description of the learning activity

The T-shirt activity is an integration-orientated social activity, introduced on the first day of the first semester for all first-year students. For many years previously, the school had hosted an informal greeting session with the aim of helping students to get to know both one another and departmental staff. Rising student numbers created a challenge to ensure that wide social interaction took place at these events, and this realisation prompted a change in format, the T-shirt activity. Each student is given a plain T-shirt and asked to represent themselves through drawing their interests and ambitions. Students form groups of mixed genders and ethnicities, based on finding others with similar drawings and using the opportunity to get to know others within their cohort. The resultant groups (around 10 students) form the basis for small group activities within the first semester. The activity provides a legitimated opportunity for students to move outside their comfort zones and make contact with students with whom they might not otherwise interact.

Step-by-step guide to running the activity

1 Provide a relaxed social environment for the activity.
2 Each student is given a plain T-shirt (you can experiment with colours – we have tried striking colours, a different colour each year, with the department name printed on them) and marker pens with clear instructions to draw representations of their interests (front) and future ambitions (back) on the shirts (*allow 20 minutes*).
3 Get students to put the T-shirt on.
4 Everyone is then instructed to search for others with similar drawings and to gather together as a group. The importance of each group containing a mix of genders and ethnicities needs to be stressed. To support this activity, staff and student ambassadors (students studying in the higher stages of the programme) can be used to move among the group to reinforce the instructions. The time required for students to

form groups can be adjusted depending on the size of the entire cohort, the size of the groups to be formed and the number of interactions required. This could be specified at the start (e.g. you must speak to at least 10 different students before you form your group) (*allow up to one hour, dependent on group sizes*).
5 Once the groups have formed, the finalised group names can be recorded on a flip chart.
6 The resulting groups can now be used for small group activities throughout the semester.

Resources required

- A T-shirt for each student.
- Marker pens.
- Flip charts to record group membership.
- Staff and student ambassadors to facilitate group formation and ensure adherence to the group formation rules. The number of staff and student ambassadors required depends on the student cohort size and the extent of direction you wish to provide. We have run these with three to five staff and three to five student ambassadors for a cohort of around 120 students, but following the initial encouragements only occasional intervention of these was used.

Ways in which it could be adapted/extended for different disciplines or levels

The exercise was already successfully tested by another institution with a cohort of criminology students. It is possible to adjust it to almost any context by setting an appropriate task/topic to draw on the T-shirt. Wearing the T-shirt provides an opportunity for meeting similar individuals, so this part is useful to retain. The task can be extended by asking the students to provide brief 'pitches' on their T-shirt drawings. We have not used this, given the cohort size, but also not to put extra stress on the 'shy' students by asking them to speak in front of the whole cohort.

Case Study 21: Peer mentoring on a Masters programme in Ghana

Ruth Cross, Diane Lowcock, Jerry Fiave, Sarah Ayiku and Grace Kafui Annan, Leeds Beckett University, Leeds, UK

Key themes: social integration, peer mentoring, retention, networking, belonging

Aim of the learning activity

The aim of the peer mentorship programme is to enhance support mechanisms for new students on a part-time Masters programme in Ghana and build a community and social network of learners with a shared identity. By linking different cohorts, opportunities to establish long-term relationships between students and alumni are created, countering the isolation some postgraduate students and practitioners experience.

Learning outcomes for students

- Build and strengthen face-to-face and online peer networks with students from different cohorts.
- Increase existing professional networks with public health and health promotion professionals to promote long-term reciprocal relationships.
- Develop an in-country alumni network.

Description of the learning activity

The peer-to-peer mentor programme was set up between different cohorts of students studying on a part-time Masters programme in Ghana. The course, delivered in-country by staff from a UK university, is supplemented by online learning between teaching visits. The student group only physically meet twice a year and are spread across a large country. From the outset, students were partners in the development of the process. The first cohort of students act as mentors to the second cohort of students, establishing the development of relationships between different cohorts, enabling new students to adapt more effectively to new ways of learning and their new identity as postgraduate students. By providing peer support systems, any potential attrition in the mentee group would be identified at an early stage and support given. In addition, students' learning and engagement for both cohorts increase. Through sharing experiences and learning with mentees, the esteem, mastery and efficacy for the mentors is raised. The project was co-facilitated by two members of the course team and two student representatives who made up the project team.

Step-by-step guide to running the activity

The project ran over 12 months as follows:

1. Establish the role of the peer mentor and the nature of the mentor/mentee relationship (peer mentoring schemes carry an element of risk as well as benefit, particularly if the different parties have different perspectives about what the nature of the relationship is or should be).

2   Set ground rules or defined role boundaries. These can be established by the student representatives from cohort 1 in discussion and negotiation with the whole student cohort to develop a shared understanding (*this reduces the risk discussed above*).
3   Allocate mentors/mentees – mentors from cohort 1 were paired up with mentees from cohort 2. Mentors and mentees were given each other's contact details (email) prior to the face-to-face visit (*consider issues such as gender, geographical location and age when making the matches*).
4   A teaching visit took place when the first cohort was in session for their final taught module and the second cohort was beginning the programme. Prior to the teaching visit, all except one set of mentors/mentees had been in touch with each other prior in some way. Some had already met face-to-face. During the teaching visit, a formal session was built into the programme for mentors and mentees to interact with one another.
5   A formal session with mentors/mentees and a social event:

    - An introduction to the programme led by the student mentors, including a discussion about role boundaries and expectations (with reference to the document produced by the student representatives in cohort 1). This part of the session was supported by the staff members.
    - A student-led Q&A session with mentors and mentees without the staff members present.
    - A formal opportunity for the mentor/mentee pairs to meet and get to know one another.
    - An informal social event also took place during the teaching visit, which provided an opportunity for more networking in a different environment. This was in the form of an evening party with food and local entertainment.

6   The mentor/mentee relationship continued as negotiated within the specified role boundaries.
7   Evaluation.

Ways in which it could be adapted/extended for different disciplines or levels

The mentorship system described in this case study could be adapted to suit many different disciplines and levels. Any programme that has a staggered intake of students, whether by academic year or otherwise, could set up mentors in the leading cohorts to mentor those starting later. It was helpful to have a clear project lead that worked with a small team (including students as co-producers) to progress the project. The nature of the role boundaries need to be established early in the process to reduce any risk.

Case Study 22: The PodMag: podcasting to promote academic community

Karen Foley, The Open University, Milton Keynes, UK

Key themes: integration, distance learning, community, inclusion, belonging

Aim of the learning activity

The PodMag, an audio news magazine developed by the Faculty of Social Sciences at the Open University, aims to provide an engaging radio magazine style broadcast to inform and engage the remote academic community. Aimed predominantly at students, associate lecturers and academic staff, it seeks to bring together the distant academic community by highlighting a variety of practice and opportunities, thereby reducing students' feeling of remoteness, promoting belonging and a sense of community.

Learning outcomes for students

- Increase awareness of ongoing activities within the faculty, including research, work with broadcasting, module production and study advice.
- Develop a holistic perspective that gives an opportunity to see the learning community in a non-modular way.
- Develop a lively sense of community for staff and students in a distance learning environment through reducing feelings of remoteness and promoting a sense of belonging.
- See themselves as part of a wider academic community outside of the university.

Description of the learning activity

The PodMag is a monthly audio news magazine from the Faculty of Social Science at the Open University. While the editorial format is continuously evolving, generally it is a 15- to 20-minute podcast that highlights work that the faculty is doing that is of interest to students and that may relate to research, broadcasting and study. It consists of news bulletins, in-depth feature interviews, research and promotional materials, providing the opportunity to include voices from across the university. Inclusivity is a priority, as well as promoting accessible options (such as a newsletter and transcripts). The PodMag welcomes contributions from students and academics, and interviews can be conducted face-to-face or remotely. The light, upbeat tone of the PodMag makes it accessible, and the flexibility of the format means that the faculty can communicate in a variety of ways. Once produced, the assets can be used in a range of ways (e.g. to promote specialised areas by embedding in websites/social media and advertising opportunities from inside and outside of the curriculum). The PodMag is an innovative way to expand, reframe and make readily accessible some of the academic work that the faculty delivers, supporting the sense of community promoted by the Student Connections Conference and faculty Facebook page.

Step-by-step guide to running the activity

Defining the editorial content

The content of the PodMag is based on the priorities of the faculty and also based on contributions from staff and students; for example, episodes have been dedicated to focuses on the nations, changes to curriculum, and focuses on topical issues such as Brexit. Once the theme is decided, a running order is established to include, for example, interviews, news, featured research, events and music to separate out sections.

Focus and planning

The focus of the interview/feature is defined and an appropriate interviewee/guest sought. Interviews are pre-planned by the interviewer, with outline questions being sent to the interviewee in advance of the recording.

Prior to recording

A brief discussion about the key focus of the interview will be held. Generally, this will take between 15 and 30 minutes for a three-minute interview. Featured guests will be given guidance on timescales, focus and the nature of the piece.

Recording

It is important to generate recordings that do not require substantial editing, hence there is a focus on planning the structure of the interview. In addition to saving time and editing fees, a tight focus also produces content that is fluid and as engaging as possible. Once the interviews are recorded, the news and linking sections are recorded in line with the running order.

Editing

The interview material is edited and put together. Music is included for an introduction and to separate sections. It usually takes an interviewer one day to plan, research and record the interviews, and an editor half a day to produce a 20-minute edition.

Approval and publication

Once approved by the key stakeholder in the faculty's Teaching and Learning Department, and by contributors, the PodMag is transcribed and published on the Open University podcast server. It is marketed via the 'Student Connections' website, the faculty Facebook page, Student Home (news board), and on news sections on the module and qualifications websites. Podcasts can also be published using an RSS feed. There are no formal ethical guidelines, but the nature of the interview is agreed between the interviewer and interviewee.

Measuring impact

Viewing figures or downloads can be tracked depending on where the podcast is embedded.

Resources required

- Audio recorder (Zoom).
- Two microphones.
- Headphones.
- Audio editing software (such as Audacity).

Ways in which it could be adapted/extended for different disciplines or levels

The editorial content can be adapted to include any discipline or level. Equally, the tone can be adapted to suit the audience for which the podcast is intended. Consideration of the best way to approach the content may be required, and other formats such as vox pops and sound bites may also be worthy of consideration, depending on the focus.

Case Study 23: Student induction and graduate attributes: the outdoor problem-solving residential

Bill Davies, Cardiff Metropolitan University, Cardiff, UK

Key themes: integration, outdoor learning, skills development, personal development

Aim of the learning activity

The informal purpose of the residential is to provide an opportunity for students to hothouse social networks, while providing an active and positive induction period that builds confidence in their ability to deal effectively with the challenges and experiences that lie ahead. More formally, it offers a stimulus for students to identify and evaluate graduate attributes such as self-management, team-working, problem-solving and communication, all important elements in their personal development planning related to employability.

Learning outcomes for students

- Develop an action plan based on a personal audit of strengths and developmental needs through an evaluation of their individual responses to a series of teamwork-related activities.
- Increase understanding of the importance and nature of transferable skills such as those characterised by graduate attributes.
- Develop greater awareness of the impact of various leadership and management behaviours on the outcome of team-based problem-solving.
- Develop social networks to assist in the transition to university.

Description of the learning activity

The residential experience offers an opportunity for students to reflect on their personal development, engage with personal development planning, and also get to know other students and staff on the undergraduate programme at an early stage. Each new entrant to the school (600 in total) experiences a two-day/three-night residential held in the first month of their first year. Based at an outdoor activity centre in the Brecon Beacons, away from the university campus, the programme is staffed by the school of sport staff and specialist activity instructors. During the residential, students work initially in small groups (7–9 in each group) and finally in a large problem-solving group (36–42 in number), predominantly in an outdoor environment with novel and challenging activities. Students are encouraged to evaluate their contribution to the processes and outcomes of these endeavours through formative self- and peer evaluation via scheduled staff- and student-led review discussions. The development of an action plan for personal development forms the basis of individual ongoing review and discussion with personal tutors when back in university.

Step-by-step guide to running the activity

Such is the range and complexity of outcomes that can be attained from a particular activity in the outdoors that it is vital that facilitating staff clearly understand the desired learning outcomes of every activity.

An illustrative framework for a residential is given below as it provides a basis to identify and illustrate some key issues relevant to planning and delivery.

Day 1

The initial afternoon is a preparatory phase comprising icebreaking and warm-up activities offering participants insight into key elements of teamwork, such as communication, decision-making, planning and use of resources. It is important that staff have a range of alternative activities to enable them to respond to the needs of individuals and groups. The first evening comprises of skills classes relevant for the next days' activities. Each small group sends delegates, who will then return to their groups equipped with these different skills.

Day 2

The second day has three elements:

1 A problem-solving journey in which each group, together with a staff member, engages in a journey around the area, on foot, by minibus and by student-built raft. At preset locations on the journey (if student navigation permits!), the group employ the skills they have previously learnt to undertake practical tasks, using rudimentary equipment. Success in these tasks increases the pool of equipment available for a final raft-building task. The group tutor is responsible for briefing students on the various tasks and facilitating a review of each activity, and as far as possible all navigational and problem-solving decisions are made by the student group. With the exception of the final aspect of the journey, the activities are designed to be cooperative small group tasks. The final activity is a rafting competition between the groups, with points being awarded, which are carried forward to the evening team challenge activity.
2 An evening competition between the groups engages all groups in the same tasks in pursuit of points for achievement. The competitive factor normally provides motivation among the sport students to engage their attention, despite their fatigue.
3 Feedback on the team challenge in the form of 'the results'. The winning team receives additional equipment for use in that night's overnight bivvy (sleeping under the stars) and a 'treat' – usually a box of biscuits. In addition to receiving these results, the groups are briefed for next day's activity, undertaking planning and finally building the outside shelter for that night's stay.

Day 3

The early morning of day 3 focuses on a whole-group activity, planned and executed by the students. This activity is based around the need to find various people and pieces of information in order to identify a final location. The main focus is on the nature of successful large group organisation. The session concludes with a debrief highlighting the differences between working in large and small groups and the transferability of any learning to other situations.

The final activity of the formal residential is a review of the individual's experience of the residential carried out in the original small working groups, led by the group tutor. This focuses on self-assessment and feedback from peers and staff, allowing collection of material for later reflection by individuals.

Points for consideration

- It is likely that the participants will have a range of experience, attributes, expectations and attitudes towards the residential. It is therefore important to have a broad range of activities to ensure all participants have the opportunity to experience working outside their comfort zones in terms of physical and/or cognitive demands, within a supportive environment.
- To foster generic learning through outdoor activities, technical demands should be simple and at the level of (adult) beginners. Activities requiring greater levels of technical proficiency not only carry higher levels of risk and objective danger, but also may take the participants' focus away from the transferable team and personal skills, placing it on the specific technical demands.
- Activities should be integrated into a coherent and progressive linear programme.
- Activities need to have flexibility in relation to the demands they make upon the group individually and collectively. The group tutor needs to judge the level and nature of challenge and support that will optimise the positive learning process.
- In an integrated programme where success in an activity impacts on the available physical resources or positive group motivation relevant to the next, failure should be tempered by the possibility of retrieval through the use of alternative or bridging activities that temper the negative effects without obscuring the learning potential of an analysis and review.
- Staff working on the delivery of the residential need to have flexibility and confidence in the role they are adopting. This has obvious implications for staff development and support.

Ways in which it could be adapted/extended for different disciplines or levels

The key to adaptation is to have a clear understanding of the potential learning outcomes for each activity, an understanding of that activity's purpose in being placed at that point of the programme, and an appreciation of the cognitive and physical resources of the participants. Most activities are flexible and adjustable to provide an appropriate balance of novelty, challenge, support, enjoyment and learning. On a broader front, the use of competition between groups can raise motivation, but in some cases a focus on internal group collaboration encourages a focus on process rather than outcome.

Case Study 24: Normalising a campus culture of safe mental health difficulty disclosure and support through mental health awareness (literacy) training: developing sport student mental health ambassadors

Mikel Mellick, Cardiff Metropolitan University, Cardiff, UK

Key themes: mental health awareness, peer support, wellbeing, student ambassadors

Aim of the learning activity

The purpose of the intervention is to increase the awareness of sport students (and staff) to 'at-risk' peers for mental health difficulties. Group dialogue, reflective discussion and 'courageous' conversations are used to develop a mental health awareness of the 'typical' signs and symptoms of sport student mental wellbeing distress, risk factors and 'appropriate' peer support approaches.

The learning experience is purposively collaborative (staff and students), providing an opportunity to develop positive staff–student and peer relationships and safe conversations around campus mental health. The learning environment is situated within a level 5 student work placement. As such, it is embedded within the curriculum, providing a valuable opportunity to promote and reinforce campus values of integration, belonging and inclusiveness. The overall approach is framed from a perspective that actively acknowledges that periods of student vulnerability are 'typical' but 'manageable' through effective coping skills, the reinforcement of mental health 'protective' factors, and in the promotion of staff and peer student support. This approach emphasises a strength through adversity model where vulnerability is seen as manageable, and not as a defining character flaw of the student.

The intervention establishes a yearly cohort of suitably trained student mental health ambassadors who actively promote campus mental health conversations and peer support.

Learning outcomes for students

- Demonstrate an understanding for, and awareness of, common mental health and wellbeing difficulties and useful protective factors for a sport student population.
- Recognise the signs, symptoms and risk factors associated with common mental health issues and challenges in sport students.
- Encourage safe conversations around mental health and engage confidently in a non-judgmental manner, and in accordance with university protocols, with a vulnerable/distressed peer (including the appropriate signposting to student services and school-based on-campus support).

Description of the learning activity

Mental wellbeing/mental health awareness training: reflective student and staff discussions (six × 1 hour)

Students and staff participate in six one-hour reflective discussions. Discussions are face-to-face and led by fellow sport students and academic staff who have been previously trained as mental health ambassadors (undergone mental health first-aid training). Discussions are framed around six reflective narrative accounts of students' real-world 'peer' support experiences and/or prepared case studies. The case studies/peer-identified situations provide a trigger for discussion and an opportunity for the students to respond constructively to feedback, experiences and learning. It also allows for the identification of areas for future learning and development, and to consider how campus-based changes or improvements in mental health awareness may be actioned in order to further promote a safe school culture of disclosure and the provision of appropriate and timely support.

Key principles

The reflective accounts are used to highlight key principles associated with sport student mental health awareness. These are briefly discussed below. These serve as 'themed' activity discussions across the six sessions.

Step-by-step guide to running the activity

Triggers for discussion are identified. Examples include:

- newspaper reports of current issues around student mental health;
- news interviews or personal stories;
- photographic montages; and
- student-led case studies of real-life experiences that they have had to deal with (e.g. student isolation, anxiety, low mood, disordered eating patterns, panic attacks before presentations).

Discussion involves the use of four different forms.

Insight discussions

The reflective discussions and courageous conversations provide for a deeper understanding of sport student mental health and wellbeing issues. It promotes an improved awareness of the participants' own mental attitudes and behaviour, and through this a greater appreciation for prevailing campus-wide issues of stigma and barriers to disclosure. The discourse within the school around mental health is discussed using ecologically valid case studies. A shared understanding of the appropriate, consistent and acceptable use of terminology when holding conversations around sport student mental health and wellbeing is agreed.

Knowledge discussions

Essential facts, information, descriptions, and skills concerning the 'typical' signs, symptoms and risk factors associated with the more common sport student mental health difficulties, crises and illnesses are explored through collaborative learning techniques.

Context discussions

Case studies highlighting particular school of sport circumstances, conditions, surroundings and factors provide important contextual information so that sport student mental health and wellbeing can be more fully explored and understood. Case studies permit an experiential learning approach.

Practice discussions

Participants discuss, develop and rehearse 'helping' peer support conversations. Students agree a 'support' flow chart – guidance by which to 'help' with confidence and appropriateness.

Ways in which it could be adapted/extended for different disciplines or levels

This intervention could be used to increase the awareness of staff and students to 'at-risk' students for mental health/wellbeing difficulties within each school discipline. This will better serve the unique needs and vulnerabilities of students associated with each of the university's academic areas. It could also be situated within year levels. This will further develop mental health literacy across the university and better facilitate the earlier recognition of 'typical' signs and symptoms of student mental wellbeing distress.

A 'within' academic school-based community approach led by appropriately trained student mental health ambassadors will better promote a shared responsibility and accountability for the support of at-risk students and those students experiencing mental wellbeing challenges.

Case Study 25: Networking approaches to integrating mid-programme entry undergraduate musical theatre students

Louise H. Jackson and Victoria Stretton, Trinity Laban Conservatoire of Music and Dance, London, UK

Key themes: social integration, multiple entry points, establishing community, student ownership

Aim of the learning activity

Musical theatre training can be perceived as a competitive and, in some cases, unsupportive 'survival of the fittest' environment. While musical theatre programmes must prepare students for the intense and competitive nature of industry, developing a supportive, networked and inclusive community of artistic practitioners is the aim of this approach.

Learning outcomes for students

- Differentiate between their own social needs and the needs of others.
- Evaluate and formulate practices that support the wider learning community.
- Recognise a variety of impacting situations that may affect an individual's integration and progression within the programme.

Description of the learning activity

The musical theatre department has developed programmes underpinned by an ethos of individuals as community, whereby the negative stereotypes of what a musical theatre performer is are navigated and exposed through an admissions process that recognises performance talent wherever it may be found, and through a teaching approach that balances the development of technique and 'grit' with clear scaffolding that nurtures and supports the student in exploring their assumptions about musical theatre.

With diversifying student cohorts, integration at all points of entry is actively explored. Students will need to work together in devising processes, choirs, rehearsals, and in performances, as well as in acting and dance classes. By embedding principles drawn from first-year experience research in an integrative, wrap-around approach within audition, induction and curriculum, and by using networking approaches students have engaged with as part of their learning, the musical theatre community is more flexible and adaptable to change. Preparing students to be responsive to the varying needs of a socially integrated community includes readying the cohort for change, to be able to adapt to occurrences such as when a student enters the programme in second year rather than during first year, or when one is injured and cannot participate in performance. Joining an already established cohort can be difficult, but it is not unusual in musical theatre performance contexts for individuals to join established casts or performance groups: we use these as models for supporting students building upon the approaches to networking that are part of their programme.

Step-by-step guide to running the activity

Our approach uses four intersecting approaches to networking that support social integration of midpoint entry students. A 'checklist' focusing on midpoint entry students ensures they receive an appropriate induction, recognising that social integration is a key feature to a successfully supportive musical theatre department.

Readying the student cohort for change

Each year group within the musical theatre department forms a unique community with its own internal dynamics. Current students gain employment on departmental open days and audition days. The department uses these as learning opportunities for students to develop a sense of the variety of backgrounds and skill sets students come to the programme with. These interactions at pre-application, audition and entry are vital for ensuring that the ethos of the department is fully understood by students. They develop an appreciation for difference, and recognise and understand how various skills manifest in individuals. There is also acknowledgment that everyone on the programme has fundamental technical skills, without which it would be very difficult to attempt any integration of midpoint entry.

Digital and performance-based networking

The department operates a Facebook page for alumni and current students, and all students are active on Twitter as part of their curriculum-guided approach to developing professional online digital footprints. When students are offered a place on one of the musical theatre programmes, they can join this Facebook page and connect via Twitter. Additionally, the programme runs a variety of performances and shows; prospective and incoming students are encouraged to attend. For midpoint entry students, the combination of connecting on social media and attending performances of their new cohort is an effective combination that empowers the student to begin integration prior to the start of the academic year.

Student-led induction day

Induction day is led by current musical theatre students to welcome all incoming students. The day is designed completely by students, but they are briefed in terms of the ethos they are attempting to embed in their work. This practical approach to inducting new students works across all levels, and utilises musical theatre games and a 'getting to know the area' event that mixes up year groups and orientates new students to the geography of the local area.

Technique analysis

Each year as part of the induction and transition process, dance classes are 'levelled' at the beginning of each academic year to allocate each student to a class appropriate to their stage of technical development. This is common practice within musical theatre and dance programmes, and students may change groups on an annual basis. However, viewing this as a transition exercise changes the emphasis as it is an opportunity to examine mid-programme entrants and what habits they may have picked up that are particular to other higher education programmes, and what areas they may need further support with. Without this intervention, students who already have a training profile within the programme would be at an advantage over those entering mid-programme.

Ways in which it could be adapted/extended for different disciplines or levels

Transition checklists are helpful to guide staff in ensuring students have a fully designed (re)induction process that includes ways to assess skills and knowledge at the point of entry. The pre-arrival use of social media enables incoming midpoint entry students to connect with their future cohort. If this is combined with invitations to attend departmental and institutional events, then a cycle of physical and virtual connections can develop. Student-led induction days involve challenging current students to lead and design a day that both orientates students to the institutional and local area but also utilises particular features of the subject.

Chapter 8

Developing self

Sue Tangney and Valerie Clifford

Introduction to the chapter

The student lifecycle has provided a thread running through this book (Lizzio, 2011). Central to students' evolving identities as they progress is the notion of *becoming* as students negotiate the stages of thinking about university, and of entering, progressing through, leaving and sometimes returning to university. Student identity typically evolves during this transition (Lizzio, 2011). In this chapter, we are taking a holistic view of the development of student identity to the graduate and the citizen that they are becoming, and we will explore the ways that purposeful interventions offered by universities could enhance students' holistic development of self.

The chapter begins by recognising who our students are, and their motivations for coming to university. It takes into account students' backgrounds and ongoing living arrangements, and the impact this has on university life. The chapter also considers students' self-belief and the interventions we can make to enhance self-belief and students' sense of their capability. It also focuses on the development of self as a socially responsible citizen, preparing students not only with skills and knowledge, but also with flexibility, creativity and moral courage for an uncertain world in the future.

Higher education environment

A number of factors have influenced the growing emphasis on students' development of self, including widening and increasing participation and attrition rates. Alongside this, there has been a shift to a knowledge-based economy (Turner, 2014), and a greater emphasis on the role of universities to produce graduates to tackle global problems such as poverty and economic disparity, environmental issues, and in particular climate change, and sustainable development. The knowledge-based economy has also brought acceleration in the creation of new job roles (Mitra, 2017), and the need for graduates to be more versatile, responsive to change, and have a wider, more global frame of reference.

Challenges to developing self

Lizzio's (2011) student lifecycle focuses on the evolving identities that accompany student transition, and the need for purposeful interventions that we as staff can make within and outside the curriculum to complement students' identity development needs. Transitioning into university is clearly the first critical stage for students, and perhaps the one that is the most challenging, as students start to identify with what it means to 'be a student', and to have a sense that they belong in university.

Four aspects of transition have been identified as students develop their sense of potential in starting university: (a) a sense of inclusion; (b) a sense of belief; (c) a sense of feasibility; and (d) a sense of aspiration (Lizzio, 2011: 8).

Inclusion

Five factors have been suggested as being potentially disadvantageous to students' sense of belonging and engagement at university. They are having a part-time job, commuting to university as opposed to living on site or close by, having caring responsibilities, not having a quiet space to study, and declaring a disability. In Thomas' (2017) study, however, having a part-time job and declaring a disability had little impact on either engagement or belonging, while commuting students, carers and those without a quiet space at home all had a lower sense of belonging than other students. There was also evidence that black and minority ethnic (BME) students in the UK had a lower sense of belonging than white students, and this was influenced by their perceptions of the relevance of the curriculum content, their prior educational experiences and their level of cultural capital (Thomas, 2017).

In phase 1 of the *What Works?* project, Thomas et al. (2017) noted that "it is the human side of higher education that comes first – finding friends, feeling confident and, above all, feeling a part of your course of study and the institution," and this was a critical factor in determining whether students succeeded at university (p. 3). While we cannot change choices such as commuting, we can engender belongingness. Induction activities (e.g. Case Study 4), early sessions with teaching staff and peers, focused on getting to know one another, and purposeful encounters with personal tutors can strengthen students' transition at this stage. We can also work to ensure that the curriculum is relevant to all students, a theme that is often stressed in the inclusive curriculum and internationalisation literature, which we will return to in this chapter.

Self-belief

In her study, Turner (2014) focused on the importance of self-belief as critical to the development of employability, and this in itself is dependent on a belief that "ability can be improved; that one has the ability to achieve one's goals; and that the environment will allow for goal attainment" (p. 592). We can assist students by ensuring that learning outcomes and assessment criteria are transparent and by dedicating teaching time to discussing these.

Feasibility

Having established the goalposts and ongoing feedback processes specific to the students' progression, exercises that enable early and ongoing success will help students see what it is feasible for them to achieve (Turner, 2014). We have to enhance students' faith in themselves and in us, that we will help them in their journey through higher education and not dampen their hopes (Barnett, 2011). Exercises should be challenging but manageable; some of the case studies in earlier chapters do this (e.g. Case Study 1, which seeks to integrate students into university culture through a try-out day before they formally arrive).

Aspirations

As students develop their sense of self-belief, we need to encourage a maturity in their understanding of their own abilities to learn, and of the concept of knowledge itself through extended learning opportunities. Conceptions of knowledge range from the least sophisticated perspective, that knowledge is either right or wrong, prompting students to see their teachers as experts and the discipline as unequivocal, to realising that knowledge is provisional and depends on interpretation and perspective, and that this personal meaning-making is tied closely to their previous experiences and understandings. Ultimately, students evolve their own personal perspectives and learning becomes transformative; an example that illustrates this is students changing their understanding of racism through engaging with intercultural studies. This transition, though, is not necessarily continuous or predictable, and students can go back and forwards on the spectrum, particularly if learning experiences are not framed around extending their conceptions of knowledge and learning (Entwistle & Peterson, 2004). Beliefs about learning are also associated with motivations for coming to university in the first place, whether this is extrinsic and around how they are perceived in their work or civic life, or intrinsic and motivated by studying for the sake of it, or wanting to make a contribution to society (Beaty, Gibbs & Morgan, 1997, cited in Entwistle & Peterson, 2004).

Making this progression explicit to students can augment their transition in other domains, and this can be enhanced through engaging students in reflective exercises alongside typical developmental academic work. Other ways students' conceptions of knowledge are extended is through engaging them in activities such as:

- contributing to assessment criteria for their course through group discussions;
- role play, real-world assignments and other engagement with the workplace;

- reading each other's assignments in small groups and giving feedback before they submit their work for assessment; and
- after assessment, reading a few of their peers' assignments to see different approaches to, and understanding of, the task.

Personal tutoring

Another way that institutions are engaging with student transition is through personal tutoring. The Quality Code for universities in the UK (Quality Assurance Agency for Higher Education, 2013) stipulates an expectation that students will be supported in their personal and professional development from entering to leaving higher education, and that this is the joint responsibility of academic staff and professional services. It was reported that 80 per cent of 96 universities surveyed in 2008 have some form of personal tutoring in place in the UK (Universities UK, 2015).

Personal tutor programmes can be reactive or proactive, structured or unstructured, available to all or just to those in need, and lean towards pastoral and/or providing professional service and/or focused in the curriculum (Thomas, 2006). All programmes have a role in assisting students in the development of self. Typically, the personal tutoring involves an ongoing relationship, often over the duration of a student's degree, and holistic support, including both academic and personal guidance (Grant, 2006). Personal tutors also act as a referral service to other specialist services in the university, such as disability support or counselling. Frequent contact is important to build trust between tutor and student to ensure the student feels comfortable talking about the challenges they face. Alongside seeking professional help if necessary, the personal tutor is generally instrumental in assisting students to engage in purposeful personal development planning to meet their aspirations (Grant, 2006).

Personal tutors are often key in reinforcing Turner's (2014) ideas that ability can be improved, that students can harness their ability to achieve aspirational goals, and that the university environment will enable goal achievement. Personal tutors have the capacity to encourage students to consider "Who am I becoming?" which is a central organising principle in Lizzio's model of transition (Lizzio, 2011: 5).

Associated with personal tutor systems, universities may also adopt peer-assisted learning opportunities, sometimes focused on the most difficult modules within a programme of study (e.g. Plymouth University, n.d.). Student leaders from former cohorts undertake support sessions with students, which typically are around discussing content, related study skills, and solving problems together (Dawson et al., 2014) (e.g. Case Study 21). Student leaders are generally trained for the purpose, and have to attend the same lectures their mentees are attending. While it is acknowledged that the research into the benefits of peer-assisted systems is perhaps limited, there appears to be gain in terms of grades, lower failure and withdrawal rates for the recipients (Dawson et al., 2014), and improved self-efficacy for the student leaders (McPhail, Despotovic & Fisher, 2012).

Fitness for purpose of the curriculum

Despite the increasing emphasis on employability, one of the greatest challenges teaching staff face is that we are developing students for a rapidly changing world. The future job market, as stated earlier, is uncertain. Skills needed to increase students' employability are constantly evolving, and this is perhaps reflected in other associated drivers for change in the curriculum (e.g. internationalisation, sustainability, enterprise and entrepreneurship). As noted in Chapter 5, Barnett's solution for an uncertain future is to foster students' will to learn, as knowledge in the contemporary world is always lagging behind the understanding needed to deal with global issues (Barnett, 2007, 2011). This was highlighted in the global financial crisis of 2008, where it became apparent that entrepreneurship education needed to change to reflect a new values-driven approach (Rae, 2012). Rae suggests this approach should focus on active, experiential and personalised learning, with opportunities for identity development and profound personal development, in an environment of social and ethical responsibility. The key message of all these ideas for education for the future is less focus on curriculum content, and more on developing student agency through curricular and extracurricular activities. Many of the case studies associated with this chapter endeavour to do this.

Internationalisation and global citizenship

It is no coincidence that internationalisation is now often present in the learning and teaching strategies of universities. Initially, the focus was on supporting international students to understand 'how the West is done' (Doherty & Singh, 2005) and enhancing intercultural competence in all students. Quite apart from the increasing exposure workers will have to people of other cultures and the benefits intercultural learning will have on the employability of graduates, intercultural learning has the capacity to develop students' self more broadly. The more life-wide our experiences, the more potential for development as a person.

Breaking down conceptions of 'other' can be readily integrated into any discipline of study through encouraging students to reflect on their taken-for-granted cultural values, introducing case studies from alternative perspectives, enabling students to draw on prior knowledge and approach the discipline from their own cultural perspective, and through valuing alternative perspectives, using learning outcomes and assessment tools and criteria to focus students' reflections. These approaches have been well documented in the internationalisation literature (e.g. Banks, 2007; Clifford & Montgomery, 2011; Jones & Killick, 2007; Kitano, 1997; Leask, 2009). It is evident that changing one's conception of others can be transformative; students can change as a person (as described by Entwistle & Peterson, 2004) and recalibrate their values and attitudes.

Increasingly, university internationalisation programmes have focused on the purpose of a tertiary education for our citizens. While some still argue that we need to prioritise developing excellent professionals, others argue that knowledge and skills do not evolve in a vacuum. Being a citizen involves social responsibility, and moral and social development are vital to society (Clifford & Haigh, 2011). These ideas are embedded in the concept of global citizenship. Although a contested term, not least because of its association with colonialism, global citizenship draws attention to the need for the holistic development of students (Clifford & Montgomery, 2014). Global citizenship involves having a critical knowledge of oneself, one's own culture and social-historical positioning, and knowledge of other cultures and peoples and the interdependence of all (Nussbaum, 2002). The enhancement of knowledge of global issues also needs to involve the dimensions of moral sensitivity and social injustice, inequality and racism. Also, rather than being observers and analysts of these issues, global citizenship implies an active involvement to bring about social change (Clifford & Montgomery, 2014, 2017; Giroux, 1988).

Since 9/11 and the financial crash of 2008, there is an increasing focus in the internationalisation literature on values-driven drivers such as social justice, human rights, sustainability of the environment, and interdependence of people and nations (Clifford & Montgomery, 2011, 2017; Jones & Killick, 2007; Morey, 2000). This increasing focus on ethical responsibility is prevalent in social enterprise curricula, and more broadly in a groundswell of negativity towards neoliberal capitalist models (Andreotti, 2011; Pashby, 2011). Introducing students to the concept of global citizenship and engaging them in discussions about the meaning of the concept can add another dimension to their personal development. This could include looking outwards at the world and expanding their awareness of differing perspectives on issues, developing their intercultural competence, and considering their own moral values in relation to their personal community, their local community, their country and globally.

Global perspectives include critique of how disciplines are represented and understood within other cultures, so students' frame of reference is widened beyond the purely Western or secular. Intercultural competence begins with an awareness of our own culture and perspectives, and the development of the confidence to question one's own values and those of others responsibly and ethically. It also includes developing an understanding of social responsibility and active citizenship, and involving a sense of responsibility towards ourselves, others and future generations. It can enhance students' sense of empowerment and self-efficacy (Clifford & Montgomery, 2011; Edwards et al., 2003). Educating students for global citizenship requires not only a knowledge of the world, but also a concern and a willingness to act. These ideas are challenging personally and intellectually, and can cause discomfort and distress (Hellsten & Reid, 2008; Nussbaum, 2004).

Global citizenship can enter the curriculum through engagement with global issues such as climate change, pollution, sustainability, equity, justice, prejudice and discrimination, as illustrated in the case studies. Case Study 13 focuses on students visiting South Korea as part of their art and design course, and through interaction with peers in two Korean universities and well-planned cultural and political orientation activities, the students augment their awareness of their own stereotyping, and display ethical and moral sensitivity to cultural 'others'. Case Study 31 of physiotherapy students exploring community-based rehabilitation demonstrates the use of 'cultural assessors' in a creative assessment worth 25 per cent of the students' mark. The approach was so successful that it was considered that the assessment could have been used to cover all of the students' assessment requirements.

Dissonance

Exposing students to other ways of knowing and valuing these in the curriculum by embedding them in the learning and assessment processes can create dissonance. It is worth considering whether the curriculum you teach is explicitly or implicitly dominated by Western/white/straight/middle-class perspectives. Explicit enabling of alternative ways of knowing through the course documentation, the assessment tools, and the attitudes of teaching staff recognises and values greater diversity among students and staff, and provides interesting learning opportunities for all.

Dissonance is evident in many transformative experiences where students are wrestling with an issue that challenges prior thinking, or in situations where they have to think outside the box (e.g. Case Study 29). This may also be experienced by staff teaching in new and challenging areas, and may necessitate the learning of new skills to facilitate emotional discussions in the classroom and online, and the consideration of our own self-development (Clifford & Montgomery, 2015). Dissonance may be particularly pronounced with undergraduate dissertations and postgraduate study.

Conclusion

This chapter has asked us to stand back and consider the purposes of higher education in our society and how this impacts on the holistic development needs of students. It draws together many of the ideas in preceding chapters and puts a spotlight on the personal and social moral development of students as they consider their place as future citizens of the world. It moves through their knowledge and belief in themselves and how this can be enhanced, to considerations of the curriculum that we are offering students, as well as our own positionality, and the personal and professional resources we need to facilitate our students' transformative learning.

The chapter has moved us into difficult spaces, spaces not part of the current transition literature (Gale & Parker, 2014). However, Gale and Parker (2014) question whether current institutional induction and development activities are focused on moulding the student to fit the culture of the university, rather than aiding the development of the student as a future citizen. Seeing all the curriculum as about student development moves transition from an activities/epistemological focus to an ontological focus, and also asks us to consider our own development needs.

References

Andreotti, V. (2011) (Towards) decoloniality and diversality in global citizenship education. *Globalisation, Societies and Education*, 9(34), 381–397.

Banks, J. (2007) Approaches to multicultural curriculum reform. In: Banks, J.A. & Banks, C.A.M. (eds.), *Multicultural education: issues and perspectives*. 6th ed. Hoboken, NJ, John Wiley & Sons, pp. 247–270.

Barnett, R. (2007) *A will to learn: being a student in an age of uncertainty*. Maidenhead, Society for Research into Higher Education and Open University Press.

Barnett, R. (2011) Learning about learning: a conundrum and a possible resolution. *London Review of Education*, 9(1), 5–13.

Clifford, V. & Haigh, M. (2011) Graduate attributes for global citizenship. In: Clifford, V. & Montgomery, C. (eds.), *Moving towards internationalisation of the curriculum for global citizenship in higher education*. Oxford, OCSLD, Oxford Brookes University, pp. 93–118.

Clifford, V. & Montgomery, C. (2011) Introduction: internationalizing the curriculum for global citizenship in higher education. In: Clifford, V. & Montgomery, C. (eds.), *Moving towards internationalisation of the curriculum for global citizenship in higher education*. Oxford, OCSLD, Oxford Brookes University, pp. 13–24.

Clifford, V. & Montgomery, C. (2014) Challenging conceptions of Western higher education and promoting graduates as global citizens. *Higher Education Quarterly*, 68(1), 28–45.

Clifford, V. & Montgomery, C. (2015) Transformative learning through internationalization of the curriculum in higher education. *Journal of Transformative Education*, 13(1), 46–64.

Clifford, V. & Montgomery, C. (2017) Designing an internationalised curriculum for higher education: embracing the local and the global citizen. *Higher Education Research and Development*, 36(6), 1138–1151.

Dawson, P., van der Meer, J., Skalicky, J. & Cowley, K. (2014) On the effectiveness of supplemental instruction: a systematic review of supplemental instruction and peer-assisted study sessions literature between 2001 and 2010. *Review of Educational Research*, 84(4), 572–608. Available from: https://doi.org/10.3102/0034654314540007.

Doherty, C.A. & Singh, P. (2005) How the West is done: simulating Western pedagogy in a curriculum for Asian international students. In: Ninnes, P. & Heelsten, M. (eds.), *Internationalizing higher education: critical explorations of pedagogy and policy*. Hong Kong, Comparative Education Research Centre, University of Hong Kong, pp. 53–73.

Edwards, R., Crosling, R., Petrovic-Lazarovic, S. & O'Neill, P. (2003) Internationalisation of business education: meaning and implementation. *Higher Education Research and Development*, 22(2), 183–192.

Entwistle, N. & Peterson, E. (2004) Conceptions of learning and knowledge in higher education: relationships with study behaviour and influences of learning environments. *International Journal of Educational Research*, 41, 407–428.

Gale, T. & Parker, S. (2014) Navigating change: a typology of student transition in higher education. *Studies in Higher Education*, 39(5), 734–753.

Giroux, H.A. (1988) *Teachers as intellectuals: towards a critical pedagogy of learning*. South Hadley, MA, Bergin & Garvey.

Grant, A. (2006) Personal tutoring: a system in crisis? In: Thomas, L. & Hixenbaugh, P. (eds.), *Personal tutoring in higher education*. Stoke-on-Trent, Trentham Books, pp. 11–20.

Hellsten, M. & Reid, A. (2008) *Researching international pedagogies; sustainable practice for teaching and learning in higher education*. New York, Springer.

Jones, E. & Killick, D. (2007) Internationalisation of the curriculum. In: Jones, E. & Brown, S. (eds.), *Internationalising higher education*. London, Routledge, pp. 109–119.

Kitano, M.K. (1997) What a course will look like after multicultural change. In: Morey, A.I. & Kitano, M. (eds.), *Multicultural course transformation in higher education: a broader truth*. Boston, MA, Allyn & Bacon, pp. 18–34.

Leask, B. (2009) Using formal and informal curricula to improve interactions between home and international students. *Journal of Studies in International Education*, 13(2), 205–221.

Lizzio, A. (2011) *The student lifecycle: an integrative framework for guiding practice*. Available from: https://app.griffith.edu.au/assessment-matters/pdfs/student-lifecycle-framework.pdf [Accessed 25 March 2017].

McPhail, R., Despotovic, W.V. & Fisher, R. (2012) Follow the leader: understanding the impact being a PASS leader has on self-efficacy. *Journal of Peer Learning*, 5, 1–18. Available from: http://ro.uow.edu.au/ajpl/vol5/iss1/7/ [Accessed 19 June 2017].

Mitra, J. (2017) Holistic experimentation for emergence: a creative approach to postgraduate entrepreneurship education and training. *Industry and Higher Education*, 31(1), 34–50.

Morey, A.I. (2000) Changing higher education curricula for a global and multicultural world. *Higher Education in Europe*, 25(1), 25–39.

Nussbaum, M. (2002) Education for citizenship in an era of global connection. *Studies in Philosophy and Education*, 21, 289–303.

Nussbaum, M. (2004) Liberal education and global community. *Liberal Education*, 90(1), Winter, 42–47.

Pashby, K. (2011) Cultivating global citizens: planting new seeds or pruning the perennials? Looking for the citizen-subject in global citizenship education theory. *Globalisation, Societies and Education*, 9(3–4), 427–442.

Plymouth University (n.d.) *Peer assisted learning scheme (PALS): regular study sessions for students, by students*. Available from: www.plymouth.ac.uk/student-life/services/learning-gateway/learning-development/pals [Accessed 28 June 2017].

Quality Assurance Agency for Higher Education (2013) *UK quality code for higher education: Chapter B4 – enabling student development and achievement*. Gloucester, Quality Assurance Agency for Higher Education.

Rae, D. (2012) International entrepreneurship education: postgraduate business student experiences of entrepreneurship education. *Education and Training*, 54(8/9), 639–656.

Thomas, L. (2006) Widening participation and the increased need for personal tutoring. In: Thomas, L. & Hixenbaugh, P. (eds.), *Personal tutoring in higher education*. Stoke-on-Trent, Trentham Books, pp. 21–31.

Thomas, L. (2017) Building student belonging at a time of change. In: Cardiff Metropolitan University Annual Learning and Teaching Conference. *Learning together, developing understanding*. Cardiff, Cardiff Metropolitan University.

Thomas, L., Hill, M., O'Mahony, J. & Yorke, M. (2017) *Supporting student success: strategies for institutional change. What works? Student retention and success programme.* Paul Hamlyn Foundation in association with the Higher Education Academy and Action on Access.

Turner, N. (2014) Development of self-belief for employability in higher education: ability, efficacy and control in context. *Teaching in Higher Education*, 19(6), 592–602.

Universities UK (2015) *Student mental wellbeing in higher education: a good practice guide.* London, Universities UK.

Introduction to the case studies

This chapter focuses on how universities can facilitate the development of students' self. Developing self-awareness and self-monitoring skills, goal-setting, and other aspects of personal development are an integral part of this, whether they are purposeful or a consequence of other student activities and learning. Many of the cases throughout the book therefore would be relevant to this chapter. Opportunities for self-development through explicit citizenship education and creative learning environments also have the capacity to develop self.

The case studies include:

- an activity to develop purposeful professional learning while on placement;
- developing students' oral and written communication skills by interacting with wider audiences, including schools;
- using play to explore new solutions and ideas for projects;
- using wacky ideas to harness students' creativity;
- using the senses to encourage student reflection and discovery in an international mobility context; and
- developing intercultural skills through the assessment process.

Case Study 26: A picture is worth a thousand words: stimulating nursing students to reflect and make sense of their experiences in a professional context

Catarina Lobão, Health School of Leiria, Portugal; Ana Baptista, Queen Mary University of London, London, UK; and Rui Gonçalves, Nursing School of Coimbra, Coimbra, Portugal

Key themes: reflection, professional learning, personal goals

Aim of the learning activity

The activity was designed to increase nursing students' critical reflections on their experiences in a professional context, while simultaneously thinking about their personal goals and ability to address issues arising from the clinical practicum. This was also an opportunity for the students, at the final year of their degree, to think about their transition to professional life, and what it might entail for them as nurses, lifelong learners, citizens and individuals.

Learning outcomes for students

- Critically reflect on their professional practice weekly, linking it to personal attitudes and knowledge about what they need to know to provide a high-quality care practice.
- Evaluate personal and professional goals at a short term (clinical practicum) and at a medium term (after finishing the degree).
- Demonstrate critical thinking about their practices and plan their practices accordingly.

Description of the learning activity

In the seventh semester, 12 nursing students enrolled in the critical care clinical practicum were asked to choose an image that would speak for the personal and professional experience they had in each week. Simultaneously, they needed to write a short reflective paragraph to explain the meaning of the selected image. By combining images and words, this activity opened space for the students to approach their own 'issues': academic, professional, social, emotional, psychological, and so on.

In a way, the underlying principle of this activity closely relates to the construction of an ongoing reflective portfolio through the promotion of students' self-reflection about their learning experience, in this case in a professional context, but still while in a formal learning context. When choosing an image and articulating the reasons for selecting it, each student confronts themselves with the process of learning. Also, because there are no constraints in terms of what they need to approach, they have the possibility of dealing with 'unspeakable' and emotional aspects of learning, which tend to be different each week. In the short paragraph, students usually describe, reflect and meta-reflect on their personal, sequential and contextualised experiences along a time frame.

This process thus stimulates different levels of reflection and awareness, and potentiates the sharing of diverse perspectives on learning, and specifically learning through professional practice. Therefore, one underlying assumption for this activity is that the process of learning through practice and making sense of knowledge in practice in a professional context is a transitioning period that might be experienced by the students in very powerful (emotional) ways.

Step-by-step guide to running the activity

In the seventh semester, before starting the critical care clinical practicum

The academic supervisor meets up with the students and gives all instructions related to the activity. The activity was neither compulsory nor assessed. However, its importance was highlighted as a way for the students to reflect on each week and share the main 'trend' of their experience, which could be positive or negative.

The academic supervisor created an email account specifically for this activity, and the academic supervisor would send weekly feedback to the students, building a relationship between the supervisor and students.

At the beginning of each week of the clinical practicum, specifically by Monday at noon

Students send an email with the selected image and a short reflective paragraph. This was an individual activity, and there were no constraints in relation to the topic each student would choose each week, nor the emotional tone transmitted. It was nevertheless essential that the image and respective reflective paragraph mirrored the most significant 'moment' in each student's week. The image could be: (i) chosen from the web – in this case, students needed to identify the source; (ii) drawn by them; (iii) a photo taken by them; and so on. The paragraph to describe the image was around 200–250 words.

The academic supervisor, when receiving the document, would not judge. Instead, they would serve as an expert mediator/facilitator who had already gone through the same process the students were experiencing. The documents sent by each student were only shared with the academic supervisor.

This activity occurred over 10 weeks – the duration of the clinical practicum. Week after week, after receiving the document from each student, the academic supervisor replied to each one by providing individualised and timely feedback. It was interesting to note that the students continued to engage with this activity because of receiving prompt and significant feedback on what they had sent. With the input from the academic supervisor, they could thus rethink their weekly reflection from another point of view, and were motivated to think about their practice through an 'evidence-based practice' approach. Other benefits were growing confidence and better articulation between theory and practice. Students also (re)used some issues of their weekly reflections in their final summative report. The activity also promoted closer links between teaching staff and students.

Ways in which it could be adapted/extended for different disciplines or levels

This activity could be adapted and extended to any discipline, level of study and even context of study and learning due to its individual nature and focus on students' learning context and profile. It might, however, be difficult to apply this activity to more than 15–20 students because of the weekly, individualised, in-depth feedback, as well as follow-up emails/communication between each student and the academic supervisor. However, it could be adapted to a larger class by linking more closely with module formative and summative processes.

Case Study 27: The role of public engagement in enhancing transition at postgraduate level

Dudley Shallcross and Tim Harrison, University of Bristol, Bristol, UK

Key themes: communicating to different audiences, writing skills, oral skills, real world, play, outreach

Aim of the learning activity

The aim of this intervention is to improve postgraduate chemistry students' subject knowledge by communicating that knowledge to an audience that ranges in age and academic background; to improve their communication skills through interacting with a wide range of learners with and without special educational needs; and to work with postgraduates from different fields within chemistry, enhancing social and academic interactions.

Learning outcomes for students

- Gain a deeper subject knowledge in their main field and allied fields through questioning and interactions with peers outside their sphere
- Develop a range of communication strategies relevant to their research, and wider communication skills development through oral presentations and written pieces for general interest articles, website material, etc.
- Develop teamwork, planning and implementation strategies, including health and safety, through organising engagement events inside and outside the university.

Description of the learning activity

Postgraduate students work with the engagement team at the School of Chemistry at the University of Bristol to deliver outreach events to primary and secondary school students and their teachers and to the general public. In Bristol, the team is led by a School Teacher Fellow, who is generally a former secondary school science teacher on permanent secondment.

Prior to the proposed engagement, the postgraduate student will have training in science communication in collaboration with our local StemNet. Once completed, the postgraduate may write articles on their research at a level that a general audience can understand. These will be published in journals or magazines that the general public, school students and teachers may read (e.g. *Education in Chemistry, School Science Review, Chemistry Review*).

They may also devise a talk on their work augmented with demonstration activities where possible. These demonstrations will present experiments that illustrate key principles that a general audience can understand that underpin the research. These demonstration experiments are often cited as being key to making the talk intelligible and adding entertainment and play into the activity. These talks may be given at an event at the School of Chemistry or at a venue away from the university. The postgraduate may also go into a school to demonstrate practical activities (mainly for primary schools), or they will demonstrate practical activities to secondary school students in the teaching laboratories at the School of Chemistry.

This intervention has proved to have a positive impact on students' research, because spending time preparing to work with a range of learners means they really understand the material relevant to their research. In one example, this meant that the student re-evaluated their research data and found some new insights that led to a high-profile paper. In general, postgraduates report that the process sharpens up and enhances their research.

They also find that they are better communicators and more confident, and they have reported that this has helped them with their presentation skills; postgraduates that take part in this programme have won numerous awards for presentations.

Step-by-step guide to running the activity

A typical example would be a talk with demonstration experiments by a PhD student coming to the end of their PhD, and the sequence would proceed as follows:

- The PhD student would generate a talk (e.g. PowerPoint) that describes their research or a key element of it. They have often done this already as part of a presentation at a conference.
- The School Teacher Fellow, myself and other postgraduate students will listen to the talk and pull out the key messages that are interesting.
- The School Teacher Fellow and I will then work with the PhD student to identify the key scientific principles that underpin the work and map these to knowledge that the audience (typically a school audience) will know. Possible experiments that support this activity will be identified.
- The PhD student will then work on the talk, and several iterations later will have a presentation that is clear, uses appropriate language and terminology for the audience, and will have practised the demonstration experiments where necessary. Health and safety implications will be thoroughly checked.

- They will then give the presentation at the School of Chemistry during a whole-day event for school students, which will be followed by feedback from the teachers and school students attending.
- Further talks at the School of Chemistry will be given, and when the PhD student is confident and the School Teacher Fellow and I are happy, the PhD student will be invited to present at venues outside the School of Chemistry.
- At this stage, the PhD student needs to plan not only the talk, but the logistics as well, including:
    - what materials to take, and booking and returning of material;
    - a pre-visit to the venue to determine space available;
    - health and safety considerations;
    - the timing required, including time to get to the venue, parking, etc.; and
    - other contingency planning, such as whether assistance will be required, clear-away time, and facilities for cleaning glassware and equipment.

Ways in which it could be adapted/extended for different disciplines or levels

This approach is simple to extend to other disciplines as there will generally be a link, and therefore potential interaction, with school curricula. The general public also wants to know about current research and have it explained in layman's terms. In the sciences, health and safety is perceived to be a big barrier, but this is not true. Working with the Consortium of Local Education Authorities for the Provision of Science Services (CLEAPPS), we have found it is possible to conduct experiments in a safe manner without having to reduce the number of demonstration experiments.

Case Study 28: Transition as metaphor: how building with Lego helps students navigate team working for an external client

Alison James, University of Winchester, Winchester, UK

Key themes: creativity, team-working, play, real world, reflection

Aim of the learning activity

This case study outlines how building three-dimensionally as part of project, collaborative and externally situated activities can enable students to develop rounder perspectives on their ventures. From personal involvement and reports on the second-year experience, it can appear that second-year students are the group that fall off our radar; the first-year experience is an essential focus for establishing the ground for a positive university trajectory, while the third-years attract attention as we want them to graduate as successfully as possible. The second-years are often those who are deemed to have oriented themselves sufficiently, know what we want, and can cope without us.

Learning outcomes for students

- Explore and understand how teams work to a brief through the medium of building bricks.
- Use a process of building metaphorically to complement traditional forms of engagement in your discipline.
- Employ multisensory techniques such as building as a means of reflecting on experience.

Description of the learning activity

This activity can be part of any project involving teamwork and a joint outcome. Examples could be prototyping a product or service, creating a campaign for a specific cause (commercial or not-for-profit), helping a third party find new ways of working, or alternative responses to an age-old problem. Its aims are twofold: to support the team in achieving a successful outcome, and in enabling participants to understand how they can operate effectively as a collective.

To illustrate, let us imagine that the students have been asked to help a company wanting to rejuvenate an established brand that has become tired and unattractive. In groups of six, they compete to produce the best proposal to help their client refresh their offer. As part of working in their subject specialism to formulate their pitch, they engage in building activities with Lego to evaluate their progress.

The principles informing the activity are multiple and inspired by the Lego Serious Play format, as discussed in more detail in the author's HEA publication, *Innovating in the Creative Arts with LEGO* (James, 2015). Teachers and students working in an industry or business context may also be interested in Kristiansen and Rasmussen (2014), master trainers in the methodology.

For the purpose of this activity, these are summarised as follows:

- As everyone builds, shares and speaks equally, everyone's contributions are heard, not just the thoughts of the noisiest.

- In line with Papert and Harel's (1991) theory of constructionism, people learn best when they are building, and come up with two outcomes – an item and new knowledge.
- Building three-dimensionally and symbolically stimulates diverse and innovative ways of thinking.

In terms of reflective practice, this activity moves participants away from a dependency on reflection as a written evaluation of engagement, and towards one that involves construction, discussion and imagination.

Step-by-step guide to running the activity

Resources: a plentiful and varied selection of Lego bricks and tables to build on.

This activity can be run over three separate workshops, or as a stand-alone element near the start of the project soon after the groups have started to work together. It allows participants to identify a general theme or angle for their proposal, share a few ideas and allocate roles. A three-hour workshop for all students (working within their teams) is scheduled to teach them how to embody and discuss complex issues, actions, needs, people and influences through building:

1 It begins with introductory and warm-up activities that emphasise metaphorical rather than literal expression; a green spiky plant is no longer horticultural, but rather may be hair, energy, sharpness, hope, new growth, and so on. Depending on how quickly students get to grips (a metaphor!) with this shift, this stage can take 30 minutes to one hour. They pass around diverse bricks to generate associations with colour, image, symbol, texture, size, symbol and distance. They build quick, playful models (the ideal client/team, the nightmare client/team) and explain them equally quickly to unleash their ability to imagine on the spot. There is no predetermined meaning for any brick; it is up to the students to decide what a brick stands for (all pieces of Lego are referred to as bricks, irrespective of shape or form); no one can tell the builder what their creation means so no one can be wrong. The focus is also on talking through the model; therefore, the pressure is off the individual beyond telling the story of their ideas.

2 Next, students build models of themselves in their project roles and what they are bringing to the venture (5–8 minutes). Then each of them describes their model to the group (20–30 minutes). Group members can ask questions about the model but not interpret it.

3   The team think about their capacities and characteristics as evidenced in their models, and arrange them by mutual agreement so that important connections between them are visible.
4   They next build models of their project's progress and situate these together (same timings as for previous stage).
5   The team look at the array of models and start to pull out the key themes and characteristics that have been made visible; they can add in quick, additional models if they spot any gaps or important influences that they need to consider that may impact on their ability to complete their work successfully.

These activities concluded, the student teams photograph their models, which offer memorable visual records to inform the development of their proposed client response.

Variations on these builds (without the introductory activities) can be further used at a midpoint in the project to evaluate progress against objectives, and then at the end to reflect on how well they worked together as a team, and how successfully they felt they achieved their outcome. In any workshop, having one or more people to roam between tables to prompt reflective conversations and ask questions is always beneficial.

Discussion at the end of the workshop/s usually reveals that the process has shifted students' thinking or helped them round out their approach through memorable, visual elements. They usually observe that they talk about things differently and make comments (relevant to the activity) that they would not make if working with flip charts and pens.

Ways in which it could be adapted/extended for different disciplines or levels

These activities lend themselves to any situation where there is a complex issue or an issue to be explored that has no obvious or single answer. They can therefore be used just as easily with anyone; for example, in outreach activities bringing students into university (What are my expectations and how am I feeling?); by doctoral students (What exactly *is* my research question?); or academic developers (How can we motivate learning and teaching? How can we function more sustainably? How will the teaching excellence framework impact on us?).

References

James, A. (2015) *Innovating in the creative arts with LEGO*. Available from: www.heacademy.ac.uk/innovating-creative-arts-lego [Accessed 26 October 2017].

Kristiansen, P. & Rasmussen, R. (2014) *Building a better business with the LEGO® SERIOUS PLAY® method*. Hoboken, NJ, Wiley.

Papert, S. & Harel, I. (1991) Situating constructionism. In: Papert, S. & Harel, I. (eds.), *Constructionism*. Norwood, NJ, Ablex. Available from: www.papert.org/articles/SituatingConstructionism.html [Accessed 26 October 2017].

Case Study 29: Design futures: a trans-active curriculum community-based approach to the development of student self-confidence, empowerment and entrepreneurship

Stephen Thompson, Cardiff Metropolitan University, Cardiff, UK

Key themes: creativity, autonomy, self-confidence, Socratic dialogue

Aim of the learning activity

This Masters module is a model of 'slow education' that aims to build a student-directed curriculum that equips students for future contexts of doctoral research by forming a student 'reactor' that generates self-confidence, a sense of empowerment, and creativity in students.

Learning outcomes for students

- Demonstrate a clear and enhanced sense of independence, autonomy and leadership in their field.
- Demonstrate a willingness to collaborate and share ideas with others, and be open to the contribution others make to their own intellectual and creative trajectory. They may begin to form collaborative partnerships.
- Demonstrate an enhanced ability to drive ideas forward and to take command of the uncertainty offered by the future through mapping out possible technological and professional landscapes.

Description of the learning activity

The trans-active curriculum was constructed in response to a perceived problem in postgraduate education. There is a widely held assumption that Masters education should provide an opportunity to focus and enhance skills. Indeed, many Masters programmes offer specific targeted career-directed enhancement to undergraduate skills. This focus works well so long as the graduate student has a clear sense of the skills they need for a specific and targeted career. However, very few graduate students possess the necessary awareness of the changing career landscape and of the changing nature of knowledge and skills in shifting technological and social contexts.

The 'trans-active curriculum' is designed to provide a means that allows students to both reveal and invent the possibilities afforded by this shifting and fluid nature of the future in times and academic contexts that are subject to rapid and seemingly unpredictable change. The 'reactor' is the group itself, including associated teaching staff, and its capacity to support each other's generation of ideas.

The trans-active curriculum has three underlying principles:

Autonomy is uncomfortable and liable to feelings of uncertainty. In order for students to attain autonomy and creative vision, it must be accepted that students, many of whom have been denied the opportunity to own ideas thus far, need self-confidence raised to begin to centre themselves within a mutable field of ideas. The idea is to reveal the true potential of students and their ideas. Prescriptive and instrumental assessment must be avoided in favour of generative dialogue.

Democracy implies the distribution of empowerment. In order for students to own their future and to occupy its territories and negotiate its plural landscapes, they must be given the space to learn through failure and to welcome uncertainty as an opportunity. This implies a trans-active curriculum that denies any attempt at the didactic inculcation of a prescribed skill set.

Rigour comes from reference to and the re-ownership of others' ideas. In order for students to gain the necessary mastery of ideas expected at this level, they will need to become familiar with contemporary and historic scholarship and to be able to own those ideas in their own terms, though always in a manner that is respectful to their originators and to the context of the times in which those ideas were originally assembled. This 'synthetic analysis' of ideas must necessarily encourage deep reading and speculation in equal measure.

Step-by-step guide to running the activity

The trans-active curriculum requires no particular resources other than an internet connection, a simple room to meet, and a means of displaying images (either a projector or flat screen) with appropriate connection to a computer. It can be assumed that students will have a mobile phone with a camera.

The trans-active curriculum was designed to take undergraduates towards doctoral study, but can be taught at any level above level 4 and can be delivered as a standalone module, or embedded in several modules in order to scale across a whole programme. It has four sequential steps, each representing 25 per cent of the dedicated programme or optional experience time.

(De)orientation

Students should be familiarised with one another and then challenged to rethink their creative and intellectual position. This is undertaken in the form of a short project with a broad brief, out of which students will be expected to produce a one-minute movie that will be shown and explained at a concluding event. I tend to use quite cryptic briefs! For example, I have used the following in the past:

- White room, scared man, place of work – resonance – what?
- My name is 'Jenny the Slider', it's what I do, I slide, what do I do?
- 01.45 Los Angeles. 8.34 Abuja. 11.16 Freetown. 12.07 Tirana. 17.15 Doha. 21.56 Funafuti.
- The trees are plastic now, not that you would notice.

(Re)orientation

Students will be absolutely baffled, perhaps angry. Explanation should be resisted. Instead, the convening tutor should use Socratic dialogue to encourage students to think through their own initial ideas – questions such as 'What ideas does this generate for you?', 'Where might you go with this?', 'How would that pan out?'. Since there is no correct or expected answer, no critique should be undertaken, but each outcome should be used as a vehicle to draw out ideas and potentials.

(Co)orientation

Once ideas and potentials are identified, students are tasked with making their ideas more concrete. Students return to present their ideas again to others; this provides an opportunity for feedback, clarification and validation of their ideas. This is a substantive opportunity for learning. The validation might be seen in terms of a scientific or technological advancement, a philosophical context, or some form of speculative social or historical construct.

(En)visioning

Students now construct a presentation of their own envisioning of a plausible landscape of the future and place themselves within that future. If this is a stand-alone option module, emphasis should be placed upon how the students might use this experience in their studies. If this is part of an extended programme, students should be asked to 'bank' these ideas and to build upon them as the process repeats again. With each iteration, the students become more familiar and audaciously confident with the process of interpretation required, more rigorous and focused in their research, and more skilled in their presentation and means of output.

Assessment is done through students maintaining a reflective blog of their transition through the curriculum.

Ways in which it could be adapted/extended for different disciplines or levels

Since it contains no predetermined 'content', the trans-active curriculum is suitable for any discipline where speculative enquiry is valued, but is particularly suitable for art and design, speculative science contexts, and also the wider studies of history and the humanities.

Case Study 30: Designing a student-led framework for pre- and post-mobility intercultural skills development as part of the curriculum

Monika Foster, Queen Margaret University (formerly Edinburgh Napier University), Edinburgh, UK

Key themes: mobility, intercultural, cultural probes

Aim of the learning activity

The aim is to encourage a holistic approach to student mobility that focuses on the development of intercultural skills and capabilities through a student lens as part of a degree programme. The senses are used as a stimulus to capture cultural probes while students are abroad.

As a result of the activity, outgoing students are better engaged in the wider intercultural dimension of the mobility experience, and are prepared to capture their cross-cultural adaptation and to reflect on the development of their intercultural awareness. Students not involved in mobility can also benefit from 'internationalisation at home' by having access to the visual representations of the cross-cultural adaptation of the outgoing students through sharing these on student portals and posters on campus.

Learning outcomes for students

- Achieve an awareness of the potential for intercultural skills development while in mobility.

- Take ownership for how mobility experience is captured.
- Develop their own record of the development of intercultural awareness.

Description of the learning activity

A strategic objective for many UK HEIs is to grow international student mobility, especially outgoing mobility. Students at the university have the opportunity of international mobility as an integral part of the curriculum, not a stand-alone option, and the development of intercultural skills is also captured through interactive assessments.

Students who are thinking about engaging with outgoing mobility are buddied up with those who have already taken part in mobility, and through employing the use of 'cultural probes' achieve a much deeper meaning to mobility, beyond credits and the experience of being in a different country. The intervention is student-driven; students are encouraged to take ownership of how the mobility experience is captured, and through which means/ senses, so it evokes empathy and personal engagement with intercultural skills development.

The intervention involves a more reflective approach to working with students in mobility and a shift away from a mechanistic focus on systems and structures towards developing practical intercultural skills. The focus is on developing a student-led record of intercultural awareness through their mobility. In the intervention, the prospective students involved in outgoing mobility are invited to join a programme of two workshops on intercultural skills and the use of 'cultural probes' to capture cross-cultural adaptation. The self-collection, 'cultural probes' instruments, video diaries and reflective journals are completely student-led (Haque, 1997; Mertens, 2005).

During their time away, students record developing intercultural awareness through various media. Upon return, students take part in creative assessments based on the mobility experience; for example, a film or a selection of visual postcards may be presented on their interaction with the new learning environment. This cyclical process ensures that mobility is viewed as a holistic process embedded in the curriculum, beyond visa and travel issues, and that new students possibly interested in mobility can see its long-term benefits and fellow students' achievements.

Mobility is part of internationalising the curriculum, viewed in this intervention less as a 'process' (Knight, 2008: 21), and more as academic learning that blends own and other perspectives (Leask, 2016). This view of internationalisation is also congruent with the perspectives of Haigh (2009) and Sanderson (2011), who foreground the value of personal awareness in intercultural encounters in higher education. The development of intercultural competence to deal with different cultural backgrounds and with diverging ways of working or communicating is the most profound of the competencies to be gained from mobility and is well researched (Prazeres, 2013). The intervention is positioned around cross-cultural adaptation of students in mobility to inform efforts to engage students in outgoing mobility and to inform the decision-makers at universities. Using creative interventions includes cultural probes such as photos and videos (Gaver et al., 2004), which is a design-led approach to understanding others, and stresses empathy and engagement using evocative tasks to elicit inspirational responses.

Step-by-step guide to running the activity

Stage 1: before mobility

Two one-hour workshops including returning students, academics involved in supporting mobility students, and prospective mobility students:

- *Workshop 1*: Developing intercultural awareness through mobility.
- *Workshop 2*: Using student-led cultural probes to capture cross-cultural adaptation. Students are then briefed on how to keep video diaries; 'cultural probes' instruments, which can include one or more of the following selection: touch, smell, sound or friend; and reflective journals.

Stage 2: during mobility

Academic support is provided for students to develop their cultural probes using their own selected student lens of either a video or a visual postcard, choosing from the categories of a sound, a smell, a touch or a friend. During their time away, students record their developing intercultural awareness through various media.

Students are given a brief with some suggested approaches; for example, for *touch*, students can choose an object they have received from someone or use every day while abroad, photograph it against a white background, and then record a one-minute narration as to why they chose this object. Finally, they prepare an 'e-postcard' from their study abroad, including the photograph and the podcast narration, which can be shared with other students. In relation to a *sound* or a *smell* category, students can record a short video about a place that they associate with a specific sound or smell they will remember from their study abroad (e.g. a busy marketplace) and add a small written summary of why they chose this place (restricted in volume and length, e.g. no more than three-minute video). For a *friend*, the students can choose to use a podcast to describe their friend whom they met during their study abroad, and why they are special, then add a photograph of the friend.

Stage 3: post-mobility

Students undertake interactive assessments using the cultural probes to showcase their development of intercultural skills. They also participate in the two workshops outlined above with prospective students, and provide buddying for these students.

Ways in which it could be adapted/extended for different disciplines or levels

The cultural probes may require more or less instruction depending on the subject area, although we used them with business students, and they embraced them quickly and enthusiastically, with minimum instruction required.

If time is an issue, the workshops introducing the intercultural skills can be delivered in a blended approach, with some of the 'input' being offered online through the virtual learning environment and instead only one workshop held to cover the preparation for the intervention.

After the mobility, the dissemination from the intervention can be shared more broadly than just through assessment; it could be shared as part of a student conference or fed into the faculty learning and teaching development programme.

References

Gaver, W.W., Boucher, A., Pennington, S. & Walker, B. (2004) Cultural probes and the value of uncertainty. *Interactions*, 11(5), 53–56.

Haigh, M. (2009) Fostering cross-cultural empathy with non-Western curricular structures. *Journal of Studies in International Education*, 13(2), 271–284.

Haque, M.S. (1997) Incongruity between bureaucracy and society in developing nations: a critique. *Peace & Change*, 22(4), 432–462.

Knight, J. (2008) The internationalization of higher education: complexities and realities. In: Teferra, D. & Knight, J. (eds.), *Higher education in Africa: the international dimension*. Chestnut Hill, MA, Center for International Higher Education, pp. 1–43.

Leask, B. (2016) Internationalizing curriculum and learning for all students. In: Jones, E., Coelen, R., Beelen, J. & de Wit, H. (eds.), *Global and local internationalization*. Rotterdam, Sense Publishers, pp. 49–53.

Mertens, D.M. (2005) *Research methods in education and psychology: integrating diversity with quantitative and qualitative approaches*. 2nd ed. Thousand Oaks, CA, Sage.

Prazeres, L. (2013) International and intra-national student mobility: trends, motivations and identity. *Geography Compass*, 7(11), 804–820.

Sanderson, G. (2011) Internationalisation and teaching in higher education. *Higher Education Research and Development*, 30(5), 661–676.

Case Study 31: Culturally appropriate assessment strategy

Hazel Horobin, formerly Sheffield Hallam University, Sheffield, UK

Key themes: intercultural skills, professional practice, assessment, communication

Aim of the learning activity

Physiotherapy can be considered a complex sociocultural performance. The manner and scope of treatments proffered is an important aspect of professional practice that is rooted in the culture in which it is exercised. The culturally appropriate assessment strategy for the module 'Community-Based Rehabilitation' (CBR) explicitly recognises and engages with the practice contexts students have experienced in their working life prior to the course, with the intention of developing their cultural flexibility and awareness.

Learning outcomes for students

- Explore in depth the issues around community-based rehabilitation and give you an opportunity to address issues in community healthcare from a variety of methodological and philosophical frameworks and from an international perspective.
- Critique current practices in healthcare provision and discuss the strengths and weaknesses of these services when considering the health status of communities.
- Develop your cultural competency and communication skills specifically in a community setting and in relation to health promotion/education.
- Evaluate and reflect on your own practice and learning needs in order to enable you to develop innovative change in the workplace.

Description of the learning activity

Between 2005 and 2014, I was involved in the delivery of an 18-month MSc course, comprising a year of mainly compulsory academic modules about research and treatment techniques within the context of healthcare in England, followed by six months undertaking a theoretical dissertation. The 'Community-Based Rehabilitation' module formed an optional element of the programme. The cohort comprised 95 per cent international students, the majority from India. The module underwent a development where the driving forces for change were both to develop greater levels of learner-centredness and encouragement for participants to recognise local capacity in developing healthcare practices in familiar, home healthcare systems. It aimed to encourage students to bring their learning (and life) into the module assessment. This strategy was considered necessary to address employability issues associated with the loss of the 2012 post-study work visa in the UK. The removal of this facilitation to UK working shifted employment possibilities for graduates towards their home countries.

The module assessment strategy was expanded. In addition to the previous group assessment task in an earlier iteration of the module, where academic understanding of CBR issues was addressed, 25 per cent of the overall module mark was allocated to the development of an individual teaching aid. This was anything that the participant could use to promote health in a specific country context. This part of the mark was further divided:

- Poster/aid – originality and creativity (30 per cent): tutor- and peer-marked.
- A justification for the health promotion message, the community it was intended for, and the medium used to transmit the message (50 per cent): tutor-marked.
- Cultural appropriateness (20 per cent): marked by 'cultural assessors' from the identified community.

This approach to assessment was felt to be grounded more strongly in a constructivist approach to education, offering greater meaning to learning and building on what they already knew. This case study focuses on experience of the individual teaching aid rather than the assessment as a whole.

Step-by-step guide to running the activity

Preparation

The preparation for the activity began with the development of the learning outcomes and assessment criteria through revalidation that located the health promotion aid in a country or regional context. The students were free to choose how to interpret this; many focused on regions or communities. Module handbooks and assignment support sessions were developed to include support and preparation for this additional task inclusion. A single room was booked for the afternoon, large enough to hold all students (approximately 15), assessors and visitors.

Identification of assessors

Most of the difference in assessment planning was in the identification and preparation of cultural assessors. An interfaith forum that had previously had some involvement with the university helped me locate people prepared to act as module assessors who would judge the cultural appropriateness of the mode and style of health message delivery selected by the student. An introductory email to forum contacts was followed by phone calls to willing volunteers to explain the nature of their involvement. The conditions of their participation were also explained as they were contracted under the 'service user and carer' conditions of service, and paid for their time via the university's guidelines for such activity. Email was used to explain the marking schema, and the cultural assessors were also invited to a provided lunch before the start of the assessment, in which they were further briefed about the afternoon. There were three cultural assessors from India, Ghana and Saudi Arabia, which covered the nationalities of the cohort. I was also present along with another tutor from the course.

The audience

The novelty of the assessment generated interest within the course and to community contacts beyond the course. Additional people (participants' friends who wanted to support the students with their presentations) were permitted into the assessment event, and there was a briefing to all at the outset regarding expectations of non-interference.

The presentation and other assessment requirements

The justification for the teaching aid was submitted online via the virtual learning platform for the module, but any mode of delivery for the health promotion aid was possible. Students presented in different ways: posters, video clips, dolls (to represent babies, as a tool for showing helpful carrying positions) and other therapy aids, dramatic representations of practice (ululation and approaches to community discussion), and songs. Students took it in turns to present their aid and explain what it was, and a little about how it worked and why. After each presentation, following applause and questions, the appropriate cultural assessor, tutors and peers made notes and allocated marks on feedback sheets designed for this purpose.

Reflection on the assessment activity

This form of assessment appeared to have a profound effect on the morale and motivation of the cohort, resulting in creativity and originality of the teaching aids presented. The energy and enthusiasm of the afternoon was stimulating, and the room had a glass wall, resulting in a crowd of students gathering outside the room to see what was happening, adding to the sense of theatre. The demonstration of local dress and customs gave the event a truly international feel, and some of the complexity of culture was exposed through the different issues addressed within the same country. The programme's external examiner was also invited, and it gave them further insight into the assessment process to fulfil their quality assurance function.

There was considerable positive feedback from students and visitors about the assessment afternoon. There was a sense that other cultures had been respected, demonstrated through the locatedness of content, the celebratory element of the afternoon, and the presence and valuing of the cultural assessors and the external examiner.

No student achieved below pass marks for any aspect of the assignment for the first time in the module's history. Generous marking by peers and cultural ambassadors resulted in a slight inflation of marks, but this element formed a relatively small part of the assessment marking overall and was tolerated by the assessment team. On reflection, the teaching aid could have formed a much greater percentage of the assessment.

Ways in which it could be adapted/extended for different disciplines or levels

All knowledge is contextually bound, and assessment strategies that reward or acknowledge those contexts are relatively simple to create. Doing so drives the meaning of learning towards higher educational goals such as the application of knowledge and the inherent critical thinking aspects that support this. In this case, it also proved profoundly motivating to students.

Involving members of the public or those with an interest in a particular content can form a valuable audience for feedback and help to set an assessment context. University-wide support of a diverse service user strategy is a helpful support in such an activity.

Part III

Chapter 9

Evaluating the effectiveness of transition activities

Lin Norton

Introduction to the chapter

My purpose in writing this chapter is to encourage readers to think about the important issues around evaluating projects or initiatives that are designed to improve students' transition experiences. I begin with a theoretical discussion around the concept of evaluation in educational research because I want to argue that evaluation will not work if it means only focusing on the narrow technological and measurable effects of pedagogical interventions. This might seem startling in a chapter on evaluation, but my stance is that we need to incorporate the crucial aspects of professional judgment, as well as professional and personal values, together with a view of what we believe to be educationally desirable. As such, I will be suggesting that action research is one useful approach (Norton, 2009, 2014).

The chapter overall will be situated in the current global higher education context that includes, among other things, quality assurance, student satisfaction and consumer rights, the neo-liberal market economy and international competition, as well as the more recent metrics approach to teaching excellence promoted in the UK by the Teaching Excellence Framework (TEF). Such often competing imperatives require that funded projects, teaching initiatives and/or straight forward research studies need to demonstrate evidence that they have merit. How this evidence is manifest acknowledges that student transition is a 'wicked problem' (Rittel & Webber, 1973), meaning it is unstructured, making cause and effect very difficult to identify and model (Weber & Khademian, 2008). Ramley (2014) also describes it as a kind of problem that cannot be definitively defined as it changes while we study it; every problem is unique and interrelated within what is often a larger, more complex problem, so may need collaborative responses.

In the second part of the chapter, I will take a more practical focus by presenting some of the commonly used methods and tools in higher education research, set within a framework of professional judgment and how it relates to educational action. I will use the concept of a 'wicked problem' to justify the view that all attempts at solving the problem will be useful in themselves, and while they cannot offer a simple solution, they may well open up avenues to explore further. This is essentially the perspective taken in an action research approach

(Reason & Bradbury, 2008), which will form the conceptual methodological background that underpins this section. An important consideration will be the sustainability of approaches taken, which is a common issue with funded projects.

Evaluation in education

At the heart of the concept of evaluating teaching and/or learning support initiatives/interventions is the perceived need for teaching to be seen as a research-based profession, much as the medical profession is viewed. Hargreaves (1996) is generally credited with this call, as he argued in a lecture to the Teacher Training Agency:

> In education there is simply not enough evidence on the effects and effectiveness of what teachers do in classrooms to provide an evidence-based corpus of knowledge. The failure of educational researchers, with a few exceptions, to create a substantial body of evidence equivalent to evidence-based medicine means that teaching is not –and never will be – a research-based profession unless there is a major change in the kind of research that is done in education. Today teachers still have to discover or adopt most of their own professional practice by personal preference, guided by neither the accumulated wisdom of seniors nor by practitioner-relevant research.
>
> (p. 4)

While Hargreaves was referring to the UK school sector over 20 years ago, his observations still have important implications for university teaching today, and it is interesting to note his mention of practitioner-relevant research.

One of the major lacunae in presenting accounts of teaching initiatives, and my personal observation, is that solid evaluation incorporating robust evidence is frequently missing. While it is stimulating and inspirational to read or hear about teachers' work on redesigning curricula or introducing initiatives to enhance the student learning experience, the evaluation aspect can be neglected. I am often left asking myself the question '. . . so did it work?'. Sometimes it is given cursory attention by referring to students' satisfaction with the initiative. This is interesting but gives us insufficient information on which to base a judgment as to the value and sustainability of the initiative itself. It does not move us any further on if we simply find out that our students liked the initiative. Doyle et al. (2015) refer to 'real-world impact', by which they mean the influence of research on policy and managerial and professional practices, and as such they distinguish it from academic impact, meaning a contribution to scholarly knowledge. The importance of real-world impact comes from the current global imperative in higher education to demonstrate accountability. However, demonstrating what are often intangible effects of research is problematic.

A further difficulty with demonstrating the effectiveness of teaching initiatives is the significant suspicion about evidence-based practice itself. Biesta (2007), for example, suggests that Hargreaves' (1996) criticism of educational research was also directed at educational practice. Biesta calls this a double transformation of both educational research and educational practice. One of the points he makes is that evidence-based education can be subverted by a managerial agenda and an associated top-down approach to educational improvement. He proposes a model of professional action that:

> acknowledges the non-causal nature of educational interaction [and recognises that] education is a moral practice, rather than a technical or technological one . . . The most important question for educational professionals is therefore not about the effectiveness of their actions but about the potential educational value of what they do, that is, about the educational desirability of the opportunities for learning that follow from their action.
> (Biesta, 2007: 10)

The implication of his argument is that we need to think beyond a simple technical question of what works to a more nuanced and interrelated question (a 'wicked problem') of what is educationally desirable. At the same time, it would mean that projects should be thought of not as straightforward initiatives, but as opportunities to open doors and stimulate different approaches to transition, as has been discussed in previous chapters in this book.

Biesta talks about how using terms such as 'evidence-informed', 'evidence-influenced' and 'evidence-aware' practice may help to make the links between research findings, policymaking and educational practice itself. This might help address the difficulty relating to poor use of research, and is a helpful way of thinking about how to show that initiatives have a reach beyond their immediate local context. One thing we need to be acutely aware of is how to disseminate our research findings in a way that will influence or at the very least inform policy-makers (Norton, 2009). This point will be returned to in my discussion about dissemination. The issue for practitioner-researchers becomes how we can articulate the impact of our research findings. Most of us would agree that making a difference is the crux of demonstrating impact, but to do so means going beyond what can simply be measured to enabling stakeholders to understand what change has been made. It could be, for example, that awareness of the complexity of the concept of student transition has been raised among academic teaching staff so that they no longer see it as one stage when students enter university. Such a conceptual shift is difficult to capture, and is further exacerbated by the fact that it often takes time (maybe years) for habits and minds to be changed, which implies there is a need for more longitudinal studies to be carried out.

Summary

What I have argued here has been that the evaluation of initiatives to improve students' transition experiences needs to be addressed in a more nuanced and holistic way than by only using some form of technical measurements. This is not to say that robust evidence such as performance measures should not be part of an evaluation, but that they should be one component of a bigger story, one that is imbued with values that are articulated and aims that are educationally desirable. In the next section, I move on to consider the question of what the practitioner can actually do.

Some pragmatic approaches

Transition initiatives can include, among other things, induction and pre-induction activities, active engagement initiatives, student involvement in curriculum and assessment design, experiential learning, preparation for employment and active citizenship, learning to learn projects, and academic writing, many of which have been presented earlier in this book. To enable such projects to reach beyond their immediate context and to influence policy and management, they should present rigorous and robust research design, high-quality data, and interpretation informed by educational and moral values. This may seem somewhat daunting to the practitioner who has little experience of carrying out pedagogical research, which is why an action research approach can be helpful. There are many guides to action research, but I have found that the most accessible way to approach it is to think about a key question derived from the work of Jean McNiff (2017) and Jack Whitehead (n.d.): 'How do I improve my learning and teaching practice?'. A good starting point to help you to answer this question is to look at what is currently troubling you about your students. In this book, it could be about some element of transition where students are not doing as well as you hope. Action researchers are practitioners who then research some element of their own practice to help them understand the problem better and to take action. The crux of action research is that it must involve some change – it is *action* as well as research. The action research cycle typically consists of a spiral of steps, which involve identifying an initial idea, reconnaissance or fact-finding, planning, taking the first action step, evaluating, amending the plan, and taking the second action step (Lewin, 1946).

While this can be a useful way of thinking about the stages in action research, it does not give guidance on how to actually carry it out. The following five steps will help to start the process in any type of pedagogical research (including practitioner and action research) in a way that is manageable. These are:

1. Consider your research focus: students or staff or both?
2. Consider the research paradigm: quantitative or qualitative?
3. Consider the methods: single or multi-method?
4. Consider your research purpose: who to influence and why?
5. Consider the ethical issues: principles or acting ethically?

Inevitably, there is overlap between these questions, but they can be used as an overall guide or framework when designing an evaluation study. I will now explore these in turn.

Consider your research focus: students or staff or both?

This is an important consideration as it depends fundamentally on your overall research purpose. A student example may be to see if an approach (e.g. teaching or curriculum initiative) improves some aspect of the student experience or performance; a staff example, on the other hand, may be that you are interested in raising staff awareness of what is involved in transition.

Let us begin with a student focus and look at some commonly used student measures.

Student satisfaction

Imagine you have designed and carried out an intervention aimed at helping students in their first year of university develop their academic writing skills. How do you demonstrate that your intervention has actually worked?

The most typical evaluation of any type of initiative or intervention is student satisfaction. It is relatively simple to design and easy to administer (such as a straightforward survey questionnaire). The most well-known measure of student satisfaction in the UK is the National Student Survey (NSS). This is an independent annual survey that began in 2005 and was designed to assess undergraduate students' opinions of the quality of their degree programmes, with questions about different aspects of their learning experience plus an overall satisfaction score. Most countries have their own surveys, such as the American Student Satisfaction Inventory or the Australian Course Experience Questionnaire (on which the NSS was based) (see also Chapter 2).

There are, however, limitations to these types of evaluation. Metrics-based measures give us little useable information as to what worked well and why, and what still needs to be improved. However, given this is one of the most common measures of evaluation, there are several ways of capturing 'satisfaction' data, which would include questionnaires, interviews or focus groups, and/or some form of student reflections (written or spoken).

Student performance measures/outcomes of learning

Possibly a more robust measure of the effectiveness of an initiative would be to see if students' work improved. A recent concept in the UK that has been associated with the TEF has been that of learning gain. This has been defined by the Higher Education Funding Council for England (HEFCE) as: "Learning gain can be defined and understood in a number of ways. But broadly it is an attempt to measure the improvement in knowledge, skills, work-readiness and personal development made by students during their time spent in higher education" (Higher Education Funding Council for England, 2016). The HEFCE suggests ways of measuring learning gain that include standardised tests to measure skills, and grades to measure progress across selected points of time, plus a number of qualitative approaches.

Measuring improvement by analysing students' work might be one of the most convincing ways to evaluate the effectiveness of an intervention, if that is the purpose of your research, but it can be time-consuming. In my suggested intervention with academic writing skills, I might, for example, consider how I could measure evidence of critical thinking in a written piece of work, and what I would need to show that it had improved pre- to post-intervention. Other measures I might obtain could come from student-generated work such as blogs, wikis and reflective journals, but again some method of devising what was actually being measured would have to be considered. A proxy measure of improvement is that of grades either on individual pieces of work or the ubiquitous grade point average (GPA), but there are many problems with this as many other factors can affect grade improvement. An overall measure such as GPA is particularly blunt in detecting the kind of small changes that would be involved.

If we imagine another project that might be about supporting students who were struggling with the transition from first to second year, there is promise in technological methods of data collection such as learning analytics, which can measure much more sensitively things such as learner activity. Slater, Peasgood and Mullan (2016), in their review of learning analytics in higher education, define it as "the measurement, collection, analysis and reporting of data about the progress of learners and the contexts in which learning takes place" (p. 4). They suggest that learning analytics data could be used as a tool for boosting retention rates by being able to identify 'at-risk' students and then intervene with advice and support. However, this approach is a fairly new one and may be possibly beyond the scope of individual practitioners. There are, however, certain elements of student behaviour that can be captured by those who are involved in e-learning, such as capturing and analysing students' reflections on their learning experiences. Doolan and Gilbert (2016) used this method to good effect by gaining insights into how students blended their own technologies such as Skype, WhatsApp and Facebook to connect with peers in their learning tasks.

Staff professional development

Projects related to staff issues are more likely to evolve around issues such as capacity-building and raising awareness, so they tie in closely with academic development and continuing professional development (CPD) models. Practitioner research and/or action research can be one effective way of enabling staff to engage with the scholarship of teaching and learning (SOTL) and reflect on their own practice (Gibbs et al., 2016). Like all other forms of small-scale research, in order to achieve impact and sustainability, collaborative or participatory action research might also be considered; this can be with colleagues and/or with students.

Changes in attitudes

The question of whether attitudes must change before behaviours change, or whether changing behaviours engender the attitude change, is still debated in the literature (Manstead, 1996; Webb & Sheeran, 2006). While attitudes are relatively easy to capture, staff behaviours are not, and the link between enhanced student experience, or in this case easier, more effective transition, is tenuous at best. Nevertheless, some difference in a measure of staff attitudes to transition and/or potential interventions might be a useful piece of evidence.

Consider the research paradigm: quantitative or qualitative?

For many years, a dichotomy has been articulated between the two research paradigms of positivism and interpretivism. There is plenty of literature for interested readers, but the following is my simplified summary. The positivist paradigm is concerned with statistical measures and analyses, and attempts to form some cause-and-effect findings. It follows a more scientific approach to data where the aims are to be as objective as possible in order to demonstrate generalisability and reliability. This type of research is suitable for large numbers (usually 30 or more). Typical designs would include experimental and quasi-experimental research that produces quantitative data, questionnaires with numerical responses, textual analysis such as content analysis that uses codings, and observation studies involving frequency counts. Critics of such an approach, usually from the social sciences and educational research communities, argue that this type of research ignores the human aspect of the participants and reduces their behaviours to meaningless numbers.

The interpretivist qualitative approach is more closely aligned to that of subjectivity, where the goal is to describe, understand and explain phenomena rather than to seek causal explanations. This type of research tends to be more small-scale and within a localised context, where the aims are authenticity and transparency in presenting the findings. Typically, research that adopts a qualitative approach will involve interviews, focus groups and analysis of documents. Analysis can range from hermeneutic phenomenology to thematic analysis. The aim is to present a rich, thick, deep understanding of the data so numbers tend to be small; depending on the research purpose, this could range from two or three to possibly 20, but more usually the numbers would be around 10–12.

In many cases, the debate between positivist and interpretivist approaches is an obsolete argument. Allwood (2012) argues the distinction is abstract and unclear, and is therefore of limited value, and possibly the most convincing evidence is to present a multi-methodological approach. Taylor and Medina (2013) discuss a range of paradigms from positivism to post-positivism, to interpretive to critical, and most recently post-modernist. They suggest there is a case for adopting a multi-paradigmatic approach in education research by combining methods drawn from some of the newer paradigms. This is a sensible and pragmatic way forward, but it is important to understand that institutions and other policy-makers may well prefer the statistical approach as it is large-scale, objective and generally seen as more trustworthy. Knowing and being able to articulate which research paradigm you are adopting is another way of making your research findings robust and rigorous.

As discussed above, you may wish to use a number of methods that would certainly add to the persuasiveness of your evidence (think in terms of the evidence that is brought before a jury), but inevitably this makes your research more time-consuming. An approach worth considering is that of the case study (Yin, 2009). The case study research method was defined by Yin (1984) in the first edition of his book "as an empirical inquiry that investigates a contemporary phenomenon within its real-life context; when the boundaries between phenomenon and context are not clearly evident; and in which multiple sources of evidence are used" (p. 23). A case study approach could be of value when evaluating the effects of transition initiatives in a given institutional context.

Consider the methods: single or multi-method?

All the following commonly used methods could be translated into collaborative research projects where students work alongside staff. The benefits of this way of working are considerable (e.g. Cook-Sather, Bovill & Felten, 2014; Healey, Flint & Harrington, 2014), and there is a tradition in action research of involving students as researchers (Dickerson, Jarvis & Stockwell, 2016).

Interviews and focus groups

Interviews with staff or students fall into the qualitative paradigm when they are unstructured or semi-structured. In the completely unstructured version, the researcher/interviewer might ask the question 'Tell me what transition means to you'. There will be no predetermined prompts, but the interviewer will ask the interviewee to expand or explain by following the direction and the content that the interviewee is revealing. A semi-structured interview would give the interviewee plenty of room to bring out issues that are particularly salient to them but within a framework of predetermined questions and prompts devised by the researcher, known as the interview schedule. In the structured interview, the format is almost like a questionnaire that is spoken. Typically, such interviews would be recorded and transcribed, and subsequently analysed. The analysis would very much depend on the purpose of the research. If, for example you wished to understand a student's perception and experience of a transition initiative, then the appropriate form of analysis might be to carry out some sort of phenomenographical analysis (Marton, 1996), but if you wanted to demonstrate some change in behaviour or improvement in experience, then a more structured thematic analysis might be more appropriate (Braun & Clarke, 2006).

Focus groups are much the same as interviews in terms of analysis, but there is the added layer of interaction between participants. There could be real value in holding focus groups that were made up of staff and students, although this would have to be carefully managed and might work better when separate focus groups are carried out first before bringing the two groups together.

Transcribing audio-recorded interviews or focus groups is time-consuming (typically six to eight hours for one hour of recording), so this method of enquiry is less suitable for really large groups of staff or students. As a general rule of thumb, the less structured the interview, the more time it takes and the less participants you need, but the usual advice is to keep carrying out interviews until you stop getting different answers, known as data saturation (Fusch & Ness, 2015).

Surveys

Another very common method to choose is that of survey research, but here there is a distinction to be made between attitude scales, which measure some concept such as confidence, and more general descriptive questionnaires, which can be a mix of closed response and open-text responses. Attitude scales fall under the positivist quantitative approach and they take some time to construct (Likert, 1967), but briefly the necessary stages are to construct a number of items (usually from the literature as well as from practical and professional experience). These are then piloted on a small sample of people (typically about 30) to test for face validity and to make sure the instructions make sense. The draft scale would then be tested for internal reliability using split-half reliability, which looks at the extent of agreement or correlation between two halves of your scale, or Cronbach's alpha, as this tells you to what extent each item contributes to the overall measure. The final scale is likely to be much smaller than the original, which is an advantage as people in general do not like answering very long instruments. Such a measure could be used to establish if there was any change before and after an initiative. For example, a measure of academic anxiety would hopefully decrease after a pre-induction initiative.

The other more frequently used survey is a questionnaire, which can be paper-based or electronic. A questionnaire can be used effectively with staff, for example, to gauge the interest in or awareness of transition issues. A questionnaire enables you to first capture individual demographics such as age, gender and university teaching experience, followed by questions such as experiences of a specific transition initiative. Closed response scales such as a Likert scale might be used (e.g. strongly agree, agree, uncertain, disagree, strongly disagree), or possibly yes/no answers. In such cases, there is a statistical element that can be reported in bar charts or percentages, such as '87 per cent of the students who took part in the pre-induction programme felt more prepared academically'. Numbers could also be used to compare with students who had not taken the pre-induction programme using statistical tests of inference. Finally, because numbers only tell us one part of the story, open-ended questions with free-writing boxes can be used, which can be analysed qualitatively. There is, however, a danger of overusing open-ended questions as they can render a questionnaire tedious and time-consuming to complete if there are too many of them.

In terms of how many participants you need in quantitative studies, there is no clear-cut answer except to say the bigger the sample, the more likely you can have confidence in your results. When evaluating a specific transitions initiative, the higher the response rate, the better. Ideally, you should aim for 100 per cent of those who participated, but acceptable rates tend to be 50 per cent or more, with 70 per cent or more being seen as very good.

Consider your research purpose: who to influence and why?

This stage is important for many reasons, but perhaps the most salient is that of sustainability. The shelf life of pedagogical projects can be limited to the period of funding. A recent prime example was that of a national programme in the UK called the Centre for Excellence in Teaching and Learning (CETL) programme, which ran from 2005 to 2010 and was funded by the HEFCE with a total of £315 million. The aim was to reward excellent teaching practice through a competitive bidding process investing in 74 centres in England, which were then expected to impact on the wider learning and teaching community in the higher education sector. This five-year programme was the HEFCE's largest ever funded programme for teaching and learning. Currently, the German Federal Ministry of Education and Research is funding a research project called CETLFUNK (2014–2018) at the Center for Higher Education Policy Studies (CHEPS) at the University of Twente. This project is aimed at understanding the effects of the CETL programme at German universities in a comparative European context.

In the UK in 2011, the HEFCE commissioned SQW, which is an independent provider of research and analysis for the UK and Europe, to carry out a summative evaluation of the CETLs. This report concluded that:

> the legacy of the programme rests largely in individual staff, and in those institutions which have embedded CETL developments and continue to support innovation and development in teaching and learning, rather than in a general enhancement of teaching and learning across the sector. Participating staff will move between HEIs, and apply their experience and expertise elsewhere, but we do not believe the CETL programme itself has led to material changes in non-participating HEIs and across the sector as a whole.
> (SQW, 2011: vi)

As SQW's conclusion indicates, the problem with the programme was that once the funding ceased, nearly all the innovative learning and teaching work that had been done disappeared. This is a nationwide example of how essential it is to build in sustainability from the beginning of the project, even if it is very large-scale. As practitioners, we need to think how the work of our project will be continued after it is formally finished. This does not necessarily mean more funding, especially if part of the aim is to engender a culture change in pedagogy; a potential approach could be one of flexible pedagogies that would require institutional and systemic approaches to learning enhancement (Ryan & Tilbury, 2013). Action research can play a significant part as one of its avowed aims is to challenge the status quo and bring about change (Carr & Kemmis, 2006; Grogan, Donaldson & Simmons, 2007; Somekh & Zeichner, 2009).

Making a change is one of the important aspects of applied research in general, and practitioner research in particular, but in order to do this, results have to be presented and opened up to peer challenge and scrutiny. There are many forms of dissemination, and they can range from the informal, such as a chat over a cup of coffee with a colleague you would like to collaborate with or a seminar presentation within the department, to the more formal and widespread dissemination of conference presentations and peer-reviewed journal papers (still the gold standard of dissemination). When making decisions about dissemination, the following questions and Figure 9.1, adapted from my book (Norton, 2009), might be useful. How and where you disseminate your research project depends very much on what your goals are in doing the project in the first place. It can help to ask yourself these four questions:

1 What are my research goals?

- Change practice?
- Contribute to new knowledge?

2 Who do I want to influence?

- Colleagues within my organisation, profession, institution (not necessarily in your subject discipline)?
- My colleagues (team)?
- Policymakers within my organisation?
- Professionals outside my organisation?

3 What level am I aiming at?

- Institutional?
- National?
- International?

4 What do I want to change?

- Subject specific practice or new knowledge?
- Generic practice or new knowledge?
- Influence policymaking?

It might be, for example, that your research findings suggest that helping students with their academic writing actually improves retention and transition between years 2 and 3 of an undergraduate programme. The first question, then, is will these findings contribute to new knowledge, such as proposing a model of transition that is aligned to students' writing strategies? Will

Goals	Focus	Dissemination methods
Changing subject specific practice	Institutional	Presentations to: Department, school or faculty Written report circulated to subject colleagues (hard or electronic copy) Institutional repository University website Collaborating with other L&T projects (if subject-appropriate)
	National and international	Presentations/reports/workshops via: Higher Education Academy (HEA) Subject professional body Subject-specific practice-based pedagogical events/conferences Subject-specific practice-based pedagogical journals
Changing generic practice informing policymaking	Institutional	Presentations/reports to the institutional senior management team or relevant academic committees Presentations/reports/workshops via: Institutional learning and teaching events
	National and international	HEA (including the HEA annual conference) Practice-based teaching and learning conferences National practice-based pedagogical journals Press articles Newsletters Chapters in edited books (may be on education rather than specifically higher education) Authored books
Contributing to subject-specific new knowledge	National and international	National/international peer-reviewed subject-specific journals Chapters in edited books Authored books
Contributing to generic new knowledge	National and international	National/international peer-reviewed generic journals Chapters in edited books Authored books

Figure 9.1 Suggested methods of disseminating pedagogical action research

Source: Adapted from an original figure first published as Figure 11.2: Suggested methods of disseminating pedagogical action research (Norton, 2009: 196), reproduced with permission from Routledge

they help you and potentially your colleagues to change your teaching and assessment practice to encourage such writing development? This leads naturally to the next question of who you want to influence – those within your subject or maybe all year 2 lecturers from different disciplines? This second alternative would probably inform policymakers within your organisation as this would be a large-scale pedagogical change. If you were working within a discipline framework, you might want to influence your professional body or, more informally, engender a pedagogical change through disseminating at subject-specific conferences, such as, in the UK, the Higher Education Academy's Science, Technology, Engineering and Mathematics (STEM) or Humanities conferences, for instance. Here again, you need to consider whether you want to inform those within your institution, which would be perfectly valid if you wanted to work alongside the institutional context, pedagogical mission, and learning and teaching strategy. If you prefer to have a bigger reach, then you might want to aim at conferences and journals that tend to be more nationally based, or if you want to have an impact at international level, two examples of relevant conferences would be those of the International Society for the Scholarship of Teaching and Learning (ISSOTL) or the European Association for Practitioner Research on Improving Learning in Education and Professional Practice (EAPRIL).

Basically, the outcomes of projects should be disseminated in as many different ways as possible. A project, no matter how good, will wither and die without making it public, but another very important part in going public is to expose research findings and conclusions to peer scrutiny and challenge. This is how pedagogical research is refined and developed.

Consider the ethical issues: principles or acting ethically?

All pedagogical research needs to pay careful attention to the issue of ethics. Most universities will require ethical approval to be gained for any pedagogical research studies, and most of these ethical processes will require some sort of reference to published principles. For pedagogical research, the British Educational Research Association's (BERA) ethical guidelines for educational research (British Educational Research Association, 2011) are appropriate. The guidelines relate to our responsibilities to participants, and comprise voluntary informed consent, openness and disclosure (avoidance of deception), right to withdraw, children, vulnerable young people and vulnerable adults, incentives, detriment arising from participation in research, and privacy and disclosure. Each one of these responsibilities can pose dilemmas.

An example is voluntary informed consent, which can be difficult to ensure if, as researchers, we are also the university teachers who teach and assess participants' work. Here, there is an imbalance of power, and students may feel that they ought to take part for fear of offending their teacher. Another example is that of privacy and disclosure. How might you protect the anonymity of participants in your institution if you were analysing senior managers' attitudes to pre-induction activities and you wanted to interview the vice chancellor, the faculty deans and heads of subject departments? It would be important for your research to identify these specific roles, but to do so would compromise participants' anonymity. Another dilemma might occur if your research revealed that your own university was covering up several bad practices and students were being treated unfairly. Mercer (2007) points out that one of the disadvantages of insider research is an ethical dilemma when you are given information that is not part of the research. What would you do, for example, if a colleague who you were interviewing about student engagement unexpectedly told you that a certain department was inflating the coursework marks given to students to improve their standing and reputation both inside and outside the university?

Ethics can get swamped in legal language and complicated procedures to follow, as the default position is for the institution to protect itself. Guidelines and codes of practice can only help, but they are not rules or regulations. They change as society changes, and they are culture-specific. Getting ethical clearance does not absolve us of our *responsibility* to act with *moral integrity* in our research projects. This is particularly the case in action research as the direction of research frequently changes while the study is still ongoing. Macfarlane (2009) says that there is an undue focus on the negative aspects of ethics, by which he means regulatory frameworks, procedures, guidelines, committees and codes of practice. These, he argues, tend to encourage an instrumental approach to satisfy a committee, which can replace a concern for the real ethical issues. He suggests that to research with integrity means we have to be ethical involving what he calls six virtues of courage, respectfulness, resoluteness, sincerity, humility and reflexivity. These are good values to follow. Finally, good ethical applications are very closely related to good research design, so this is a process that needs time and thought.

Summary and conclusion

In this section, I have offered some guidelines and steps to consider when thinking about how to evaluate your transition project. In so doing, I have suggested an action research approach, but this is just one model, and other research approaches can be equally effective, depending on who you want to inform or influence and why. If it is your intention to seek further funding for your project, for example, it might be that you decide a positivist study would be more compelling than a practitioner study. If you wanted to extend the work you have done by involving students as co-constructors of knowledge and understanding of transition issues, you might decide a collaborative research study would be more appropriate.

Overall, throughout this chapter, my stance has been that the important hallmarks of any research that is designed to achieve impact are rigour and robustness in the design, thorough and careful analysis and interpretation of the findings, together with a scholarly understanding of the relevant literature. This is equally true of pedagogical research that is practitioner-focused, but added to this approach is our need to look at the whole picture by thinking about the 'wicked problem'. We must clearly articulate our values of what we believe to be educationally desirable. In this way, our transition project, interventions and innovations stand the best chance of being both influential and sustainable.

References

Allwood, C.M. (2012) The distinction between qualitative and quantitative research methods is problematic. *Quality & Quantity*, 46, 1417–1429.

Biesta, G. (2007) Why 'What Works?' won't work: evidence-based practice and the democratic deficit in educational research. *Educational Theory*, 57(1), 1–20.

Braun, V. & Clarke, V. (2006) Using thematic analysis in psychology. *Qualitative Research in Psychology*, 3(2), 77–101. Available from: http://dx.doi.org/10.1191/1478088706qp063oa.

British Educational Research Association (2011) *Ethical guidelines for educational research*. Available from: www.bera.ac.uk/researchers-resources/publications/ethical-guidelines-for-educational-research-2011 [Accessed 28 January 2017].

Carr, W. & Kemmis, S. (2006) Staying critical. *Educational Action Research*, 13(3), 347–358.

CETLFUNK (2014-2018) *The effects of Centers for Excellence in Teaching and Learning on the teaching function of higher education institutions in Europe*. Available from: www.utwente.nl/bms/cheps/cetlfunk/ [Accessed 2 April 2017].

Cook-Sather, A., Bovill, C. & Felten, P. (2014) *Engaging students as partners in learning and teaching: a guide for faculty*. San Francisco, CA, Jossey-Bass.

Dickerson, C., Jarvis, J. & Stockwell, L. (2016) Staff–student collaboration: student learning from working together to enhance educational practice in higher education. *Teaching in Higher Education*, 21(3), 249–265.

Doolan, M.A. & Gilbert, T. (2016) Student choice: blends of technology beyond the university to support social interaction and social participation in learning. In: *E-Learning, E-Education, and Online Training: Third International Conference, eLEOT 2016*, Dublin, Ireland, 31 August–2 September 2016, Revised Selected Papers, Springer International Publishing, pp. 95–102.

Doyle, J., McDonald, L., Cuthill, M. & Keppell, M. (2015) Digital futures research and society: action, awareness and accountability. In: Australasian Society for Computers in Learning and Tertiary Education: Ascilite 2015 conference, 29 November–2 December 2015, Perth, pp. 429–433. Available from: https://eprints.usq.edu.au/28364/9/Doyle_McDonald_Cuthill_Keppell_PV.pdf [Accessed 28 January 2017].

Fusch, P.I. & Ness, L.R. (2015) Are we there yet? Data saturation in qualitative research. *The Qualitative Report*, 20(9), 1408–1416.

Gibbs, P., Cartney, P., Wilkinson, K., Parkinson, J., Cunningham, S., James-Reynolds, C., Zoubir, T., Brown, V., Barter, P., Sumner, P. & MacDonald, A. (2016) Literature review on the use of action research in higher education. *Educational Action Research*, 25(1), 3–22.

Grogan, M., Donaldson, J. & Simmons, J. (2007) *Disrupting the status quo: the action research dissertation as a transformative strategy*. Available from: http://cnx.org/content/m14529/latest/ [Accessed 28 January 2017].

Hargreaves, D.H. (1996) *Teaching as a research-based profession: possibilities and prospects.* The Teacher Training Agency Annual Lecture 1996. Available from: https://eppi.ioe.ac.uk/cms/Portals/0/PDF%20reviews%20and%20summaries/TTA%20Hargreaves%20lecture.pdf [Accessed 28 January 2017].

Healey, M., Flint, A. & Harrington, K. (2014) *Engagement through partnership: students as partners in learning and teaching in higher education.* York, Higher Education Academy.

Higher Education Funding Council for England (2016) *Learning gain: policy guide.* Available from: www.hefce.ac.uk/lt/lg/ [Accessed 28 January 2017].

Lewin, K. (1946) Action research and minority problems. *Journal of Social Issues*, 2, 34–36.

Likert, R. (1967) The method of constructing an attitude scale. In: Fishbein, M. (ed.), *Attitude theory and measurement.* London, John Wiley, pp. 90–95.

Macfarlane, B. (2009) *Researching with integrity: the ethics of academic inquiry.* New York, Routledge.

McNiff, J. (2017) *Jean McNiff.* Available from: www.jeanmcniff.com/ [Accessed 28 January 2017].

Manstead, A.S. (1996). Attitudes and behaviour. In: Semin, G.R. & Fiedler, K. (eds.), *Applied social psychology.* London, Sage, pp. 3–29.

Marton, F. (1996) Phenomenography. In: Postlethwaite, T.N. & Husen, T. (eds.), *The international encyclopedia of education.* 2nd ed. Oxford, Pergamon Press, pp. 4424–4429.

Mercer, J. (2007) The challenges of insider research in educational institutions: wielding a double-edged sword and resolving delicate dilemmas. *Oxford Review of Education*, 33(1), 1–17.

Norton, L. (2009) *Action research in teaching and learning: a practical guide to conducting pedagogical research in universities.* London, Routledge.

Norton, L. (2014) The case for pedagogical action research in psychology learning and teaching. *Psychology Teaching Review*, 20(2), 3–11.

Ramley, J.A. (2014) The changing role of higher education: learning to deal with wicked problems. *Journal of Higher Education Outreach and Engagement*, 18(3), 7–21.

Reason, P. & Bradbury, H. (2008) *The Sage handbook of action research: participative inquiry and practice.* 2nd ed. London, Sage.

Rittell, H.W.J. & Webber, M.M. (1973) Dilemmas in a general theory of planning. *Policy Sciences*, 4, 155–169.

Ryan, A. & Tilbury, D. (2013) *Flexible pedagogies: new pedagogical ideas.* Available from: www.heacademy.ac.uk/system/files/resources/npi_report.pdf [Accessed 28 January 2017].

Sclater, N., Peasgood, A. & Mullan, J. (2016) *Learning analytics in higher education: a review of UK and international practice – full report.* Available from: www.jisc.ac.uk/sites/default/files/learning-analytics-in-he-v3.pdf [Accessed 28 January 2017].

Somekh, B. & Zeichner, K. (2009) Action research for educational reform: remodelling action research theories and practices in local contexts. *Educational Action Research*, 17(1), 5–21.

SQW (2011) *Summative evaluation of the CETL programme: final report by SQW to HEFCE and DEL.* Higher Education Funding Council for England. Available from: www.hefce.ac.uk/media/hefce/content/pubs/indirreports/2011/RE,1111,Eval,of,CETL/rd11_11.pdf [Accessed 2 April 2017].

Taylor, P.C. & Medina, M.N.D. (2013) Educational research paradigms: from positivism to multiparadigmatic. *The Journal of Meaning-Centered Education*, 1. Available from: www.meaningcentered.org/educational-research-paradigms-from-positivism-to-multiparadigmatic/ [Accessed 28 January 2017].

Webb, T.L. & Sheeran, P. (2006) Does changing behavioural intentions engender behaviour change? A meta-analysis of the experimental evidence. *Psychological Bulletin*, 132, 249–268.

Weber, E.P. & Khademian, A.M. (2008) Wicked problems, knowledge challenges, and collaborative capacity builders in network settings. *Public Administration Review*, 68(2), 334–339.

Whitehead, J. (n.d.) *A living educational theory (living theory) approach to research and life.* Available from: www.actionresearch.net/ [Accessed 28 January 2017].

Yin, R.K. (1984) *Case study research: design and methods.* Beverly Hills, CA, Sage.

Yin, R.K. (2009) *Case study research: design and methods.* 4th ed. London, Sage.

Chapter 10

Student stories

Introduction to the chapter

Throughout this book, you have been offered the frameworks around transition in, through and out of university and related themes. We have gathered practical advice from practitioners across the globe to provide you with 'off-the-shelf' case studies that can be adapted to your own contexts and disciplines. This chapter presents you with the final piece of the jigsaw, bringing you student stories of the lived experience of these various transitions, providing insider insight to challenge your perceptions and shed light on what students value. We have not themed these in any way, but presented them alphabetically, as we think that they are powerful in their original form, speaking for themselves, and are a fitting conclusion to the book.

Ed Butler, UK

I entered my final year of university with some reluctance as I had enjoyed my placement year and the structure it gave me. I particularly found the pattern of Monday to Friday 9 to 5 working life useful in that I knew when I needed to be working and when I could switch off and enjoy some free time.

My final year was challenging in terms of transitioning back to university, which in my opinion was a far less structured lifestyle to the one I had experience on placement. What I have realised is the importance of structure to me in relation to my wellbeing, as it provides a scaffold for my day, allowing me to plan life accordingly. From early on in the first term, I was considering my next steps and finding it difficult to know where I wanted to be post-graduation.

My first thought was to apply for graduate jobs. This led to also thinking about further study or voluntary work. Because of the uncertainty, I decided to 'push some doors' and see what happened as a result. I found some graduate jobs that looked interesting, so I applied for those and made the assessment day for a graduate scheme, which was a good experience, but unfortunately did not progress any further. At a similar time, I was meeting with tutors from several universities to discuss Masters level study in various subjects, such as supply chain and sustainability. These one-to-one meetings were really valuable and helped me understand whether my interest was worth pursuing. Having had little success in securing a job and feeling that it probably wasn't the right time for a Masters, I felt a bit lost as to what and where my next move was going to be. These feelings were exaggerated by the fact that a lot of my course mates were securing graduate roles while I didn't know where I was going.

Not long after, a voluntary internship was being advertised at my local church to work with students, which seemed interesting. I felt it may be a good time to try something a bit different, and in doing so not feel obliged to follow the standard path of work into full-time employment. This would also provide me with a bit of breathing space to learn more about myself and my career aspirations, while doing something that was valuable and added to my CV.

The application and interview went well, and I was offered and accepted a role. Looking back, I feel this was a worthwhile decision as it gave me great opportunities to develop my skills in leadership, building relationships and public speaking, which have been transferable to my current job. I was also able to develop new skills in areas such as community work and sports coaching. I realised that full-time church work wasn't for me in the long term, but had welcomed the opportunity to have this experience and time to regroup, which helped me figure out my next steps.

I am now working for the NHS in an area more related to my degree, which I am enjoying. I hope to stay with the NHS for the foreseeable future and progress to management level in the coming years.

Lynda Camilleri, UK

I finished school in 1992 after attaining A level grades U and E – an exact reflection of the work I put in! I was a bright child but was not engaged in education at all at that time, with my priority being my social life, and more importantly at that time my boyfriend. I had moved in with him – out of my family home – at age 17, and took a variety of part-time jobs to pay my way while finishing school (badly!). My first child arrived a year or so later, followed by three more over the subsequent years (and a wedding in among them!). I loved being a stay-at-home mum, and feel so privileged to have been able to do so. However, with all my friends graduating from their university courses and moving on with their careers, my self-confidence was low, and there was always a niggling desire to achieve more academically.

I enrolled at my local college to embark on psychology and law A levels during this time, but struggled with the busyness of four small children and the mental capacity to hold concentration on barely any sleep. Needless to say, I did not complete the course again, and instead when all the children were in school I worked, filling any spare time with chauffeuring the children around, cooking, homemaking, and all the other mind-numbing chores that come alongside family life!

As the time approached for my youngest to start high school, I began to look more seriously at further education, BSc Psychology in particular, and I went along to an open day at my local uni. I was incredibly nervous. I felt old (39 at the time), I felt frumpy, I felt insecure in any abilities I may have, and wondered if I was again setting myself up for failure. Would I have the time to be able to commit to study? Was I clever enough? Would I be rejected because of my previous grades? Could I afford to leave work and survive on student finance? Would I fail? Would I be the oldest person there (sounds silly but was actually one of my biggest concerns)? The university offered a foundation phase to the degree, which promised to ease me in gently, and so I applied. Following an interview (and maths test!), I was accepted, and began the life change from working mum to mature student. It was terrifying, and when I told friends what I was doing I sensed they thought I was mad, although their words of encouragement I am sure were genuine.

There were some all-nighter sessions as I fought to meet deadlines, as there always seemed to be so many obstacles leaking into my time: sick children home from school; multiple appointments for dentists, doctors and school activities; wider family responsibilities some distances away; and the usual chores. Despite this, I shocked myself by achieving a distinction on the foundation degree, and going on to achieve a 1:1 in BSc Psychology – I now have letters after my name! I am now embarking on an MSc in Forensic Psychology with the intention of becoming a professional in the field.

It has been (and is!) a thoroughly difficult yet exhilarating journey, which, although may have been easier in my early twenties, really is happening at the best time for me. I feel a strong sense of achievement and self-pride, and cannot wait for what lies around the corner. Now I just have to figure out how to pay off the £30,000+ student debt . . .

Elyce du Mez, New Zealand

The decision to study towards an undergraduate degree at university was an obvious and possibly expected choice for me. I excelled in biology, chemistry, mathematics and English, and in 2007 won the prize for the top student in my high school. A science forum for high school students piqued an interest in microbiology, and alongside a lifelong love of the natural world I set off to study health sciences at a well-known New Zealand university. Little consideration was given to other vocational possibilities at this stage in my life. Also, minimal guidance was provided to help me understand the potential of my intended career path or other suitable possibilities.

University life and studying towards an undergraduate degree was a highly enjoyable time in my life; however, it took me at least two years of study to begin to achieve grades similar to those I had achieved in high school. However, in third year, I was offered a position in an honours degree course in my chosen major of microbiology/immunology. This additional year was very challenging for me, particularly the internal examination component, which was predominantly oral exams and presentations, not well-suited to my moderately introverted personality. My honours dissertation was completed in a human immunology research group under the supervision of a strong advocate of women in science, who at regular intervals along my fourth year of study encouraged me to recognise that the extroverted classmates I was intimidated by were achieving similar grades to me overall.

Despite obtaining a first-class honours degree, and receiving support from my supervisor to pursue postgraduate study, I was originally underwhelmed by this idea. I obtained a job with an analytical testing laboratory as a laboratory technician. I found the skills I had obtained during my degree were useful and enabled me to move to a second-level technician quickly. However, the laboratory tasks were unstimulating, and the most challenging aspect of the job was dealing with unhelpful members of the administrative team. After a year working there, I made the decision to further my academic career by studying towards a PhD in cell biology. This decision was driven by my honours supervisor's persistent support and a desire to keep learning.

I quickly began a PhD project designed by my current supervisor and funded by a charitable trust. Now that I am in the write-up stage after three years of experimental research, I can reflect back on the challenges of my PhD. A major hurdle has been learning how to design and conduct research independently and how to monitor success as grades are not handed out along the way like in undergraduate study. Throughout my project, I have had a few small successes but many setbacks, and keeping optimistic about the purpose and relevance of my work has been challenging. Being the only PhD candidate of my laboratory group means I have had no benchmark or exemplar to emulate or compare data with. I have also struggled to ask others for help in my wider research field as I have often felt they have no vested interest in my research project. This has been a major hurdle in my PhD, as up until now I have been able to succeed academically without requiring help from anyone else. I have also observed the difficulties of my friends studying towards PhDs. Collectively, it seems all of us frequently doubt our intelligence, worry about the opinion our supervisors have of us, and are concerned about the contribution we are making to our research field. More than one of my friends has suffered from disruptions in mental health during the course of their PhD, due in part to these issues.

However, I am glad I chose to study towards a PhD as it has fulfilled my initial desire to continue learning, and I am now friends with a group of highly motivated and inspiring people. I have also discovered many strengths of my character of which I was previously unaware, including a willingness to persevere and a high tolerance for stress. I also feel that despite the setbacks of my experimental research, I now possess the skill set to conduct research independently and efficiently, which I believe should be the aim of postgraduate study.

Sian Ford, UK

My decision to come to university was, like many other 18-year-olds, a spontaneous and unprepared one. Despite always knowing I wanted to go to university, what I wanted to study was ever-changing and unrefined. I felt as though my teachers and personal tutor (who I met several times) were encouraging me to only be involved in one subject; I challenged this as I was interested in many subjects, including music, art, maths and literature. I remember feeling pressured to choose a subject and choose it fast, thus my choice to study accounting and finance in 2015. I was playing to my strengths; I excelled in mathematics at A level, and subsequently thought this was the course for me.

I started the course with reluctance as my decision to do it was made so quickly. I did not know what to expect from the course or from university in general, and had no real plans post-graduation. During the course, I most enjoyed quantitative methods, in which I achieved 100 per cent in several papers. The core modules (management accounting and financial accounting) I found laborious and dull, and I received the lowest grades for those two modules over all others. I found the lecturers uninspiring and I was unmotivated by the classes. I knew I did not love the course from the beginning, but just continued with it due to the knowledge of the price I was paying for university and pressures from lecturers and peers to continue.

Nevertheless, during the course, one of the modules that sparked an interest in me was a law module. I looked forward to each lecture and seminar, and began studying law in my spare time. I would read up on environmental law cases and watched lectures on YouTube. To me, this was just a fascinating pastime additional to my studies, and I put any contemplation into switching course on hold until I received my summer results.

It was only when I had a conversation with my brother during the summer of 2016 that I was encouraged to switch course. He reminded me of the importance of studying something in which you not only excel in, but also have a passion. My brother went through a similar experience at university, switching from journalism to linguistics. He supported and assisted me in a transition that was quite stressful, with lecturers trying to persuade me to continue and becoming irritated when I persisted with the idea that I wanted to switch. When I had completed the process of changing courses, I felt as though I had lifted a huge burden from myself that I had not realised I carried.

I am now in my second year of law, stimulated by the course, and am enthusiastic about my prospects for the future. I was also awarded a scholarship in classical music at the beginning of 2017 from the university (after I joined two choirs recreationally) – singing and studying music is my coping mechanism.

The whole experience has made me realise that studying something that you love is extremely important. I was disinclined to change course at first because of the anxieties that I knew would come with it. Looking back, changing courses was one of the best things I have done, as law has introduced me to so many different areas of academia, which suits me as a person perfectly. I am constantly learning and have plans for when I leave university. This experience has also allowed me to grow as a person; I have learnt how to deal with different emotions, stubborn people and stressful situations, using my love of music to help me develop. These lessons will be transferable for many parts of life that I will encounter, work or otherwise. I endeavour to continue learning and changing; I am certainly not the same person I was when I was 18.

Nicola Harrison, Barbados

Being immersed in an environment with students of several different nationalities and cultural backgrounds, none of which were similar to my own, I felt myself fading into the background, and the excitement and anticipation of coming to the UK to study quickly faded. In the initial stages, integration was minimal as people clung to their own ethnic and cultural groups, and because of the colour of my skin I was automatically adopted by the African students. It was almost as if I had lost my cultural identity. Culture shock!

Initially, coping with this reality was challenging, but with the support in my host university I was able to overcome this. The university helped by providing useful information and suggestions to help with settling into UK university life comfortably. It also coordinated several events, activities and familiarisation trips that created the type of multicultural interaction necessary to encourage integration. Within a few weeks, I had made some really great friends, taken up a job within student services, joined the volunteering committee, and could barely keep up with my new overactive social life.

My course was very diverse, with students from the Middle East, Africa, Asia and Europe. I had no real expectations of what it would be like studying in a British university; I was just excited about the experience and the opportunity. Within a few weeks, my enthusiasm turned into frustration for a number of reasons. First, it was a Masters course that attracted students from a range of undergraduate degrees, and I was the only person on the course with a background in the discipline, so a lot of the content I had already covered at undergrad level. The teaching style was also completely opposite to the intense and rigorous approach to which I was accustomed, and the information was not stimulating enough to arouse my attention; as a result, I became a bit bored in some classes. Further to that, working on assignments in groups with people whose first language was not English was not an easy feat.

It took being elected as course representative for me to cope with this new learning environment. Representing my classmates gave me an understanding of the challenges they too were facing in the classroom through transitioning to a British university. Looking back, in my view, tutors could have capitalised on the diversity of the class. There could have been more focus on student-centred seminars, which would have fostered an environment for an exchange of perspectives on different topics across cultures and created discussion where the class could all learn from each other.

Overall, transitioning to a British university was a very eye-opening experience of great value to my personal development especially. I was able to develop a mindset to allow me a level of awareness and understanding of other cultures, how similarities and differences could impact on my personal transition experience academically and socially, and how to adapt to these situations.

Esther Osarfo-Mensah, UK/France

For years, I had dreamt of taking part in an Erasmus programme. In secondary school, our language classrooms were plastered in posters, begging students to consider the usefulness of learning a second language. During particularly dry lessons, I would stare at one poster over and over again. If you learnt another language, you could get the chance to spend a year abroad. While I loved my home, my family and my friends, I longed to escape and explore an entirely new way of life. Perhaps this was my way out.

Finally, at the age of 20, here I was in France, alone, ready to begin my study year abroad and the next chapter of my life! The first thing I realised was that August in this part of France was nothing like August in London. The air was humid, and the sun beat down relentlessly as I excitedly dragged my increasingly heavy luggage to the airport's taxi rank. My excitement, however, was short-lived once I arrived at the crumbling, dilapidated building where I would be expected to spend the next 10 months of my life.

Inside didn't get any better. Walking along the corridor to my room reminded me of a disused asylum in a horror film, where every now and again I'd hear disembodied voices drifting from behind the closed doors. The room itself was in a very sorry state. What had I done? Why did I come here? I tried to gather myself and searched my bag for the card my mum had given to me at the airport before kissing me goodbye. Opening the London-themed card, I read and re-read her loving words, describing how proud she was of me for making my dream come true. I had to make this work. After camping out in the reception over several afternoons and raining complaints on all who would listen, I was finally upgraded to the flats next door and escaped the cockroaches that had commandeered my floor.

While moving helped to improve things, going to my first lectures in French was a very bewildering experience in itself. Years of learning how to discuss French politics in school definitely did not prepare me for the perpetual confusion and frustration I was about to endure. Luckily, it transpired that I had already studied most of the topics in the UK, and so my main mission was to translate everything I heard. It was also at this point I realised that if I was to survive, I needed to find the nerdiest students and befriend them. Looking around my lectures in the next week, I noticed that the students at this university were very different from those back home. Everyone looked so classy – some actually wore full make-up to lectures! This was a world away from the 'just rolled out of bed' look I was used to encountering. It wasn't easy to make friends with them. I later realised that many of them didn't initially want to interact with me because they were worried that they would have to speak English. After many assurances that I was far more interested in French conversation, making friends suddenly became a lot easier!

And so for the first couple of weeks, it felt like I was walking in a perpetual fog. Going into labs, lectures and even grocery stores meant playing a constant game of 'What is going on now?'. As the months passed, I found that patience, study and realising that no one cared that my French wasn't perfect was the key to clearing the mist. I went to book stalls at markets and bought my favourite novels in French. We'd go to the cinema and watch Hollywood blockbusters in French. I'd wake up to French radio and sing along to French songs. I even began to dream in French. By the time our assessments rolled around, I felt more confident than ever before.

As my year abroad came to a close, I'd proudly think about how far I'd come. In those rare times I spoke in English, people would stare at me in amazement. They always assumed that I had been raised a staunch Frenchwoman!

Lina Téllez, Colombia

I did my undergraduate study in the UK. As a Colombian citizen, I would say it is a significant challenge to study abroad, not only economically, but also academically. When attending several university fairs to study abroad, tuition fees and academic requirements were always two aspects that I really needed to take into consideration to make my dream of studying abroad come true.

The first challenge is that the economy of Colombia is not at its best point and it has not been as developed as other countries; therefore, not many locals have the possibility of going abroad for their studies. For instance, the minimum wage in Colombia (currently 820.857 COP, or 207 GDP, per month) is just enough to cover rent, food, health and transport; thus, the additional costs of tuition fees, accommodation and living costs studying abroad is not really an option to think about for most.

On the other hand, when applying to universities in the UK through UCAS, I realised that I needed an academic qualification equivalent to the required UCAS entry points, and a good level of English obviously. In my case, I had the benefit of studying in one of the best schools in both the capital city, Bogotá, and the country itself, which stands out due to the possibility of graduating with both a national high school diploma (which is a requirement in Colombia) and the International Baccalaureate diploma. I simply believe that without my International Baccalaureate, I would not have achieved the UCAS points required, and would not have done my degree abroad, and maybe I would have had to either: (1) study a completely different undergraduate course and later apply for a postgraduate course instead; or (2) start a course in a university in Colombia to have the equivalent points required and study abroad as an exchange after a couple of years.

As a humble conclusion, I am completely grateful for having the benefit of studying in a school that gave me all the necessary knowledge and tools to study abroad in a country where the academic culture is very similar to the one taught throughout the International Baccalaureate programme, and where my level of English was good enough to do a course that I truly wanted to study, and which allowed me to communicate with both locals and other foreign individuals. Otherwise, I would not have had the additional opportunities offered by studying abroad because the academic culture in Colombia (not considering schools with an IB programme) is completely different to the one in the UK.

My only possible advice for future students is to consider all aspects when going abroad to study in a university, and to lecturers, that not all students have the same academic background and knowledge of local students, and that sometimes even the most basic and obvious things can be a massive new topic for us. My experience studying in the UK was the best decision I have taken in my entire life.

Alex Thomas, UK

The tentative process of securing an industrial placement begins midway through the first year of university. It is sold to you as 'the key to open the door to the wider world of employment'. This key allows you to apply the theoretical knowledge gained over the first two years to practical scenarios, thus widening your knowledge of your subject area. The key also promotes self-development in a professional environment.

The process formally began in October of my second year. We had to complete a module all about career skills, including how to create the 'perfect' CV, interview skills, 'peeling the onion' on potential jobs, how to improve or create a LinkedIn profile, and how to ascertain the qualities desired for the job you wish to apply for. This module was a quick-fire-type module to get you up to speed on how to apply for industrial placements and secure them. Once this module was completed, our course-specific careers tutor began to drip-feed potential industrial placements to us.

The first industrial placement advert came out in mid-November; I applied for this and made it through to the interview stage. This moment in time was a rather stressful one due to pressures to do well at interview, the need to complete ongoing modules and revise for January exams (which, as it happened, were conducted the week before my interview), meaning little preparation time for the interview, and finally something I like to call life pressure. Life pressure is the pressure unwittingly applied to you by people who surround you: parents, partners and friends. I found it particularly hard to juggle everything at times, and especially with a difficult group piece of coursework to submit, it nearly became overwhelming. However, my saving grace was that I was successful in my first placement interview. This was a massive weight off my shoulders in a physical and mental sense.

From a student's perspective, securing an industrial placement is a big deal; being allowed to work in a professional environment and develop professionalism midway through your university studies can only help you grow you as a person. However, this process can be make or break. Thoughts of 'What if I mess up the job or I don't like my colleagues?' certainly crossed my mind the closer I got to my starting date. I met up with my employer before the start date, and this really helped put my mind at ease and helped my integration. I would really advise others to do this.

The university focus appears to have been on securing the placement, and once secured support is less evident. The involvement I have had from the university is a visit from a tutor to ensure that I am doing some work. I have five pieces of coursework that must be completed during the placement year; this is challenging when trying to settle into a new environment, getting into the cycle of a working lifestyle, looking presentable, and producing high-quality pieces of work. More support to enable this transition and meet the demands would be useful in reducing the associated stress of industrial placement.

Universities need to ask students about their overall experience to understand what students find stressful and how they could target support. Having to complete coursework while on placement is stressful when trying to get to grips with a working week and develop as a professional. Maybe these competing demands need to be given more consideration by the university. The ability to negotiate the timing of submissions, together with additional support, might help ease the pressure. However, despite all these pressures, I am seizing the opportunity to learn first-hand and enjoying learning new skills.

Contributor biographies

Stuart Abbott

Stuart Abbott has worked as part of the Learning and Teaching Development Unit at Cardiff Metropolitan University since 2014, having previously worked in a variety of learning and teaching roles in central units at higher education institutions in South Wales. Stuart has contributed to a number of innovative projects addressing curriculum development, graduate outcomes and learner identity development. During his career, he has also researched, taught and published in the field of religious studies.

David Aldous

David Aldous, PhD, is a Senior Lecturer in Pedagogy in the Cardiff School of Sport and Health Sciences. His research interests have focused on understanding the ways people experience and provide meaning to their transitions within and across a range of education, sport and physical cultures. David continues to publish around the interrelated themes of policy and curricula change, pedagogy and transitional experience.

Grace Kafui Annan

Grace is the Head of the Health Promotion Department of the Ghana Health Service and the Local Coordinator in Ghana of the MSc Public Health Promotion programme in Ghana run by the Health Promotion Department of Leeds Beckett University. Grace trained as a public health nurse and has over 30 years' experience in health promotion practice and policymaking. She holds an MSc in Health Education and Health Promotion obtained from Leeds Beckett University (formerly Leeds Metropolitan University).

Tanefa Apekey

Dr Tanefa Apekey is a Senior Lecturer in Nutrition. She is also a Registered Nutritionist (Public Health). Her research interest is in public health nutrition, with particular focus on migrant health.

Sally Ashton-Hay

Dr Sally Ashton-Hay is Manager Academic Skills in the Centre for Teaching and Learning at Southern Cross University in Australia. Her teaching experience includes academic literacy, English as an additional and foreign language, internationalisation of the curriculum, English literature, drama and poetry, as well as conducting English language teacher training internationally. Sally was a Senior English Language Fellow sponsored by the US Department of State and reviews for several journals. She has published on peer collaboration, student voice and inclusive education.

Sarah Ayiku

Sarah Ayiku was Course Representative for the first cohort on the MSc Public Health Promotion delivered by Leeds Beckett University in collaboration with the University of Health and Allied Sciences, Ho, Volta Region. Sarah co-facilitated the peer support project. Sarah graduated with an MSc Public Health Promotion in July 2017, having secured a Commonwealth Scholarship to undertake the programme. Sarah's current research interests are community empowerment, social development and creating positive health literacy among rural communities in Ghana.

Jake Bailey

Jake Bailey is a Principal Lecturer in Sports Coaching in the Cardiff School of Sport and Health Sciences at Cardiff Metropolitan University. He is a Senior Fellow of the Higher Education Academy, and is interested in participatory and collaborative learning approaches. Jake has used problem-based learning, action research and participant observation as pedagogical tools to create modules that help sports coaching students make meaningful links between theory and practice.

Ana Baptista

Ana is a Learning and Teaching Advisor working in Learning Development but in close collaboration with the Engagement, Retention and Success team at Queen Mary University of London. She has been participating in research projects on academic success and higher education pedagogies, delivering CPD training for higher education academics, and also developing one-to-one collaborations with higher education academics from several disciplines and levels of experience. Ana's research interests are clearly related to teaching, learning and assessment. She has co-edited books and is (co-)author of dozens of articles and book chapters.

Gareth Barham

Gareth Barham is a Principal Lecturer in the Cardiff School of Art and Design at Cardiff Metropolitan University, where he is Programme Director for the

International Design Programme and Academic Lead for recruitment and partnerships. A Senior Fellow of the Higher Education Academy, his research interests focus on internationalising the curriculum. As a practising product designer, he has award-winning products to his name and successful grant-funded partnerships with the design and manufacturing industry.

David Brown

David is a Reader in the Sociology of Sport and Physical Culture at Cardiff Metropolitan University. His research interests concern the development of interpretive sociological understandings of the body–self–society relationship in the fields of sport and physical culture. Currently, his principal research foci are on Eastern movement forms as body–self transforming practice and the changing relationships between physical cultures and sustainability. Previous research has included enquiry into a range of sporting and physical cultures, including male bodybuilding identity and body projects, the corporeal (and gendered) socialisation in surfing culture and higher education sports cultures, and physical education teacher education.

Sally Brown

Sally is an Independent Consultant and Emerita Professor at Leeds Beckett University (where she was formerly PVC, Academic), and a Visiting Professor at Plymouth, South Wales and Liverpool John Moores Universities. She is a UK National Teaching Fellow, Principal Fellow of the Higher Education Academy and a Senior Fellow of the Staff and Educational Development Association. She undertakes consultancy and publishes extensively on teaching, learning and particularly assessment.

John Butcher

John is Associate Director (Curriculum & Access) in Learning and Teaching at the Open University. He is responsible for the university's Access programme and leads the Access Observatory, which coordinates research on widening access and success. He has previously led learning and teaching centres at the Universities of Derby, Northampton and Falmouth. His research publications focus on barriers faced by part-time learners, inclusive assessment, adult access to higher education, academic development, and mentoring in teacher education. John published *Developing Effective 16–19 Teaching Skills* and co-edited *Leading Professional Development in Education* for RoutledgeFalmer. He is an experienced doctoral supervisor and a review coordinator for QAA.

Robyn Cetinich

Robyn Cetinich is an International Student Adviser at Southern Cross University in Australia. She has a Master of Applied Linguistics (TESOL), and her teaching experience includes English for academic purposes and English as an additional and foreign language. She was the principal contributor of an Australian Education International funded project, supported by Universities Australia, which was aimed at enhancing the international student experience.

Samantha Child

Samantha is a Research and Evaluation Officer in widening access to higher education at Bath Spa University. She previously completed an ESRC-funded MPhil and PhD (2015) in Educational Research, specialising in learners who face barriers to education. Her research interests focus on the entire student lifecycle, from widening access to university for under-represented groups to what universities can do to support student retention and graduate progression. Samantha is now at Plymouth University.

Valerie Clifford

Associate Professor Valerie Clifford has worked in academic development in New Zealand, Fiji, the UK, South Africa, Malaysia and Australia. Her posts have included Head of the Academic Development Unit at Monash University, Director of the Centre for the Enhancement of Learning and Teaching at the University of the South Pacific in Fiji, and Deputy Head of the Oxford Centre for Staff and Learning Development. Over the last decade, her teaching, research and publications have focused on internationalisation of the curriculum.

Debby Cotton

Debby is Head of Educational Development in the Pedagogic Research Institute and Observatory (PedRIO), Plymouth University. She is a Principal Fellow of the Higher Education Academy and a National Teaching Fellow. Debby has a doctorate in Education from Oxford University and has published widely on a range of higher education topics. She is a popular invited speaker, and has delivered invited workshops and keynotes in the UK, China, the US and South Africa.

Josie Crawley

Josie is a Senior Lecturer in Nursing at Otago Polytechnic. She is a registered nurse and her Masters in Education is endorsed in counselling. She has particular interests in communication, narrative pedagogy and health promotion. Her current research activities include storytelling in nurse education and sustainable nursing practice.

Ruth Cross

Dr Ruth Cross is Course Director for Health Promotion in the School of Health and Community Studies at Leeds Beckett University and Course Leader for the

MSc Public Health Promotion delivered in Ghana and Zambia. Ruth's current pedagogical research interests are around student engagement at a distance and the value of rural fieldwork in Sub-Saharan Africa for personal and professional development. Ruth has published widely on issues in health promotion, including co-authoring two key postgraduate texts on health promotion and health communication.

Bill Davies

Bill is Principal Lecturer in the School of Sport, Cardiff Metropolitan University, and a Senior Fellow of the HEA. He was awarded a University Teaching Fellowship to investigate the potential of reflective journals for postgraduate research students and has continued to collaborate with other institutions in developing 'soft skills' training for research students. His present teaching and research interests include the use of the outdoors to facilitate team-building and self-assessment, and the use of visual ethnography to explore the student experience and guide programme development.

Sam Davis

Sam is Course Leader and Senior Lecturer in Public Health and Health Promotion at Leeds Beckett University. She was made a Fellow of the Higher Education Academy in 2015. Her research interests centre on inequalities, transformational education and empowerment. She is the co-author of *Health Communication: Theoretical and Critical Perspectives*, published by Polity Press, 2017.

Henry Dawson

Henry is a Lecturer in Housing, Health and Safety and Public Health from the School of Health Sciences at Cardiff Metropolitan University. He is a Fellow of the Higher Education Academy and recently received his institution's Student-Led Teaching Fellowship Award. In addition to teaching, his area of research interest is in the governance of the private rental housing sector. He is currently engaged in developing distance learning programmes for delivery in the UK and abroad.

Chris Dennis

Chris Dennis is an Academic Skills Specialist at Cardiff Metropolitan University. Prior to taking on this role, he worked as a tutor in the history department at Cardiff University, where he gained a PhD in 2012. He is currently editing an essay collection looking at the application of 'flexible pedagogies' in higher education and is working on several history-related publications. He is an Honorary Research Fellow at Cardiff University.

Liz Ditzel

Liz is a Principal Lecturer in Nursing at Otago Polytechnic. She received a National Tertiary Teaching Excellence Award in 2017 and is a member of the Ako Aotearoa Teaching Academy. Previous research has investigated mentoring experiences and the relationship between nurses' job stress, psychological sense of community and burnout. Current research interests focus on immersive learning through simulation and creative teaching in nurse education.

Stuart English

A specialist in design innovation, Dr Stuart English is Director of Technology Enhanced and Online Learning at Northumbria University. His work on relational problem framing has initiated new methods, new products and new IP through an inclusive approach based on design-led enterprise. The concept of multiple perspective problem framing developed by English as part of a PhD by publication provides the foundation for the development of ongoing academic collaboration, new postgraduate curricula, intellectual property and commercial value for business both through contract research and CPD.

Jerry Fiave

Jerry Fiave was Course Representative for the first cohort on the MSc Public Health Promotion delivered in Ghana by Leeds Beckett University in collaboration with the University of Health and Allied Sciences, Ho, Volta Region. Jerry co-facilitated the peer support project. Jerry graduated with the MSc Public Health Promotion in July 2017 and was winner of the Dean's Award for academic excellence, achieving a distinction in his dissertation. Jerry's interests are in school health and activities geared towards improving child health and survival.

Karen Foley

Karen Foley is a Lecturer in Learning and Teaching Innovation at the Open University. As part of her work engaging students in a distance learning environment, Karen works closely with the faculties, for example with Arts and Social Sciences on the PodMag. She created the concept of the Student Hub Live (studenthublive.open.ac.uk), an online interactive platform that is used to facilitate academic community in a distance learning environment, which was shortlisted in for the 2016 Times Higher Education award for outstanding support for students.

Monika Foster

Professor Monika Foster is Head of School of Business, Enterprise and Management at Queen Margaret University. She was awarded Principal Fellow of the Higher

Education Academy in 2014. Her research interests focus on international student transitions, student study destination choices, cross-cultural challenges for students in transition and internationalisation of higher education. Monika has co-edited a special issue of *Journal of Perspectives in Applied Academic Practice* on internationalisation of the curriculum, as well as co-edited a book on *Innovations in Learning and Teaching*.

Jarka Glassey

Jarka is a Professor of Chemical Engineering Education at Newcastle University (UK). She was awarded a National Teaching Fellowship in 2013 and became Principal Fellow of HEA in 2014. She is the Editor in Chief of the *Education for Chemical Engineers* journal and the Chair of the Education special interest group of IChemE. Her research interests focus around active learning, assessment and feedback, and professional competency development. Jarka has published widely on these topics in pedagogical literature.

Rui Gonçalves

Rui is an Associate Professor at Coimbra Nursing School, and Researcher in the Health Sciences Research Unit: Nursing (UICISA:E) hosted in Coimbra Nursing School, Portugal. He has received awards in national and international research conferences. Currently, Rui is the President of the Nursing Council for the Central Region of Portugal. Among other topics, his research interests focus around innovative teaching, learning and assessment practices. Rui has co-authored and contributed to several research papers and book chapters.

Tim Harrison

Tim Harrison, a former teacher, is a Reader in Chemistry, the Director of Outreach and School Teacher Fellow at Bristol ChemLabS in the School of Chemistry, University of Bristol. Tim was awarded the Secondary Education Award by the RSC in 2005 and the Hauksbee Award from the Royal Society in 2010. Tim has a passion for the promotion of chemistry, and has authored dozens of articles aimed at secondary students and teachers, and performs hundreds of lectures and demonstrations per year for schools.

Hazel Horobin

Hazel Horobin is a Senior Lecturer in Physiotherapy at the University of Brighton. She won a University Inspirational Teacher Award in 2012 and was awarded a UK-India Education and Research Initiative grant the same year. This enhanced her doctoral study, which explored transnational education.

Her research interests now focus on the challenges of engaging with diversity in teaching and learning. Hazel has contributed to a book addressing critical perspectives relating to internationalising the curriculum.

Victoria Hurth

Victoria is an Associate Lecturer in Marketing and Sustainability at Plymouth University. She is Faculty Lead for Student Satisfaction in the Faculty of Business and a Fellow of the HEA. Her research focuses on business purpose, and how business can help lead a shift to a sustainable society. She designed and has been the module leader of an immersive module for first-year marketers for three years. This module integrated the innovation detailed in Case Study 2.

Louise H. Jackson

Louise Jackson is Head of Learning Enhancement at Trinity Laban Conservatoire of Music and Dance. She was awarded a National Teaching Fellowship in 2013. Her research is focused on inclusive pedagogical practices and widening participation in the arts in higher education, and the neo-liberalisation of social justice and its impact on higher education.

Alison James

Alison is Director of Academic Quality and Development and Head of Learning and Teaching at the University of Winchester. This dual role looks at supporting courses with best practice in learning and teaching, overseeing a central team concerned with academic professional development, TeL and student engagement and the quality assurance and enhancement processes of the university. A National Teaching Fellow and Principal Fellow of the Higher Education Academy, her principal interests are in identity and self-construction in learning, alternative, creative and playful pedagogies, and the place of play in higher education. She is the author, with Professor Stephen Brookfield, of *Engaging Imagination: Helping Students Become Creative and Reflective Thinkers*.

Wendy Johnston

Wendy Johnston is the Programme Leader for Food Development and Nutrition at Liverpool John Moores University. Wendy was awarded a National Teaching Fellowship in 2015 for her work supporting the student experience, with a particular emphasis on collaboration, and is a Senior Fellow of the Higher Education Academy. Her research interests focus on collaborative partnerships, students as partners, problem-based learning, active learning techniques, communities of learning, creativity and pedagogy.

Stella Jones-Devitt

Stella Jones-Devitt is Head of Student Research and Evaluation at Sheffield Hallam University. She is a National Teaching Fellow and Principal Fellow of the Higher Education Academy. In 2017, Stella was appointed as one of two national Ambassadors for Teaching Excellence in Higher Education. She is presently convenor of the sector's Flexible Learning Community of Practice, working in partnership with the HEA. Her wider academic interests include exploring new approaches to impact evaluation methodologies, flexible pedagogies and applied critical thinking.

Martin Khechara

Martin is a Senior Lecturer in Biomedical Science specialising in medical microbiology. His main research interests are in the use of technology in the classroom and the pedagogy of public engagement. He has been using video for learning since 2009, and actively researches the use of novel video capture technology and the flipped classroom for teaching, and increasing student and public engagement in the healthcare sciences and science technology and maths subjects (STEM) areas as a whole.

Pauline Kneale

Pauline Kneale is Pro Vice-Chancellor Teaching and Learning at Plymouth University, Director of the Pedagogic Research Institute and Observatory, and a National Teaching Fellow. Research interests include inclusive teaching, learning and assessment approaches, and matters relating to the student experience at Masters level.

Alf Lizzio

Professor Alf Lizzio is the Dean (Learning Futures) and Director of the Centre for Learning Futures at Griffith University. He has published widely on topics related to higher education and has led a number of whole-of-institution processes in areas such as student success, professional learning and programme renewal. His expertise as a university educator has been acknowledged through national citations and awards for university teaching and programme development.

Catarina Lobão

Catarina is an Associate Professor at Leiria School of Health Sciences, Researcher in the Health Research Unit (UIS) hosted at Leiria School of Health Sciences, and also in the Health Sciences Research Unit: Nursing (UICISA:E) hosted in Coimbra Nursing School, Portugal. Catarina is the President of the College of Medical Surgical Nurses of the Portuguese Nursing Council. Her research interests focus around innovative teaching and learning approaches in nursing teaching. Catarina has co-authored and contributed to several research papers and book chapters.

Diane Lowcock

Dr Diane Lowcock is a Senior Lecturer in Health Promotion in the School of Health and Community Studies at Leeds Beckett. She teaches using blended and online modes of study. On the MSc programme in Public Health and Health Promotion, Diane leads teaching within epidemiology, evidence-based practice and research methods with the context of public health. Pedagogically, she is interested in application of threshold concepts to design curricula and enhancing the processes of learning and teaching.

Ruth Matheson

Ruth is the Head of Learning, Teaching and Student Experience in the Faculty of Life Sciences and Education at the University of South Wales. She was awarded a National Teaching Fellowship in 2012 and a University of Wales Teaching Fellowship in 2010. Her research interests focus around student as partners, belonging, problem-based learning, creativity and pedagogy. Ruth has co-edited and contributed to a book on *Problem-Based Learning in Health and Social Care*.

Mikel Mellick

Mikel Mellick is a Senior Lecturer in Athlete Mental Health and Lead on Sport Student Mental Health at Cardiff Metropolitan University. He was awarded a University Student-Led Teaching Fellowship in 2015. His practitioner work and research interests focus around mental health and wellbeing vulnerability in high-performance environments. Mikel is also a Registered Practitioner Psychologist with the HCPC, a Chartered Sport Psychologist and an Associate Fellow of the British Psychological Society.

Richard Morris

Richard is a Principal Lecturer in Product Design and the Associate Dean Enterprise in the School of Art and Design. He has 24 years' experience working in academia and the design industry, and is a Fellow of the Higher Education Academy. Richard trained as a furniture designer, and has experience in batch, mass and one-off manufacturing processes, and is most recently investigating the opportunities offered by digital fabrication techniques. Richard is currently Programme Director for the MSc Advanced Product Design programme, which focuses on user-centred design, research methods, product innovation, and design for manufacture.

David Morrison

David is a Researcher in Educational Development at Plymouth University's Pedagogic Research Institute and Observatory. He has worked on several large-scale projects addressing institution-wide curriculum change for interdisciplinarity, internationalisation, assessment and feedback, and retention and the student experience. His research focus is on new models of interdisciplinary collaboration across subjects, focusing on assessment and graduate attributes.

Loretta Newman-Ford

Loretta Newman-Ford is an Academic Development Specialist in the Learning and Teaching Development Unit at Cardiff Metropolitan University, and is a Senior Fellow of the Higher Education Academy. Her research interests include factors that influence student retention and success, enhancing student engagement, improving student engagement with feedback, and developing practice in the design and delivery of work-based learning.

Lin Norton

Lin Norton is Professor Emerita of Pedagogical Research at Liverpool Hope University, and a National Teaching Fellow. She is on the editorial board of *Innovations in Education and Teaching International*. A psychologist by background, she has had throughout her career a strong interest in pedagogical action research. She has written numerous publications, given conference papers and run workshops in this area (www.linnorton.co.uk/). Her current research interests are in all aspects of higher education pedagogy.

Liz O'Gara

Dr Liz O'Gara is a Principal Lecturer in Employability in the Faculty of Science and Engineering at the University of Wolverhampton. She has extensive teaching experience across a diverse range of abilities, including delivery of theoretical, practical and research-based modules. During her career, she has focused on the embedding of employability skills within awards. She has been a member of the biomedical science placement team for most of her teaching career, preparing students for and supporting students in the workplace.

Katie Peck

Katie is a Registered Dietitian, Senior Lecturer in Nutrition and Dietetics and Course Leader for the MSc Clinical Nutrition programme at Leeds Beckett University. She gained Senior Fellow with the Higher Education Academy in 2013. Her research interests focus on transitions to Masters level study, between academic and practice settings, and into the post-registration workplace. Katie is studying for a professional doctorate in education and working with student alumni to explore how values are performed in post-registration dietetic practice. Katie is now at Sheffield Hallam University.

Dudley Shallcross

Professor Dudley Shallcross was the first National Teaching Fellow in Chemistry in the UK and has been a Co-Director of the Bristol ChemLabS Centre for Excellence in Teaching and Learning, and is currently CEO of the Primary Science Teaching Trust. He has won national and international awards for his contributions to science education, and his interests include transition from primary to secondary and secondary to tertiary education, the use of appropriate contexts, e-enhanced learning, and the use of practicals in learning.

Sara Smith

Sara has worked for over 20 years in the field of biomedical science as a Registered Biomedical Scientist, Training Officer and Training Centre Manager before becoming a Senior Lecturer in Higher Education. Sara has conducted research into supporting the development of practitioner capability and integration of work-based placements in higher education awards. As a practitioner-researcher, Sara has collaborated with colleagues in NHS Trusts on innovative projects focusing upon the use of videos and capture technology to enhance the student learning experience and support continual professional development.

Sebastian Stevens

Sebastian is a PhD Candidate in Medical Education at the Peninsula Schools of Medicine and Dentistry (Plymouth University). He has been involved in higher education pedagogy research across a number of disciplines, with his most recent research exploring aspirations to higher education participation for vocational students in the South West. He is also an Associate Lecturer of Social Research and Fellow of the Higher Education Academy.

Victoria Stretton

Victoria Stretton is Programme Leader for the BA in Musical Theatre Performance and Head of Musical Theatre. Initially training as a dancer at North London Dance Studios, Victoria's professional career has enabled her to combine her passion for teaching, choreography and performing. Victoria has considerable experience within education and training, particularly in relation to curriculum development, timetable management and leadership.

Mark Sutcliffe

Mark Sutcliffe is a Senior Lecturer in Strategic Management, and Postgraduate Programme Director at Cardiff School of Management, Cardiff Metropolitan University. He was awarded Senior Fellow of the Higher Education Academy in 2014, and a University Student-Led Teaching Fellowship in 2015. Mark's research interests focus upon ways to enhance student belonging, especially at the postgraduate level, and developing creative and innovative approaches to teaching, learning and assessment.

Sue Tangney

Dr Sue Tangney is an Academic Developer and Principal Lecturer at Cardiff Metropolitan University. Her work and research interests include student-centred pedagogies and assessment, internationalisation of the curriculum, inclusive teaching and inclusive curricula, and the professional development of academic staff. She is also a Principal Fellow of the Higher Education Academy.

Stephen Thompson

Dr Stephen Thompson started his career working for a number of design consultancies in Europe before establishing his own design practice and moving into a career as an academic with a reputation as both a transdisciplinary theorist and an expert in transdisciplinary education. While Deputy Dean, Stephen built upon this expertise to develop and implement the radical curriculum of Cardiff School of Art and Design, and prior to that the Design Futures programme at Newport. Stephen is a designer-theorist, concerned with the interplay of the body and technologies in the enacting of cognition.

Alastair Tomlinson

Alastair Tomlinson is Senior Lecturer in Environmental and Public Health at Cardiff Metropolitan University. He is a Chartered Environmental Health Practitioner and a Fellow of the Higher Education Academy. His professional background is the interface of environmental health and public health practice, including communicable disease control, smoke-free public places and public health policy, and strategy development. His pedagogic research interests are effective curriculum design for professional qualifications in public health and environmental health, in particular the role of problem-based learning and work-based learning.

Rebecca Turner

Rebecca is an Educational Developer with the Pedagogic Research Institute and Observatory (PedRIO), Plymouth University. In addition to undertaking research into the first-year student experience, Rebecca is also interested in examining the role of research and scholarship in college-based higher education and the contribution evaluation can make to educational development practice. She is also a Senior Fellow of the HEA.

Leoniek Wijngaards-de Meij

Leoniek is both Associate Professor and Director of Education of the Department of Methodology and Statistics at the Faculty of Social and Behavioral Sciences at Utrecht University. She has successfully initiated, guided and completed several educational innovation projects; for example, the project on improving the alignment within curricula by visualising learning trajectories, for which she received an educational innovation grant. Her research interests focus around student–program fit, counsel and advice for study choice, and alignment within curricula.

Index

Abbott, Stuart 113–138
academic culture 31
academic integration 34, 42, 113–138; assessment 116–117; case studies 121–138; definition of 114–115; developing academic literacy 116; diversity of students 113–114; measurement of 118–119; partnership in learning 117–118; peer relations 143; reflection 115; retention linked to 7
academic integrity 67, 69
academic self-concept 32
academic skills 13, 21, 113, 115–116, 118; assignment feedback 135; induction 53, 54; learner empowerment 38; Masters carousel 67; *Passport to Success @ SCU* 66; patchwork assessment 130; transition tube 91; *see also* skills
accommodation 18, 65, 145
accountability 200
action learning 80
action research 199–200, 202, 209; dissemination of research findings 210; ethical issues 212; peer-supported video intervention 100; professional development 204–205; reflective practice 97–99; research methods 206
active citizenship 202
active learning 40, 81–82, 83, 94–95, 103, 170
adaptability 23, 81, 100
adjustment 11
advice services 76
agency 81, 86, 90, 115, 170
Aldous, David 71–74
Aljohani, O. 7
Allwood, C.M. 205
alumni 42, 67, 139, 152

Anglia Ruskin University (ARU) 53, 127, 129
Annan, Grace Kafui 151–153
anxiety 12, 33, 145
Apekey, Tanefa 67–70
applicant days 75
apps 95
argument 23–24
Ashton-Hay, Sally 63–67
aspirations 10, 36, 83, 122, 168–169
assessment: academic integration 116–117, 118, 119; assessment literacy 22, 116, 117, 119, 121, 127–128; authentic 6, 8, 12, 23, 28, 55, 82; biscuit game 127–128; culturally appropriate 172, 192–195; formative 8, 11, 62, 70, 84, 116, 117; grading criteria 127–128; intercultural awareness 189, 191; international students 24; mature students at the Open University 122, 123; patchwork 115, 129–132; peer 24, 194–195; prior experience of 22; problem-based learning 105; screencast 136–137; social integration 145; SPICE International 125; student involvement 168, 202; summative 62, 80, 105, 110, 116, 117; timing of 117; trans-active curriculum 188; visioning 39; viva voce 109
assignments: assignment design for students on international mobility 107–112; feedback 26, 135–138, 169; grading criteria 127–128; international students 24
assumptions 25–28
'at-risk' students 144, 160, 162, 204
attendance 27
attitude change 205
attitude scales 207

audio news magazine 154–156
Australia: graduate attributes 6; retention 141; student surveys 18, 203; widening participation 6
Australian Learning and Teaching Council 13–14
autonomy 185, 186
Ayiku, Sarah 151–153

Bailey, Jake 113–138
Bandura, A. 41
Baptista, Ana 176–179
Barham, Gareth 107–112
Barnett, R. 86, 170
Baron, R. 10–11
Barron, P. 142
Baumeister, R.F. 32
becoming 14, 31, 42, 83, 85, 146, 166, 169
Beetham, H. 23
behaviour change 205
belonging 11, 31–45; academic integration 115; dialogic activities 85; flipped classrooms 96; international students 51; mental health awareness training 160; *Passport to Success @ SCU* 64; PodMag 154; sense of inclusion 167; social capital 34–35; social integration 140, 141, 143, 144, 145; student engagement 83, 90; student lifecycle 35–42; student surveys 118; transition tube 91; trust 33–34
benevolence 33–34
Biesta, G. 200–201
Birkbeck College 20
biscuit game 127–129
black and minority ethnic (BME) students 19, 167
Born, M. 32
boundary-crossing 40–41, 86
Bourdieu, Pierre 34–35, 140
Bovill, C. 39
Bowl, M. 14
Bridges, S. 12
Bridges, W. 12
'bring your own device' 96
British Educational Research Association (BERA) 211
Brooman, S. 140
Broughan, C. 113
Brown, David 71–74
Brown, Sally 17–30, 127–129
Bryson, C. 83

BTEC students 19, 20
buddy schemes 126
building with Lego activity 181–185
Burke, P.J. 33
Burnett, L. 10, 12
Butcher, John 121–123
Butler, Ed 216–217

Callender, C. 17
Camilleri, Lynda 217–218
Camtasia Studio 136–137
capabilities 22, 23, 42, 86; intercultural 107–111, 146, 170, 171, 188–191; sense of capability 31, 38; transformative 40, 86; *see also* skills
Cardiff Metropolitan University: assignment design for students on international mobility 107–112; assignment feedback 135–138; mental health awareness training 160–162; 'Mind Your Own Business' project 77–80; outdoor problem-solving residential 156–160; problem-based learning 103–107; storytelling-as-pedagogy 71–74; trans-active curriculum 185–188; transition tube 90–94
Cardiff School of Art and Design 77–80, 107–112
career pathways 54–55
caring responsibilities 145, 167
Carroll, J. 25
case studies: academic integration 121–138; engagement 90–112; self-development 176–195; social integration 149–165; student expectations 58–80
case study research method 206
Centre for Curriculum Internationalisation 111
Centre for Excellence in Teaching and Learning (CETL) 208
Cetinich, Robyn 63–67
Chalmers, D. 6
charters 52–53
cheating 25
Child, Samantha 60–63
China 19
choice 8, 17, 83
Christie, H. 142
classification 71, 72
Clifford, Valerie 166–195

clubs and societies 141, 142, 144, 145; *see also* extracurricular activities
collaboration 36, 40–41, 114; collaborative autobiographies 72, 73; collaborative research 212; collaborative spaces 14; outdoor problem-solving residential 160; trans-active curriculum 185
Colombia 223–224
communication skills 23, 132, 179, 192
communities of practice 41, 85, 98, 99
community 31, 38, 76, 154
competence 33–34
competitiveness 5
complaints 18
confidence: academic integration 113, 115, 119; assessment 116; belonging 33; lack of 121; learner empowerment 38; 'Mind Your Own Business' project 77; nursing students 178; outdoor problem-solving residential 156–157; *Passport to Success @ SCU* 64, 66; patchwork assessment 131; social integration 140, 143, 145; trans-active curriculum 185, 186; transformative capabilities 40
confusion 11, 12
connectedness 31, 32, 34, 42
constructionism 183
constructivism 34, 83, 84, 100, 193
consumers, students as 17–18, 50
contact hours 27, 49, 50
Cook-Sather, A. 39
Cooke, S. 14
Cotton, Debby 60–63
course organisation 49
coursework 225
Cousin, G. 100
Covey's matrix 69
Crawley, Josie 132–135
creativity 31, 81, 90, 166; culturally appropriate assessment 194; groupthink 42; 'Mind Your Own Business' project 78; social capital 35; trans-active curriculum 185
critical reflection 67, 69; *see also* reflection
critical thinking 27, 67, 68, 72, 81, 100, 195; graduate capabilities 23; measurement of 204; nursing students 177; patchwork assessment 129, 130; problem-based learning 104
cross-cultural adaptation 188, 189, 190
cross-cultural competence 108, 109–110; *see also* intercultural capabilities

Cross, Ruth 151–153
Cullen, J. 113–114
cultural awareness 14
cultural capital 18, 167
cultural differences 37, 51
cultural integration 146
'cultural probes' 189, 190–191
cultural values 107, 108, 111, 170
culturally appropriate assessment 172, 192–195
culture shock 65, 221
curriculum 6, 31, 37–38; authentic 8; co-designed with employers 55; decolonising education 40; dissonance 172; early engagement 11; fitness for purpose 28, 170; induction 37; internationalisation 189; learner empowerment 38, 86; postgraduate students 13; relevance 167; social integration 142; student development 173; student involvement 40, 85, 87, 202; trans-active 185–188; transnational 68

D'Annunzio-Green, N. 142
Darwent, S. 140
Davies, Bill 156–160
Davis, Sam 67–70
Dawson, Henry 135–138
The Dearing Report (1997) 5
debate 23–24, 84
decolonising education 39–40, 86, 146
demographics 7, 19–20
demonstration experiments 180–181
Dennis, Chris 113–138
development 14, 31
Devlin, M. 34
Dewey, J. 68
dialogic activities 85
digital technologies 25
direct entrants 142, 144
disabled students 7, 25, 167
discrimination 107, 108, 146, 171–172
dissertations 172
dissonance 172
distance learning 51, 54, 143, 146, 154–156
Ditzel, Liz 132–135
diversity 11, 13, 51, 85, 172; academic integration 113–114; decolonising education 39–40; social integration 141
Doherty, C.A. 170

Dong-A University 110
Doolan, M.A. 204
Doyle, J. 200
Drew, S. 140
drop-out rates 20, 140–141, 143; *see also* withdrawal
du Mez, Elyce 218–219
Dunn, L. 39

e-portfolios 55
elite universities 6
employability 5–6, 8, 82, 85, 170; contextualisation 100; expectations 55; 'Mind Your Own Business' project 78; outdoor problem-solving residential 157; self-belief 167; social capital 35; student engagement 83; Teaching Excellence Framework 18; UK visa changes 193
employers 6, 18–19, 55
employment: during study 50, 65, 167; industrial placements 224–225; 'Mind Your Own Business' project 77; preparation for 202; student stories 216–217; transition to 54–55
empowerment 38–39, 86, 117, 171; academic integration 114; trans-active curriculum 185, 186
engagement 8, 37–38, 81–112; active 58, 83–84; assignment feedback 135, 136; case studies 90–112; connectedness 34; decolonising education 40; expectations about 27; focus on becoming 85; holistic view of 10; induction 37, 144; learner empowerment 38, 39; pre-arrival information 36; public 179–181; reflection 84–85; sense of belonging 31; social integration 140, 141, 142, 145; student expectations 50; transition for the future 86–87; Utrecht University orientation programme 59
English as a second language 8, 37
English, Stuart 97–99
entrepreneurship 6, 77–80, 170
Entwistle, N. 25
envisioning 39, 86, 87, 187–188
equal opportunity 5, 85
equity 107, 108, 171
ethical issues 202, 211–212
ethical responsibility 170, 171
European Association for Practitioner Research on Improving Learning in Education and Professional Practice (EAPRIL) 211
evaluation of transition activities 199–215; ethical issues 202, 211–212; evaluation in education 200–201; focus of research 202, 203–205; purpose of research 202, 208–211; research methods 202, 206–208; research paradigm 202, 205–206
evidence-based practice 28, 178, 200–201
examinations 24, 27–28; *see also* assessment
expectations 6, 8, 9, 18, 34, 49–80; academic integration 114; attendance and engagement 27; case studies 58–80; changing nature of 50–51; employers 55; gap with reality 35, 49; induction 10; 'institutional habitus' 140; international students 23, 24; peer learning 53; personal tutoring and personal development planning 53; postgraduate students 54; pre-entry 10, 36, 51–52; reorientation and reinduction 12; skill sets 21–23; SPICE International 124; student charters 52–53; student engagement 83; transition to employment 54–55
experiential learning 40, 67, 68, 130, 170, 202
extracurricular activities 6, 10, 36, 37–38, 170; decolonising education 40; social integration 145; social learning 41; structured timetables 62; T-shirt induction activity 145; *see also* clubs and societies

Facebook 35–36, 41, 75, 145–146, 155, 156, 164, 204; *see also* social media
feasibility 168
feedback: academic integration 117, 118–119; assessment literacy 22; assumptions about 26; culturally appropriate assessment 194, 195; early 8, 11; flipped classrooms 95, 96; impact on achievement 28; international students 24–25; mature students at the Open University 122–123; middle years 12; nursing students 178; peer 169; screen recording software 135–138; social integration 145; transition tube 91, 93; Utrecht University orientation programme 59–60; 'Virtual Experience Labs' 54

feedforward 12, 95, 110, 123
fees 18, 19, 51
Felten, P. 39
Fiave, Jerry 151–153
finances 65, 141, 142
first-year experience 11–12, 82
flexibility 6, 40, 74, 87, 166
Flexible Pedagogies Framework 38–42
Flint, A. 38
flipped classrooms 82, 94–97
focus groups 207
Foley, Karen 154–156
Ford, Sian 220–221
Forrester, G. 51
Foster, Monika 124–127, 188–191
framing 71–72, 73
France 222–223
Franiel, Dominic 18–19, 23
Freeman, S. 95
friendships 11; Liverpool John Moores University support programme 76; *Passport to Success @ SCU* 64; social integration 139, 140, 141, 143, 145; social media 35–36; student stories 222–223; *see also* relationships
funding 208–209
future-facing education 39, 86
Fyvie-Gauld, M. 141, 145

Gale, T. 11, 13–14, 31, 81, 146, 172–173
gender 51, 150
Germany 208
Ghana 151–153, 194
Ghoshal, S. 35
Gilbert, T. 204
Glassey, Jarka 149–151
global citizenship 12, 37, 81, 85, 107, 108, 171–172
global perspectives 108, 109, 146
globalised economy 5–6
goals 122, 177
Gonçalves, Rui 176–179
Goodenow, C. 32
grade point average (GPA) 204
graduate attributes 8, 13, 82, 85; employability 6, 55; middle years 12; outdoor problem-solving residential 157; problem-based learning 104; *see also* skills
graduate premium 18–19
Gray, R. 146
group work: future-facing education 39; 'Mind Your Own Business' project 77–80; outdoor problem-solving residential 158–159; *Passport to Success @ SCU* 64; problem-based learning 104; reflection 84; social integration 143, 145; structured timetables 62; T-shirt integration activity 150–151; 'thinking outside the square' 132–133
groupthink 42

Hagerty, B. 32
Haigh, M. 189
Hamshire, C. 141
Harel, I. 183
Hargreaves, D.H. 200
Harrington, K. 38
Harrison, Nicola 221–222
Harrison, Tim 179–181
Harvey, L. 140
Healey, M. 38
health and social care education 130–131, 192–195
health issues 65; *see also* mental health issues
hierarchy of needs 32, 64
Higher Education Academy (HEA) 22, 127
Higher Education Funding Council for England (HEFCE) 203–204, 208
Higher Education Statistics Agency (HESA) 140
Hockings, C. 14
homesickness 11, 145
Horobin, Hazel 192–195
Hunt, L. 6, 113
Hurth, Victoria 60–63

identity 9, 10, 81, 167; academic 13, 114, 115, 116, 119; becoming 31; belonging 32, 33; development 14; induction 37; learner empowerment 38, 39; patchwork assessment 131; positive student identity 11, 37; postgraduate students 13; pre-arrival activities 35; professional 31, 37, 41, 42, 85, 102, 139; reflective exercises 115; student lifecycle 8; timing of assessment 117; transformative capabilities 40; *see also* self-development
images 177–178
inclusion 7, 10, 140, 146, 154, 160, 167
independence skills 81, 85, 90
independent study 12, 27, 49, 53, 60–63, 100
India 19, 192, 194

induction 10–11, 14, 31, 50, 172–173; academic skills 54; active 34; assumptions about 26; belonging 36–37, 167; evaluation of 202; evidence-based practice 28; immersive 144; international students 24; Liverpool John Moores University support programme 75–76; mental health awareness training 146; midpoint entry students 164–165; outdoor problem-solving residential 156–160; pre-arrival 35; social integration 143, 144; SPICE International 124–127; structured timetables 62; student expectations 52, 53; transition tube 92; vulnerability to withdrawal 145
information literacy 116
informed consent 211–212
initiative 100
institutional culture 87
'institutional habitus' 140
integration 7, 8, 36, 76; see also academic integration; social integration
integrative framework 8
integrity 33–34, 212
intercultural capabilities 107–111, 146, 170, 171, 188–191
interdisciplinary education 40–41, 67, 68, 86, 87, 106
International Baccalaureate 223
international mobility 107–112, 188–191
International Society for the Scholarship of Teaching and Learning (ISSOTL) 211
international students 20, 23–25; belongingness 51; culturally appropriate assessment 192–195; middle years 12; *Passport to Success @ SCU* 63–67; social integration 142; SPICE International 124–127; student stories 221–222, 223–224; transition tube 90–94
internationalisation 86–87, 111, 170–171; 'at home' 188; curriculum 167, 189; Kitano Model 108
interpersonal skills 23, 81
interpretivism 205–206
interviews 206–207
isolation 11, 51, 140, 141, 142, 152

Jackson, D. 55
Jackson, J. 17
Jackson, Louise H. 163–165
Jackson, N. 86
James, Alison 181–185

Jin, L. 51
Johnston, Wendy 74–76
Jones-Devitt, Stella 129–132

Kandiko, C.B. 50–51, 53, 55
Kember, D. 23
Khechara, Martin 94–97, 99–103
Kitano, M.K. 108, 111
Kneale, Pauline 60–63
knowledge: active learning 83; belonging 33; conceptions of 168; context of 195; dissemination of research findings 210; learner empowerment 38; learning gain 203–204; perceptions about 21; prior 103, 170; problem-based learning 104; tacit 116–117; 'thinking outside the square' 132; transition stages 82
knowledge-based society 5, 166
Kolb, D. 68
Kookmin University 109–110
Kristiansen, P. 182

Lave, J. 41
leadership 28, 85, 131, 157
learner empowerment 38–39, 86; see also empowerment
learning: academic integration 114–115, 118, 119; active 40, 81–82, 83, 94–95, 103, 170; authentic 55; changes in perceptions about 20–21; connectedness 34; experiential 40, 67, 68, 130, 170, 202; first-year experience 11–12; international students 23; learner empowerment 39; learning analytics 204; learning gain 203–204; mature students at the Open University 122–123; opportunities for 201; partnerships 117–118; *Passport to Success @ SCU* 66; peer 53, 54, 76, 100, 102, 169–170; prior 84; problem-based 55, 103–107; professional practice 177; social 41–42, 86, 114, 115, 119; storytelling-as-pedagogy 71; structured timetables 61–62; student-centred 14, 82, 115, 119; transformational 40; transition in 81–82; see also online learning
learning communities 41–42; formative assessment 117; Liverpool John Moores University 74, 75; National Student Survey 18; online 54; PodMag 154
Leary, M.R. 32

Leeds Beckett University 67–70, 151–153
Lego 181–185
Leung, D.Y. 23
library support 53
Lightfoot, Martha 133
literacies 22, 27, 116
Liverpool John Moores University 74–76
living at home 20, 142, 143, 145, 167
Lizzio, A. 8, 10, 39; becoming 169; 'senses' 31; social integration 139; student identities 35, 37–38, 42, 81–82, 167
Lobão, Catarina 176–179
loneliness 142
Longden, B. 50
Lowcock, Diane 151–153

Macfarlane, B. 33–34, 35, 212
Madge, C. 36
maieutic models of learning 21
Marton, F. 82
Maslow, A. 32, 33, 64
Masters programmes: international students 20; Masters carousel 67–70; peer mentors 151–153; student stories 216–217, 221; trans-active curriculum 185–188; transition tube 90–94; see also postgraduate students
Matheson, Ruth 5–16, 31–45, 139–165
Matthews, D. 19
mature students: digital technologies 25; Open University 121–123; social integration 143, 145; student stories 218; widening participation 19; withdrawal 7, 20
Mawer, M. 50–51, 53, 55
May, V. 32
McAllister, M. 73
McNiff, Jean 202
Medina, M.N.D. 205–206
Meeuwisse, M. 32
Mellick, Mikel 160–162
mental health issues 76, 146, 160–162
mentors 53, 85; Liverpool John Moores University 75, 76; peer mentoring in Ghana 151–153; work placements 55
Menzies, J.L. 10–11
Mercer, J. 212
metacognitive skills 84, 94, 114, 115, 137
Mezirow, J. 40
mid-programme entry 163–165
middle years 12, 54, 182
'Mind Your Own Business' project 77–80
minority groups 19, 167

mobile devices 95, 102, 186
mobility 107–112, 188–191
Model of Institutional Departure 7
Moodle 137
moral courage 166
moral integrity 212
Morgan, M. 7, 10, 12, 13
Morris, Richard 77–80
Morrison, David 60–63
motivation: extrinsic 168; intrinsic 34, 104, 168; learner empowerment 39
Mullan, J. 204
musical theatre students 163–165

Nahapiet, J. 35
National Student Survey (NSS) 18, 118, 203
networking 150, 163–165; see also peer networks
Newcastle University 149–151
Newman-Ford, Loretta 49–80
Nicol, D. 85
Northumbria University 97–99
Norton, Lin 199–215
NSS see National Student Survey
nursing students 141, 176–179

O'Donnell, V.L. 8, 36, 38, 54
O'Gara, Liz 99–103
online learning 42, 54, 96, 137; culturally appropriate assessment 194; flipped classrooms 82; intercultural skills 191; *Passport to Success @ SCU* 64, 66; SPICE International 124–126; see also technology
open days 75
Open University 20, 121–123, 154–156
orientation 11, 14, 53, 63–66, 76; see also induction
Osarfo-Mensah, Esther 222–223
O'Shea, H. 34
Otago Polytechnic 132–135
outdoor problem-solving residential 156–160
outreach events 179–181
Oxford Brookes University 108, 111

Panopto 95
Papert, S. 183
Parker, S. 11, 13–14, 31, 81, 146, 172–173
Parkinson, G. 51
part-time study 18, 19–20, 130–131, 142, 143

participation: induction 37; learning communities 41–42; widening 5, 6, 19–20, 166
partnerships 21, 38–39, 40, 87, 114, 117–118, 119
Passeron, J. 140
Passport to Success @ SCU 63–67
patchwork assessment 115, 129–132
PBL *see* problem-based learning
PDP *see* personal development planning
Peasgood, A. 204
Peck, Katie 67–70
pedagogies 6, 14, 31, 87; academic integration 115; active learning 81–82; culture change 209; decolonising education 146; Flexible Pedagogies Framework 38–42; storytelling-as-pedagogy 71–74
peer assessment 24, 194–195
peer learning 53, 54, 76, 100, 102, 169–170
peer mentors 53, 75, 76, 85, 151–153
peer networks 141, 143, 144, 145–146, 150, 152; *see also* social networks
peer support 12; mental health awareness training 160, 161, 162; patchwork assessment 131; peer mentoring in Ghana 152; social integration 143, 145–146; SPICE International 124–125, 126
Penguin Random House UK 19
performance measures 202, 203–204
Perry, W.G. 82
personal development planning (PDP) 53, 55, 90–91, 94, 123, 157, 169
personal tutoring 53, 144, 145, 169
personalised learning 131, 170
physiotherapy 192
placements 12, 55; nursing students 176–178; peer-supported video intervention 101, 102; student stories 219, 224–225
plagiarism 21, 25–26, 69, 125
planning 97–98
Plymouth University 60–63, 169
PodMag 154–156
policies 5
positivism 205–206, 207, 212
postgraduate students 8, 36, 38; academic capabilities 38; academic integration 114; dissonance 172; Masters carousel 67–70; *Passport to Success @ SCU* 66; peer mentoring 151–153; public engagement 179–181; reinduction 12, 13; student stories 219; transition needs 54; *see also* Masters programmes
pre-arrival/pre-entry 10, 35–36; expectations 51–52; social integration 143; SPICE International 124–127; Utrecht University orientation programme 58–60
predictability 33–34
prejudice 107, 108, 171
presentations 110, 180–181, 194, 210
prior knowledge 103, 170
prior learning experiences 84
prioritisation 67, 69
privacy issues 211, 212
problem-based learning (PBL) 55, 103–107
problem-solving: active 21; graduate skills and capabilities 23, 81; 'Mind Your Own Business' project 80; outdoor residential 156–160; *Passport to Success @ SCU* 65; peer-supported video intervention 100; 'thinking outside the square' 132–135
professional development 130–131, 169, 204–205
professional judgment 199
professional practice 177, 200
professional services 53, 144–145
public engagement 179–181
purpose 31, 39, 42

qualifications 19, 223
qualitative research 202, 205–206
Quality Assurance Agency for Higher Education (QAA) 11, 50, 86
Quality Code 169
quantitative research 202, 205–206, 207, 208
Queen Margaret University 124–127, 188–191
questionnaires 207–208

Rae, D. 170
Ramley, J.A. 199
Rasmussen, R. 182
'real-world impact' 200
'real-world' problems 103, 104, 168
'reality shock' 55
referencing 67, 70, 115, 116, 119, 125
reflection 84–85, 90; academic integration 115, 118; assignment feedback 136, 137; graduate capabilities 23; mature students at the Open University

122–123; nursing students 176–178; patchwork assessment 129, 130, 131; 'thinking outside the square' 132, 135; transition tube 91
reflective learning 68
reflective practice 40, 97–99, 183
reinduction 12, 13, 54
relationships 31, 37; academic integration 118; flipped classrooms 96; *Passport to Success @ SCU* 64; peer mentoring programme 152; social integration 140, 145; student engagement 83; student-staff 31, 33–34, 38, 83, 90, 140, 143–144, 145; *see also* friendships
reorientation 12
research: dissemination of findings 201, 209–211; ethical issues 211–212; evidence of effectiveness 200–201; focus of 202, 203–205; PhD students 219; purpose of 202, 208–211; research methods 103, 104, 202, 206–208; research paradigm 202, 205–206; research skills 66
residential experiences 156–160
resilience 23, 42, 81, 85, 121
resourcefulness 31, 39, 42
resources: assumptions about 26; problem-based learning 104, 106; SPICE International 125; transition tube 92
responsible citizenship 108, 111
retention 6–7, 36; academic integration 114; belonging linked to 32; early engagement 11; induction linked to 10, 28; social integration 140–141, 146; student engagement 83; student expectations 50; Teaching Excellence Framework 18; *see also* withdrawal
returning students 12, 144
Richardson, D. 54
The Robbins Report (1963) 5
Royal Roads University 54
Rubin, M. 141–142
Russell Group 20
Ryan, A. 38, 39, 86, 146

safety issues 65
Saljo, R. 82
sample size 208
Sanderson, G. 189
satisfaction 8, 18, 49–50, 144; assignment feedback 136; evaluation of interventions 203; student engagement 83
Saudi Arabia 194

scaffolding 12, 104, 105–106, 122
scenario-based learning 55
schemata 83
schools 180–181
Sclater, N. 204
Scoggins, J. 131–132
Scott, G. 50
screen recording software 135–138
SCU *see* Southern Cross University
self-awareness 39, 40, 97, 99, 100, 115, 176
self-belief 23, 140, 167–168
self-concept 32
self-development 42, 166–195; case studies 176–195; challenges 167–169; curriculum 170; dissonance 172; Flexible Pedagogies Framework 38; global citizenship 171–172; higher education environment 166; internationalisation 170–171; peer-assisted learning 169–170; personal tutoring 169; placements 224
self-directed enquiry 11–12, 22, 104
self-efficacy 27, 152, 169–170, 171
self-esteem 64, 152
self-regulation 61, 62, 81
sense-making 83, 84, 90
'senses' 31
settling-in sessions 65
Severiens, S. 32
Shallcross, Dudley 179–181
Sheffield Hallam University 129–132, 192–195
Singh, P. 170
skills 13, 18–19, 81; academic integration 113, 115–116, 118; assignment feedback 135; changing expectations about 21–23; cognitive 81, 82, 84; graduate 82, 85; induction 53, 54; learner empowerment 38; learning gain 203–204; Masters carousel 67–70; Masters education 185–186; mature students at the Open University 122, 123; middle years 12; 'Mind Your Own Business' project 77, 78; musical theatre 164; outdoor problem-solving residential 157, 158; *Passport to Success @ SCU* 66; patchwork assessment 130; peer-supported video intervention 100; postgraduate students 13, 54; SPICE International 124; storytelling-as-pedagogy 72, 73; structured timetables 62–63; transferable 13, 157, 159; transition tube 91, 92, 93; *see also* capabilities; graduate attributes

Skype 126, 204
Smith, M. 140
Smith, Sara 94–97, 99–103
Snyder, W. 41
social capital 18, 34–35
social integration 8, 9, 34, 37, 42, 139–165; case studies 149–165; cultural integration 146; definition of 140; lack of 141–142; Masters carousel 67; mental health 146; responsibility for 142–145; retention linked to 7, 140–141; transition tube 92
social interaction 37
social justice 5, 6, 107, 108, 171
social learning 41–42, 86, 114, 115, 119
social media 35–36, 143, 145–146, 164, 165; *see also* Facebook
social networks 35, 145–146, 156–157; *see also* peer networks
social responsibility 170, 171
social skills 85
socio-economic status 7, 20, 141–142
Socratic dialogue 21, 187
Socrative 95
South Korea 107–112, 172
Southern Cross University (SCU) 63–67
SPICE (student pre-arrival induction for continuing education) 124–127
staff: academic integration 119; dissonance 172; mental health awareness training 160, 161; nursing students 178; outdoor problem-solving residential 159; partnerships with 38–39, 117–118; PodMag 154–155; professional development 204–205; social integration 142, 143–144; student engagement 83; student-staff relationships 31, 33–34, 38, 83, 90, 140, 143–144, 145; T-shirt integration activity 150, 151; *see also* tutors
stages of transition 9–13, 82
stereotyping 107, 108, 110, 172
Stevens, Sebastian 60–63
storybooks 133–134
storytelling 54, 71–74
stress 11, 225
Stretton, Victoria 163–165
structured timetables 53, 60–63
Student Adjustment Model 10–11
student-centred learning 14, 82, 115, 119
student charters 52–53
student lifecycle 6, 7–9, 81, 139; academic integration 114; belonging 35–42; self-development 167; student expectations 54; timing of assessment 117
student numbers 5
student pre-arrival induction for continuing education (SPICE) 124–127
student stories 216–225
student unions 142
student voice 18, 40, 142
study skills 137–138, 169
summer schools 51
support 6, 11, 12, 27; academic integration 114; independent study 49; international students 24; learner empowerment 38; library 53; Liverpool John Moores University 74–76; *Passport to Success @ SCU* 63, 64; postgraduate students 13; resources 26; social integration 142, 144–145; SPICE International 124, 125; student expectations 18; student-staff relationships 34; student stories 221, 225; 'value for money' 50; *see also* peer support
surveys 18, 52, 118, 144, 203, 207–208
sustainability 107, 108, 171, 208–209
Sutcliffe, Mark 31–45, 90–94, 139–165
switching courses 220–221

T-shirt integration activity 145, 149–151
tacit knowledge 116–117
Tangney, Sue 81–112, 166–195
Taylor, P.C. 205–206
teaching: changes in perceptions about 20–21; learner empowerment 39; quality of 49; structured timetables 61–62; student expectations 51; 'teaching intensity' 27
Teaching Excellence Framework (TEF) 17–18, 199, 203
team-work 6, 104, 157, 179, 182; *see also* group work
technology 50, 204; assumptions about 25; distance learning 54; flipped classrooms 94–97; *Passport to Success @ SCU* 65; screen recording software 135–138; *see also* online learning; virtual learning environments
TEF *see* Teaching Excellence Framework
Téllez, Lina 223–224
'thinking outside the square' 132–135
Thomas, Alex 224–225
Thomas, L. 11, 31, 141, 143–144, 167

Thompson, Stephen 185–188
Tilbury, D. 38, 39, 86, 146
time management 27, 60, 62, 79, 92, 125
timetables 53, 60–63
Tinto, V. 7, 113–114, 145
Tobbell, J. 8, 36, 38
Tomlinson, Alastair 103–107
'touchpoints' 114
trans-active curriculum 185–188
transformative capabilities 40, 86
'transition shock' 55
transition stages 9–13, 82
transition tube 90–94
trends 17–23
Trinity Laban Conservatoire of Music and Dance 163–165
trust 33–34, 75, 122; future-facing education 39; induction 36, 37; learning communities 42; Liverpool John Moores University support programme 76; partnership in learning 117; personal tutoring 169; social capital 35; social learning conditions 114
Turner, N. 167–168, 169
Turner, Rebecca 60–63, 144
tutors: academic integration 117–118, 119; connection with 85; mature students at the Open University 122–123; outdoor problem-solving residential 157, 158, 159; personal tutoring 53, 144, 145, 169; pre-entry activities 52; SPICE International 125–126; support from 12; trust 34; see also staff
Twitter 164

uncertainty 12, 36, 86, 119, 170, 185, 186
United Kingdom: Centre for Excellence in Teaching and Learning 208; graduate attributes 6; international student stories 221–222, 223–224; National Student Survey 18, 118, 203; personal tutoring 169; Teaching Excellence Framework 17–18, 199, 203; widening participation 6, 19; withdrawals 7; work visas 193
United States: academic integration 114; graduate attributes 6; student expectations 51; student surveys 18, 203
university choice 8
University of Adelaide 104–105
University of Bristol 179–181
University of Reading 52
University of Winchester 181–185
University of Wolverhampton 94–97, 99–103
Utrecht University 51–52, 58–60

'value for money' 50
values: cultural 107, 108, 111, 170; educational desirability 213; integrity in research 212; internationalisation 171; 'Mind Your Own Business' project 79, 80; pre-arrival information 36; trust 34; values-based learning 85
video: assignment feedback 136; 'cultural probes' 190; peer-supported learning 99–103; trans-active curriculum 187; transition tube 93
'Virtual Experience Labs' 54
virtual learning environments (VLEs) 101–102, 105, 191; see also online learning
visioning 39, 187–188
Vygotsky, L.S. 41

web conferencing 54
Wenger, E. 41
WhatsApp 204
Wheelahan, L. 72
Whitehead, Jack 202
Wibberley, C. 141
'wicked problems' 199, 201, 213
Wijngaards-de Meij, Leoniek 58–60
Wilcox, P. 141, 145
Willgoss, T.G. 141
Wilton, N. 55
Winn, S. 141, 145
Winter, R. 131–132
withdrawal 11, 20, 61, 140–141; diversity of students 113–114; lack of belonging 32; peer-assisted learning 169–170; reasons for 7, 36, 141; vulnerable times 145; see also retention
women 19
working-class students 141–142
workloads 12, 27, 53, 61
Wright, C.L. 141–142
writing skills 92, 115, 116, 119, 179, 202, 204

Yin, R.K. 206
Yorke, M. 7, 50

Zammit, M. 8, 36, 38